GERHART HAUPTMANN
AND THE
NATURALIST DRAMA

German Theatre Archive
A series of books edited by David Hill, University of Birmingham, UK

Volume 1
Gerhart Hauptmann and the Naturalist Drama
John Osborne

Forthcoming
Samuel Beckett in Germany
Julian Garforth

This book is part of a series. The publisher will accept continuation orders which may be cancelled at any time and which provide for automatic billing and shipping of each title in the series upon publication. Please write for details.

GERHART HAUPTMANN AND THE NATURALIST DRAMA

John Osborne
University of Warwick, Coventry, UK

LONDON AND NEW YORK

Originally published in 1971 by Manchester University Press. This second, revised and updated, edition copyright © 1998 by OPA (Overseas Publishers Association) Amsterdam B.V. Published under license under the Harwood Academic Publishers imprint, part of The Gordon and Breach Publishing Group.
Reprinted 2004
by Routledge,
2 Park Square, Milton Park, Abingdon, Oxon, OX14 4RN

Transferred to Digital Printing 2004

All rights reserved.

No part of this book may be reproduced or utilized in any form or by any means, electronic or mechanical, including photocopying and recording, or by any information storage or retrieval system, without permission in writing from the publisher.

British Library Cataloguing in Publication Data

Osborne, John, 1938 –
 Gerhart Hauptmann and the naturalist drama. – Rev. and updated ed. – (German theatre archive; v. 1)
 1. Hauptmann, Gerhart, 1862–1946 – Criticism and interpretation 2. German drama – 19th century – History and criticism
 I. Title II. The naturalist drama in Germany
 832.8

ISBN 90-5755-006-7

Cover illustration: Gerhart Hauptmann by Lovis Corinth.
Courtesy of the Städtische Kunsthalle, Mannheim.

CONTENTS

Introduction to the Series   vii

Preface   ix

PART I   History and Theory

1   The first steps to Naturalism   3
2   Naturalism and the theatre: From Heinrich Hart to Otto Brahm   27
3   Naturalism in theory: Arno Holz   43
4   Naturalism and Socialism   63

PART II   Gerhart Hauptmann in Context

5   *Vor Sonnenaufgang*   87
6   *Das Friedensfest*   101
7   *Einsame Menschen*   119
8   *Die Weber*   135
9   The Naturalist comedy   149
10   Some later dramas   159
11   The dramatic style of Naturalism   175

Appendix I
    Plays presented by the Freie Bühne   193
Appendix II
    Plays presented by the Volksbühnen, 1890–5   195

Select Bibliography   199

Index   213

INTRODUCTION TO THE SERIES

The *German Theatre Archive* makes available to a worldwide anglophone readership books about the traditions of German Theatre from the medieval period to the present. Included are translations of plays with introductions that elaborate their contexts, as well as monographs about the major dramatists and other important figures or aspects of theatre in the German-speaking world.

David Hill

PREFACE

The present study is a comprehensively revised and updated version of the author's earlier book, *The Naturalist Drama in Germany* (Manchester University Press, 1971). In the intervening years there have been a number of publications which have significantly affected both the accessibility of the subject and the interpretative methods which have been applied to it. However, the work of revision and the consequent engagement with more recent scholarship confirm the sense that in its original form the book contributed in some measure to this process of reappraisal, that the lines of investigation which were pursued in it have continued to prove fruitful, and that many of its basic insights remain valid.

    The two-part structure of the earlier version is therefore retained. The opening chapter provides a survey of the reaction of the Naturalists to the preceding generation of writers over a broad front. It concludes with an examination of the confrontation between fathers and sons in response to the challenge presented by the work of Zola, noting certain revisionist tendencies in the reception of the theory of the French novelist which opened the way to the recovery of subjectivity by German Naturalism. The following three chapters consider the further development of Naturalism in Germany with reference to the institutional, theoretical and political context in which this development took place. A consequence of the broadening of literary studies which has taken place over recent years, and the shift of focus away from canonical figures and into cultural studies, has been that the importance of these matters in their own right has come to be recognised. There now exist comprehensive and detailed investigations into such previously neglected subjects as the development of the institutions of 'high' and popular theatre on which the dramatists depended for the performance of their texts, the significance of the theorising of Arno Holz for the development of narrative forms and techniques in literary modernism, the political issues involved in the encounter between German Naturalism and organised Socialism, and the relationship between Naturalism as an aesthetic theory and as an ideology. The updated bibliography shows just how decisively the study of German Naturalism has moved into these fields, corroborating some previously tentative conclusions, and indicating ways in which other insights might have been, or indeed might still be, developed further.

The second part of this study consists of critical analyses of the practice of the Naturalist dramatists. At the time the book was first written the extent to which the work of Gerhart Hauptmann, the canonical Naturalist, was considered alongside the work of his contemporaries, marked a significant departure from what was then current practice. Nevertheless the strategy was based on an (unchanged) belief that the close analysis of a limited number of representative texts was the only legitimate way of complementing the more general approach adopted in the first part. This strategy was also influenced by the wish to state firmly a particular (and likewise unchanged) view of the special importance of the Naturalist impulse in the work of Gerhart Hauptmann. To do justice to the wider claims which today's reader might feel are implied by the original title would have involved major rethinking, if not a completely new book. The change of title is an attempt to regularise the situation without losing sight of the purpose of a revised edition.

As is indicated above, in the years since my first serious engagement with German Naturalism the subject has inspired a large amount of scholarship, including much work of distinction, from which the present book has profited. I have endeavoured to acknowledge this in the appropriate way, but wish to record a special debt to three scholars who have come to occupy positions at the very forefront of studies in German Naturalism: Roy Cowen, Edward McInnes and Helmut Scheuer. Their example, encouragement and friendship have contributed much to the endurance of my own interest in this subject.

When referring to the work of Gerhart Hauptmann I have, where possible, used the centenary edition: *Sämtliche Werke*, Centenar-Ausgabe, edited by Hans-Egon Hass and Martin Machatzke, 11 vols, Frankfurt a.M. and Berlin: Propyläen, 1962–74. References to this edition take the form of volume and page numbers only and follow quotations in parentheses.

PART I
HISTORY AND THEORY

1
THE FIRST STEPS TO NATURALISM

The Naturalist movement in German literature got off to a late start. Not until 1878, ten years after the appearance of Zola's preface to the *second* edition of *Thérèse Raquin*, did the indefatigable Hart brothers begin to publish the *Deutsche Monatsblätter*, the first of the many literary journals associated with their names. This same year also saw the first German performance of Ibsen's social drama, *Pillars of Society*; and in the long run this was to be of greater significance for the development of the dramatic genre. It would, however, be wrong to assume a close connection between these two events, and regard this also as the beginning of Ibsen's breakthrough in Germany. It was some time before Ibsen came to be recognized by the German Naturalists as an ideological ally, and some time before they came to regard his dramas of social realism as their model. It is true that in certain quarters (with the Harts for instance) the drama was very soon recognized as the ultimate citadel, but in the early years the aspirations of the Naturalists found more ready expression in the form of criticism and theory, novel and lyric. Despite achieving fairly considerable public success with *Pillars of Society* and *A Doll's House* (which was known in Germany as *Nora*), Ibsen was, until 1887, a neglected dramatist, and the German Naturalists' great foreign model was Zola.

The ten or so years which preceded the real breakthrough of Ibsen (with *Ghosts* in 1887) and Gerhart Hauptmann (with *Vor Sonnenaufgang* in 1889) are a very confused decade. Ten years is probably too long a period for any but the smallest and tightest literary circle to preserve its identity, and the term Naturalism, in the context of German literature, describes a very loose coalition within which no single figure or group succeeded in securing a dominant position, not even the slightly older Hart brothers. It was only in the early years of the movement, when the principal task was a negative one, that there was any very wide degree of agreement between the factions which went to make up the coalition.

The first task was the overthrow of contemporary idols, and the Harts took this up with the zeal of pioneers, and some polemical skill. Soon they had the support of Otto Brahm, the most perceptive of the Naturalist critics, and the more strident chorus of Alberti, Bleibtreu, Conrad, and others. The achievement of these writers is mixed. With the exception of Brahm, their positive contribution to the future of German literature was insignificant. They undoubtedly contributed to, and expressed, a growth of confidence among the younger generation, and, in certain instances they cleared the ground of over-esteemed minor figures – this is especially true of the Hart brothers – but it is easy to be misled by the sound and fury of their polemic into regarding them as genuine revolutionaries or innovators. The view that since the eighteenth century German literature has alternated regularly between contrasting movements such as *Aufklärung* and *Sturm und Drang*, Classicism and Romanticism, is a misleading, but tenacious one; and the belief that Naturalism fits into such a pattern (at either end of its life) is in need of considerable qualification.

The period immediately preceding the Naturalist era, the decade following the proclamation of the Second German Empire (the *Gründerzeit*), is a period whose distinct character has, thanks in particular to the pioneering work of Jost Hermand, become more widely understood.[1] There is a certain unity underlying the work of such apparently diverse writers as Nietzsche, Meyer, Heyse, Storm, Anzengruber, Ernst von Wildenbruch, Carl Spitteler, Wilhelm Jordan, Felix Dahn, Hermann Lingg, Adolf Wilbrandt, Arthur Fitger, Albert Lindner, Franz Nissel, Georg Ebers, Heinrich Kruse, Julius Wolff, Ernst Eckstein, Heinrich Leuthold, Richard Voß, Wilhelm Jensen, Robert Hamerling, Eduard Grisebach, Graf Schack, and Martin Greif. Yet the preceding list consists of a curious mixture of writers who were singled out for special praise or special criticism by one or other of the pioneers of the German Naturalist ovement; it is therefore difficult to define German Naturalism in terms of its attitude to its predecessors. The fact that many of the writers named above wrote in a decidedly nationalistic manner, and that some of them were subsequently attacked by the self-styled revolutionaries of the next generation, has lent weight to the assumption that they represented a kind of literary establishment in this period. In many respects their work can indeed be seen to embody an attempt at self-legitimation by the new German *Reich*; but behind the great figures who stride through the dramas, epics, and *Novellen* of the *Gründerzeit* there lurks an ill concealed resentment of the political reality of Bismarck's state, and the place of the artist in it. In the face of an increasingly prosperous and increasingly materialistic bourgeoisie, the politically impotent artist finds self expression in wish-fulfilment, in the fanciful flight into a Utopia, in which the great creative individual grandly asserts himself, with a supreme unconcern for the resistance of social reality.

---

[1] Jost Hermand, 'Zur Literatur der Gründerzeit', *Deutsche Vierteljahrsschrift für Literaturwissenschaft und Geistesgeschichte*, 41 (1967), 204. See also Richard Hamann and Jost Hermand, *Epochen deutscher Kultur von 1870 bis zur Gegenwart*, 5 vols (Munich: Nymphenburger Verlagshandlung, 1971–73), I, *Gründerzeit* (1971).

The socialism and the socialist attitudes with which the German Naturalist movement was closely associated should not blind us to the fact that many of the seemingly incompatible views held by the preceding generation were not jettisoned by the Naturalists; among these were the belief that the artist belongs to an elite, an 'aristocracy of the spirit', and with this a certain distaste for political realities and political action. The socialism of the Naturalist writers is itself something which is not fully understood. In fact the Naturalists were never able to find a real home for their political aspirations, and they eventually withdrew from the political arena, muttering the same sort of slogans as the generation of writers they had once criticized.

There is in the literary memoirs of Heinrich Hart considerable evidence of sympathy for the kind of *Gründerzeit* attitudes outlined above. Heinrich Hart claims to have perceived an upsurge of optimism and idealism in German literature around 1870, which was, he says, soon replaced by disappointment, as economic and material interests were seen to be playing a predominant role in the politics of the age.[2] He describes the theatre of this period as particularly empty and imitative, particularly conscious of the box office; but in other fields of literature he notes the following 'outstanding' works: Wilhelm Jordan's *Nibelungen*, Robert Hamerling's *Ahasver in Rom*, and Paul Heyse's *Kinder der Welt*. The figure whom Heinrich Hart singles out for special criticism, both here and in the earlier *Kritische Waffengänge*, is the Berlin critic and dramatist, Paul Lindau, who remained the Naturalists' principal whipping-boy for some years. Gerhart Hauptmann writes of an encounter with Lindau in 1889 as follows:

Paul Lindau als Novellist, Dramatiker und auch Kritiker war damals wohl der, meistgenannte Name in Berlin und der einflußreichste unter den Schriftstellern. Bei uns Jungen – Gott mag wissen warum – war er zugleich der meistgehaßte. Er war, ich habe es später erfahren, durch und durch Liebenswürdigkeit. Er kam bei diesem Diner auf mich zu, schenkte mir laute und herzliche Worte, wünschte Hals- und Beinbruch für meine	Paul Lindau, the writer of Novellen, dramas and criticism, was at that time the most famous name in Berlin, and the most influential man of letters. Among us young men – God alone knows why – he was the most detested. He was, as I discovered later, a thoroughly charming person. He came up to me at this dinner, addressed me cordially, wished me the best of luck for the

---

[2] 'Literarische Erinnerungen. 1880–1905', *Gesammelte Werke*, edited by Julius Hart, 4 vols (Berlin: E. Fleischel, 1907), III, 27ff.

kommende Aufführung und sagte, er werde die Daumen halten. Wird man es glauben, daß ich, der junge Neuling, dem alten Herrn mit frostigem Hochmut antwortete und gleichsam wie einen begossenen Pudel fortschickte?[3]	coming performance, and said he would be keeping his fingers crossed. Is it credible that I, the young novice, answered the respected old man with chilly pride, and sent him away like a naughty schoolboy?

Along with writers like L'Arronge, Lubliner, and Blumenthal, Paul Lindau was the leading exponent of a kind of drama which dominated the Berlin theatres from about 1870 onwards; he was seen as the leader of a group of writers whose hold had to be broken before the younger generation could penetrate the theatre. The style these writers cultivated was a moderate social realism; they specialized in the 'well made play', the *pièce à thèse* in the manner of the French dramatists, Dumas *fils*, Augier, and Scribe, and the young Naturalists had no hesitation in appealing to nationalistic sentiments in their criticism of this foreign influence. The principal feature in the works of these writers was a tendentiousness which sought the causes of personal misery in social conditions and conventions. Lindau explained that in his play *Marion* he wanted to show

> how prevailing conditions alone are enough to bring about this tragedy, that the two decisive factors in human life, education and the way in which marrriage is entered into and the family established... lead inevitably to the weakening of the family and the moral and physical destruction of the individual.[4]

These works were, it would seem, intended to display that same belief in social determinism which is such a dominant factor in the Naturalists' own writings. What, then, were the young Naturalists' objections? If, for the moment, we overlook the fact that the Naturalists were by no means uniformly fervent in their adherence to a creed of scientific determinism – and Heinrich Hart, for one, praises Goethe for tempering the modernity of his outlook with 'germanic sensibility' – then there remain certain other significant differences between Lindau, Dumas, and the rest, on the one hand, and their Naturalist successors, on the other. The earlier dramatists are decidedly bourgeois

---

[3] 'Das zweite Vierteljahrhundert', *Die großen Beichten* (Frankfurt a.M.: Propyläen, 1966), p. 645.
[4] *Dramaturgische Blätter*, 2nd edition (Stuttgart and Leipzig: Simon, 1877), I, 209.

dramatists, and the restricted scope of their work seems to imply a conviction that bourgeois conventions and prejudices are indeed the most serious problems in human life. Furthermore, the authenticity of the moral purpose proclaimed by these writers is called into question by their evident reluctance to treat social problems which are less attractive, in a superficially theatrical sense, than that of the 'fallen woman'. Looking back in 1893, Julius Hart wrote:

aus den glänzenden Salons und parfümierten Boudoirs, in denen unsere Alten vor ein und zwei Jahrzehnten daheim waren, flüchtete die Kunst, wie von einem jähen Ekel ergriffen vor der tanzenden, lachenden und soupierenden Welt des 'ancien régime', um in den Hütten der Armen und Unterdrückten einzukehren.[5]	art fled from the elegant salons and perfumed boudoirs, in which our elders were at home ten or twenty years ago, as if seized with a violent disgust for the dancing, laughing, dining-and-wining world of the 'ancien régime', in order to enter the homes of the poor and the oppressed.

When faced as a critic with the working-class drama, *Vater Brahm*, by Heinrich Schaufert, Lindau concedes the gravity of the social problem being treated, but argues that such problems are not the concern of the dramatist. He is satisfied that the minds of the 'most distinguished international specialists' are being applied to the subject, and is content to leave it to them to find a solution. Such a play, he concludes, is only likely to encourage discontent, and increase class hatred.[6]

This desire to avoid material which might be politically or morally offensive to a theatre-going public in search of undemanding and undisturbing entertainment is an aesthetic principle for which the critic, Lindau, is severely taken to task by Julius Hart in the *Kritische Waffengänge*. Views like these, of course, made Lindau one of Zola's most hostile German critics in the 1880s; and because such views were widely shared by Lindau's generation, they gave rise to a running fight on the subject of art and morality which lasted throughout the Naturalist period.

When the Hart brothers left their native Westphalia to settle in Berlin in 1880, they immediately saw themselves in direct confrontation with Lindau; and among the Naturalists they remained the most consistent in their rejection of Lindau's type of drama. Others were less

---

[5] *Freie Bühne für modernes Leben*, 4 (1893), 593.
[6] *Dramaturgische Blätter*, I, 226–33.

doctrinaire; on occasion Otto Brahm was prepared to praise the skill with which such dramatists presented their theses, even if he happened to disagree with them; and one German exponent of the form, Richard Voß, was highly regarded by the Munich circle of Naturalists. The form itself was taken over with little modification by such Naturalist dramatists as Sudermann and Ludwig Fulda; and although Ibsen's social dramas are immeasurably more original and more powerful, a distinct formal debt to the French salon drama is still recognizable. In this context it is interesting to note that both Lindau and the social novelist, Friedrich Spielhagen (another writer severely criticized in the *Kritische Waffengänge*), were among the earliest German admirers of *Pillars of Society* and *A Doll's House*, at a time when Otto Brahm was still criticizing Ibsen for his tendentiousness, and the Harts' praises were directed towards the early Ibsen of *Brand* and *Peer Gynt*.[7] All of which serves to illustrate the point that there is a modest degree of continuity between the work of the Naturalists and one of the trends they were consciously seeking to displace; it is also a typical illustration of the confusion of the whole period.

After Berlin, the great literary centre of Imperial Germany was Munich, and here too the Naturalists made a bid for power under the leadership of Michael Georg Conrad. In 1885 Conrad founded the literary periodical, *Die Gesellschaft*, which remained the Naturalists' leading journal until the launching of the *Freie Bühne für modernes Leben* in Berlin in 1890. In the Munich of this time the dominant literary tone was still that which had been set by the *Münchener Dichterschule*, a circle of writers established under the patronage of Maximilian II, and led by Emanuel Geibel and (after his death) Paul Heyse. Munich was emphatically the home of the grand style in literature and the theatre, the historical drama and the historical epic being the genres especially favoured. In this context the historical drama, it should be noted, does not mean the drama of Hebbel, nor, on the other hand, does historical epic mean something resembling Freytag's *Bilder aus der deutschen Vergangenheit* or Riehl's *Die deutsche Arbeit*. Hebbel's historical dramas, particularly *Agnes Bernauer*, may be said to correspond to the historiography of the Hegel-Ranke school, in that they are concerned predominantly with the state, or the great individual as the embodiment of the state. The withdrawal of a disillusioned bourgeoisie from political activity in the years after 1848 was accompanied by a decline of interest in ideological history, and this is at least one probable reason for the neglect of Hebbel's work during his own lifetime. In the first instance

---

[7] Lindau, *Nur Erinnerungen*, 2 vols (Stuttgart and Berlin: Cotta, 1917–19), II, 317; Spielhagen, *Westermanns Monatshefte*, 49 (1881), 665.

ideological history was replaced by the 'non-political', cultural history, as the middle classes sought some consolation for political failure; in the words of Riehl: 'in the fifties the People [*Volk*] were a popular and favoured subject of study because the life of the State was so flat and wearisome and political discussion so futile. Consolation was sought in the People, so that hope for the State was not lost.'[8]

Romantic, conservative, and selective they may have been, but Freytag and Riehl were concerned to depict a definite social reality in fairly considerable detail. This is not true of the historical literature of the *Gründerzeit*; the great heroes do not face political dilemmas, and they are not placed in any real historical context; they strike the sublime attitude of truth to their own inner selves in a world chosen primarily for its spectacular quality.[9] Thus Lindau criticizes *Die Nibelungen* precisely because Hebbel's figures aspire to representative (i.e. political) grandeur, contrasting it unfavourably with Geibel's *Brunhild*, in which the historical-political dimension is submerged in a story of love and jealousy; and Heinrich Laube, the director of the Burgtheater, attributes Hebbel's failure to the lack of visual appeal in his dramas, for this was an age which liked to see its history presented as in the dynamic, colourful, and theatrical paintings of Karl von Piloty.[10]

The weakness of the *Gründerzeit* for the superficially decorative, for painters such as Piloty, Makart, and Kaulbach, was nowhere more evident than in the field of theatrical production. The Meiningen Court Theatre owed much of its enormous popularity to this weakness. It was a period which saw and encouraged rapid advances in the skills and techniques of theatrical decoration; much was imported into Germany from London's Princess Theatre, where Charles Kean had been the director. Theodor Fontane, who as theatre-critic of the *Vossische Zeitung* had visited the London theatres, wrote of the meticulous accuracy which was the dominant principle behind Kean's productions, suggesting in a mildly ironic fashion that accuracy in such matters is often less relevant than visual effect. At the Burgtheater Laube had been regarded as something of a Spartan in such matters; but his views on Hebbel make it clear that he did value the visual side of theatrical production, and he is said to have paid a great deal of attention to such things as the visual effect of groups of actors; nevertheless Laube had always stopped short of elaborate decorations, feeling that they could distract the audience

---

[8] Quoted from Fritz Martini, *Deutsche Literatur im bürgerlichen Realismus, 1848–1898*, 3rd edition (Stuttgart: Metzler, 1974), p. 450.

[9] Cf. Hermand on Conrad Ferdinand Meyer ('Zur Literatur der Gründerzeit', p. 219) and Martini on Paul Heyse (*Deutsche Literatur im bürgerlichen Realismus*, p. 222).

[10] See Heinrich Bulthaupt, *Dramaturgie des Schauspiels*, 4 vols (Oldenburg and Leipzig: A. Schwartz, 1897–1902), IV, *Ibsen, Wildenbruch, Sudermann, Hauptmann* (1901), p. 211.

from the words of the dramatist. In 1876, however, the Burgtheater was taken over by Franz von Dingelstedt, who, as director of the Munich Hoftheater, had been closely associated with the *Münchener Dichterschule*. With his arrival the decorative style took over in Vienna. In acting, as in production, the emphasis seems to have been on externals; Fontane wrote that Klara Ziegler 'acted Kaulbach'; and the theatre-historian, Max Martersteig, has described the Viennese actress, Charlotte Wolter, in similar terms, comparing her acting with that of another celebrated contemporary history painter, Hans von Makart.[11]

Once again it would be an oversimplification to pretend that the young Naturalists responded to this trend with outright rejection. On the one hand there is the *critic*, Karl Bleibtreu, who attacks in the most outspoken manner the historical school: 'Our healthy realistic age demands rigorous accuracy from the historical novel. The result of this is...that pseudo-poets try to exploit costume in order to cover up the deficiencies of their sham-poetry';[12] on the other hand there is the *dramatist*, Karl Bleibtreu, who cultivates the genre of the historical costume drama with undiminished enthusiasm in such plays as *Harold der Sachse, Ein Faust der Tat, Das Halsband der Königin*, and *Schicksal* (1888). Well into the 1880s the Berliners Otto Brahm and Arno Holz remained declared admirers of Heyse and Geibel respectively; whilst Gerhart Hauptmann was strongly influenced by Felix Dahn and Wilhelm Jordan, and his early drama, *Germanen und Römer*, was very much in their style. In *Vor Sonnenaufgang*, it will be recalled, Dahn's best-selling historical novel, *Ein Kampf um Rom* (1876) is recommended by Loth to Helene as more worthy of her attention than the work of Zola and Ibsen. There is even reason to believe that this had been Hauptmann's own view in the 1880s.[13] The subject matter of the historical drama of the early Naturalist period does, however, reflect a change of outlook. A renewed political interest, which was centred on class conflicts, makes the French Revolution (Bleibtreu's *Weltgericht* [1888]; Franz Held's *Ein Fest auf der Bastille* [1889]) and the Peasants' War (Conrad Alberti's *Brot*; Julius Brand's *Thomas Münzer*; and later Hauptmann's *Florian Geyer* [1896]) the most favoured topics. But motivation in these dramas still tends to arise from individual passions rather than social-historical circumstances.

---

[11] Theodor Fontane, 'Grillparzer, "Medea"', in *Werke, Schriften und Briefe*, edited by Walter Keitel and Helmuth Nürnberger, 20 vols (Munich: Hanser, 1962-94), Abt. II, *Aufsätze, Kritiken, Erinnerungen*, ii, *Theaterkritiken*, edited by Siegmar Gerndt (1969), p. 77; Max Martersteig, *Das deutsche Theater im neunzehnten Jahrhundert: Eine kulturgeschichtliche Darstellung*, 2nd edition (Leipzig: Breitkopf und Härtel, 1924), p. 512.

[12] *Revolution der Literatur*, edited by Johannes J. Braakenburg, Deutsche Texte, 23 (Tübingen: Niemeyer, 1973; reprint of 3rd edition, Leipzig: W. Friedrich, 1887), p. 22.

[13] See Frederick W.J. Heuser, 'Frühe Einflüsse auf Gerhart Hauptmann', *Gerhart Hauptmann* (Tübingen: Niemeyer, 1961), p. 16.

In Alberti's play the political conflict is subordinate to the romantic theme, the love of Thomas Münzer and Gerlind.

It is hardly necessary to emphasize that German unification and national pride at the outcome of the Franco-Prussian war tended to foster the creation of a national tradition, and so the cult of the historical drama. As I have already suggested, certain of the young Naturalists were not unaffected by such pride, among them Heinrich and Julius Hart, and the former did, in fact, write a drama entitled *Sedan*.[14] Their early agitations, which heralded the beginnings of the German Naturalist movement, were an open statement of their disappointment that the national revival seemed to lack a spiritual dimension; in their more pedestrian way they, like Nietzsche, lament the extinction of German spiritual life in favour of the German *Reich*.[15] It is, however, a strange accident of literary history that the Harts, and a number of German writers like them, should have come to be associated with a movement so cosmopolitan in character as Naturalism, for their nationalism is more than just skin-deep, more than just a stick with which to beat Paul Lindau and the epigones of the French salon-dramatists. The open letter addressed to Bismarck in the *Kritische Waffengänge* of 1882 declares that literature, like every other field of activity, must draw its strength from the national state in which it is based. Nationalist criteria are an important factor in their literary judgement, responsible for their praise of the work of Graf Adolf von Schack (remembered now only for his collection of paintings, housed in Munich's Schack-Galerie), and the dramas of Ernst von Wildenbruch – which many detached observers might regard as a symptom of precisely that spiritual decline of which Nietzsche complained. Nationalism is equally in evidence in the pronouncements of the Munich writers, Bleibtreu, Conradi, and Conrad, who frequently criticized the international repertoire of the *Freie Bühne*. Through one of its regular contributors, the anti-semitic Fritz Lienhardt, the periodical, *Die Gesellschaft*, is linked with the development of *Heimatkunst*; and Conrad, it appears, was one of the first to raise the subsequently notorious cry for a literature of 'blood and soil'.[16] Conrad Alberti, a prominent member of this circle and himself a Jew, not only argued in the pages of *Die Gesellschaft* for the complete assimilation of the Jews into the German nation, but conducted his argument in a particularly virulent anti-semitic tone.[17] We need not here concern

---

[14] *Sedan: Eine Tragödie* (Leipzig: O. Wigand, 1882).

[15] *Unzeitgemäße Betrachtungen*, I, *Werke*, Kritische Gesamtausgabe edited by Giorgio Colli und Mazzino Montinari, 30 vols (Berlin and New York: de Gruyter, 1967–78), III/i (1972), 155–56.

[16] See Hans Schwerte, 'Deutsche Literatur im wilhelminischen Zeitalter', *Wirkendes Wort*, 14 (1964), pp. 265f.

[17] 'Judentum und Anti-Semitismus', *Die Gesellschaft*, 5 (1889), 1719.

ourselves further with this particular tendency, except perhaps to remark that the movement we know as German Naturalism contains distinct elements of a romantic nationalist ideology which are barely compatible with the Enlightenment values and critical thinking normally associated with European Naturalism.[18] In this respect German Naturalism is decidedly untrue to the spirit of one of its masters, Emile Zola, who, because of his role in the Dreyfus affair, came to be regarded as the principal exponent of the Western European liberal-progressive tradition.[19]

Among the theatres which cultivated the historical-decorative style a very special place is occupied by the Meiningen Court Theatre; indeed, this theatre occupies a very special place in the development of the modern European theatre.[20] In 1866 Georg II von Sachsen-Meiningen, the 'theatre duke', came to power. He was a devotee of the historicist culture of his age; but at the same time he was a man of considerable artistic talent.[21] His overriding interest was with the theatre, and with the assistance of his wife (a former actress) and Ludwig Chronegk, a middle ranking actor from his company, he soon assumed personal responsibility for the running of the theatre of his own court. In the first instance it was the Duke's special contribution which won the company its reputation; it became renowned for the splendour and authenticity of its costume and decor. But the real importance of the Meiningen theatre lay in its use of all the fashionable paraphernalia to implement a radical reform in theatrical production. The Court Theatre of a small state could scarcely afford the services of the best-known star actors of the day, but this deficiency was turned to good account as it became necessary to look elsewhere than to individual talents for artistic and commercial success. The Meiningen team came to assume the function of the modern director, asserting its authority over the actors, designers, and all aspects of production so as to approach the drama as a coherent whole. Particular attention was paid to ensemble-playing

---

[18] See Theo Meyer, 'Einleitung', in *Theorie des Naturalismus*, edited by Theo Meyer (Stuttgart: Reclam 1973), p. 5. For an account of the seamless development of Johannes Schlaf from radical exponent of consistent naturalism to fellow-traveller of National-Socialism see Dieter Kafitz, *Johannes Schlaf – Weltanschauliche Totalität und Wirklichkeitsblindheit: Ein Beitrag zur Neubestimmung des Naturalismus-Begriffs und zur Herleitung totalitärer Denkformen*, Studien zur deutschen Literatur, 120 (Tübingen: Niemeyer, 1992). Kafitz argues that both Schlaf's naturalism and his subsequent ideological development have their source in a monistic world-view which also enjoyed wide currency among his contemporaries (p. 99).

[19] See Heinrich Mann, 'Zola', *Die weißen Blätter*, 2 (1915), 1312–82.

[20] See John Osborne, *The Meiningen Court Theatre, 1866–1890* (Cambridge: C.U.P, 1988).

[21] *Georg II. und der Historismus: Ein Kulturideal im Zweiten Deutschen Kaiserreich* (Exhibition catalogue, Staatliche Museen Meiningen, Schloß Elisabethenburg; [Meiningen], 1994).

and crowd-scenes, where professional actors were used instead of off-duty soldiers or other makeshift personnel. This is not to say that the company never employed first-rate actors – when on tour they would engage well-known performers like Ludwig Barnay or Emmerich Robert, and for a time the young Josef Kainz was a member of the company (although this was before he became famous) – but in general the successes of the Meiningen company were greater in those plays or scenes where stage-direction could conceal or compensate for the performers' inadequacies.

The repertoire of the company bears out this impression. Among their most popular productions were *Julius Caesar* and *A Winter's Tale*; Schiller's plays, especially *Die Jungfrau von Orléans* and *Wilhelm Tell*, figured prominently; and the company did a great deal to popularize the work of Kleist with their productions of *Das Käthchen von Heilbronn* and the then little performed *Die Hermannsschlacht*, and *Prinz Friedrich von Homburg*. As even this cursory glance indicates, the Meiningen Court Theatre was a company whose importance lies in the field of theatre history rather than the history of literature. They introduced very few new works to the public (though among those they did introduce were Ibsen's *The Pretenders* and *Ghosts*), but concentrated on the serious, classical drama, at a time when the public theatre was given over to rather more frivolous fare. They owe their importance to the manner of their presentation and the scope of their influence rather than the plays they produced.

This influence was very largely won by the tours which the company undertook between 1874 and 1890, which took them as far afield as London, Moscow, Brussels, and Copenhagen, as well as to many German and Austrian cities. In the 1880s their style was recognized to be having considerable influence on the theatres of Berlin, especially L'Arronge's new *Deutsches Theater*.[22] In Vienna, where Dingelstedt had already introduced the more superficial and spectacular elements of the style, the company had less impact, and this may be one reason why Naturalism was slow to overcome the resistance of the Austrian capital. Of much greater moment was the long-term influence of the Meiningen theatre on Antoine in France, Stanislavsky in Russia, and, in the German theatre, Otto Brahm. These three men, the great Naturalist directors, are the direct heirs of the authoritarian Chronegk, but they were committed to a literary tendency in a way he was not. As Naturalists they carried to its logical conclusion a process of which their predecessor – if his

---

[22] Otto Brahm, *Kritische Schriften*, edited by Paul Schlenther, 2 vols (Berlin: S. Fischer, 1913–15), I, 40. For a full account of the reception of the Meiningen company see *Die Meininger: Texte zur Rezeption*, edited by John Osborne (Tübingen: Niemeyer, 1980).

repertoire is anything to go by – had only a dim awareness. They applied his style to new subject matter in such a way as to show that the day of the great star-performer, the great individual, was past. In the Naturalist drama the hero is no longer an eloquent, articulate figure, capable of comprehending his own destiny, and standing out against an aesthetically appropriate backcloth; he is subordinate to external forces beyond his control, and most evidently to the milieu represented in the stage-set. The Naturalists went further than the Meiningen company in the representation of relationships between setting and action, basing their practice on contemporary theories of determinism which played little part in the project of Duke Georg II.

The belief in determinism is widely and, I believe, correctly regarded as one of the key features of Naturalist theory; it is a conviction which grew very rapidly in the latter part of the nineteenth century. One field in which this growth can readily be traced is the field of historiography. Hegel can be seen as standing at the turning-point between an idealist view of history which saw an idea behind historical phenomena and actions, and a materialist view, which tended to explain historical change by external reasons, ideas by circumstances. I have already spoken briefly of the development of cultural history, in the first place by ideologically conservative writers such as Freytag and Riehl in the period after 1848. The methods of such historians could readily be carried into other territories; and though, with few exceptions, literature held out for a while, there arose rapidly a school of historians who began to concentrate on the investigation of material causation. Marx's influence made economics a particularly important field of study, and in the 1870s Roscher, Schmoller, and Inama-Sternegg wrote and lectured on the economic history of Germany. In a wider European context the positivism of Taine, Comte, and Buckle assumed even greater importance.

The advance of cultural history did not proceed without any resistance; there was, for instance, the Gothein-Schäfer controversy of 1888–91; and Karl Lamprecht's *Deutsche Geschichte* (1891) met with some severe criticism.[23] On the whole, though, the study of history seems to have passed more smoothly through this period; the historians seem to have been more progressive and tolerant of new ideas than many of the literary historians and critics.

The treatment of the revolt of the Silesian weavers in 1844 provides an interesting parallel case. Hauptmann's *Die Weber*, completed in 1892, split the literary world into two camps, progressives and reactionaries; the play was not released for unhindered public performance until

---

[23] See George P. Gooch, *History and Historians in the 19th Century*, 2nd edition (London: Longmans and Green, 1920), pp. 586–93.

after the turn of the century. Yet this same weavers' revolt had for some time been a respectable subject of historical investigation: in 1873 Gustav Schmoller had written a study of the weaving industry which covered it; and in 1885 a pupil of Schmoller, Alfred Zimmermann, published his study of the same subject, *Blüthe und Verfall des Leinengewerbes in Schlesien*, from which Hauptmann drew extensively in writing his play. Moreover both historians are distinctly less equivocal than Hauptmann about the apportionment of blame: Schmoller expresses the view:

> that the crisis was much more serious and severe than it need have been, that it was not brought about solely by irresistible forces, and that, if there can be any question of guilt, this does not reside with the individual weaver, but is to be sought in those higher circles where there were people better placed than the weavers to see the true situation;

and Zimmermann quite explicitly attributes the revolt to conditions rather than people:

> The unreasonableness of the manufacturers, together with the rapidly rising cost of food, had caused a great deal of bad feeling in the Reichenbach area.... Industrial progress... had brought along with it the evils of mass industry, particularly since there was no factory act to impose restraint on the capitalists.[24]

Both these accounts and Hauptmann's play make an interesting contrast with the reports which had appeared in the *Vossische Zeitung* of 1844. Here the weavers' revolt was attributed to such things as hatred, the desire for vengeance, the effects of alcohol, the stubborn insolence of the Langenbielau workers, and discontent caused by agitators; the report dated June 10 asserts: 'As far as anyone can see, there is no deeper basis for these disturbances.'

The comparison between a professional social historian of 1885 and a conservative journalist of 1844 exaggerates the change of outlook which took place in the intervening years, but change there undoubtedly was. Where the two sides are not simply indulging in empty abuse, these changes are what the controversy surrounding the emergence of Naturalism is about. The younger generation of writers begins to display a scepticism about the accuracy of the picture of reality presented by its elders in their literary work. The older, idealist generation continues,

---

[24] Gustav Schmoller, 'Die Entwicklung und die Krisis der deutschen Weberei im 19. Jahrhundert', *Deutsche Zeit- und Streitfragen*, II (Berlin, 1873), p. 32. Alfred Zimmermann, *Blüthe und Verfall des Leinengewerbes in Schlesien* (Breslau: Korn, 1885), p. 350.

for its part, to reject the principles of the new positivist thought, protesting that it takes insufficient account of the freedom of the will, treating Man as if he were on the same level as animals and demands that such a pessimistic view of life should be excluded from the field of art. Johannes Volkelt, a generally tolerant academic critic, insists that the primary purpose of art is the manifold and exhaustive representation of that which is of human significance, and he goes on to specify that it should not therefore merely demonstrate material causation.[25] The younger generation protests that this kind of selectivity excludes whole areas of life where such causation is believed to be of major importance; and not surprisingly these, the areas which contain the great social problems of the day, are the areas which most interest the Naturalist writers. Bleibtreu voices the typical protest: 'It is as if the dreadful social problems of the present did not exist for German writers.'[26]

One of the first tasks of the Naturalist theorists, then, was to overcome prejudices against certain types of material. The aesthetic and moral objections raised by the various critics of Naturalism are countered time and again with an appeal to 'Truth'; sometimes with an appeal to the proposition that no material is intrinsically unpoetic; and occasionally a writer will go further than this, and defend an author's right to be gratuitously provocative:

Beleidigt Zola in seinen Romanen unser angeborenes Anstandsgefühl, auch dort, wo es die Dichtung nicht verlangt, aus bloßem Mutwillen, so kann ich ihn für einen ungehobelten, ungebildeten Menschen halten und für was sonst noch, aber seine dichterische Bedeutung schmälert das in keiner Weise, der dichterische Wert des Romans wird dadurch in nichts gedruckt.[27]	If, in his novels, Zola offends our innate sense of decency, even when it is not artistically necessary, out of sheer wantonness, then I can consider him a coarse and uncultured man, and much else besides – but it does not lessen his aesthetic importance by one jot, the aesthetic merit of the novel is in no way reduced.

This pronounced emphasis on the subject-matter of the work of art is typical of early Naturalist theory – just as a certain sensationalism

---

[25] *Ästhetische Zeitfragen* (Munich: Beck, 1895), pp. 15f.
[26] *Revolution der Literatur*, p. 12.
[27] 'Für und gegen Zola', *Kritische Waffengänge*, 2 (1882), pp. 35, 47.

in the choice of material is typical of the practice – but it is not really typical of the Harts, who were in no sense and at no time radical representatives of the newer literary trends. They still consciously preserve a residue of the idealist tradition, and will not see it replaced by scientific rationalism:

Wir müssen wieder anknüpfen an den jungen Goethe, den Schöpfer des Goethe, Werther und Faust, denn da ist nicht nur Wahrheit wie bei Zola, da ist poesiegetränkte Wahrheit. Nur dann wird unsere Poesie die rechte Mitte finden zwischen erdfrlschem Realismus und hoher Idealität, zwischen kosmopolitischer Humanität und selbstbewußtem Nationalismus... nur dann wird sie das Höchste erreichen, nämlich aus dem vollen Born der Gegenwart schöpfend ursprüngliche, individuell gefärbte Natur zum Ideal verklären.[28]	We must look back again to the young Goethe, the creator of *Werther* and *Faust*, for there one finds not only truth, as in Zola, but truth imbued with poetry. Only then will our literature find the middle way between fresh, earthbound realism and high idealism, between cosmopolitan humanity and self-assured nationalism... only then will it reach the summit of artistic achievement and, drawing from the source of the present, transfigure original, individual nature to an ideal.

In the later years of Naturalism Heinrich and Julius Hart still remain true to their 'idealistic realism', dissociating themselves from what they regarded as the extreme theories of Arno Holz, and the rigid policy of Otto Brahm at the Deutsches Theater. In the 1890s they enthusiastically embraced the new 'subjectivism' or 'impressionism' practised by such writers as Dehmel, Bierbaum, Liliencron, Arne Garborg, and Przybyszewski:

In diesem Kreise regten sich zuerst oder doch wenigstens am stärksten und nachhaltigsten jene Stimmungen, welche über die Epoche des Naturalismus, Pessimismus und Sozialismus hinausstrebten. Man hatte sie satt, übersatt, die graue Nüchternheit der Elendsliteratur,	It was in this circle that there were the first, or at least the most powerful and enduring stirrings of the desire to overcome the epoch of naturalism, pessimism, and socialism. They had had enough, more than enough, of the drab solemnity of the

---

[28] 'Für und gegen Zola', pp. 54f.

die engbrüstige Moral der Massenprediger, den herrschenden Rationalismus und die herrschende Politisiererei.²⁹	literature of misery, the narrow moralizing of the mass preachers, the dominance of rationalism and the dominance of politics.

The cautious and basically conservative attitude of the *Kritische Waffengänge* is widely shared in the early 1880s. In 1882 Brahm expresses much the same reservations about the inter-relationship of science and literature and, far from proclaiming a rigid and doctrinaire Naturalism, he rather timidly advances the work of Gottfried Keller as a model for the writers of the future:

Die Vereinigung dieser beiden Elemente, des Realistischen und des Phantastischen, macht den hervorstechenden Zug in Kellers Wesen aus. Hier liegt der Weg, welchen die Dichtung der Zukunft wird beschreiten müssen, wenn sie sich nicht einseitig bescheiden will entweder auf das spezifisch 'Poetische' zu verzichten, oder auf die Gestaltung des spezifisch 'Modernen'.³⁰	The combination of these two elements, the realistic and the fantastic, constitutes Keller's most prominent characteristic. This is the way that the literature of the future will have to go if it is not to make a one-sided renunciation of the specifically 'poetic' or of the specifically 'modern'.

The common concern among the more thoughtful representatives of the pro- and anti-Naturalist camps (among whom Brahm, Volkelt, and Heinrich Hart must be included) is the problem of art in an increasingly scientific climate, and the question of whether it can be preserved both as art and as a vehicle of truth. As confidence in biological, psychological, and sociological diagnoses increases, as the scientist becomes surer of his ability to discover the laws of the universe, the artist feels called upon to justify his imaginative creation, to ask himself the sort of questions Schiller (for instance) was asking himself a century earlier, and in a similar climate of scientific and philosophical discovery: 'What meaning can literature still have for the modern world?'[31] The answer which was most usually offered by the Naturalists was that, in order to continue to be a meaningful activity, literature would have to

---

[29] 'Literarische Erinnerungen', *Ges. Werke*, III, 92.
[30] 'Gotttried Keller', *Kritische Schriften*, II, 140.
[31] The title of an article by Wolfgang Kirchbach, *Litterarische Volkshefte*, 6 (1888), 14–44.

assimilate the techniques of the sciences. Such a view is incorporated in many of the programmatic writings of this period; thus in the introduction to his *Die naturwissenschaftlichen Grundlagen der Poesie* (1887) Wilhelm Bölsche characteristically asserts: 'what I hope to see in the work of the rising generation of writers is the skilful application of improved knowledge in the field of psychology, more precise observation, and healthier sensibility; the basis for this resides in the natural sciences'. Nevertheless the discussion which surrounds this issue deserves a closer scrutiny, for it tells us a good deal about the uncertainties of the German Naturalists, and the conflict between their theoretical confidence in science and their more traditional beliefs.

The basis to the discussion about the relationship of literature and science, as indeed the Naturalist answer to the problem, is provided by Zola, in *Le Roman expérimental*. Now the simplified view that German resistance to Zola came only from the older generation is a mistaken one, for many of the younger writers had immense difficulty in coming to terms with his works and theories. In the essay 'Für und gegen Zola' Heinrich Hart is inclined to explain away the heavy scientific emphasis in Zola's theory as a reaction against the excesses of French Romanticism; this analysis is quite erroneous, for while Zola did reject Romanticism, he also praised the movement for its contribution to artistic freedom, and so for its contribution to the development of Naturalism; for him the romantic drama represented a first step towards the drama of Naturalism.[32] Heinrich Hart goes on to argue somewhat implausibly that the German literary tradition (and presumably German Romanticism) would not have called forth in Zola a reaction so violent, that it is likely to exclude the spiritual dimension from literature altogether:

Geschichtlich ist die Entstehung des französishen Naturalismus leicht erfaßlich, er ist aus dem bewußten Widerstreben gegen die Romantik, gegen die Unwahrheit und den Schwulst der Viktor Hugo, Dumas, Sue, hervorgegangen, aber die Reaktion ist so stark, daß die Literatur in Gefahr steht, unmittelbar in das entgegengesetzte System geworfen zu werden und auf diese Weise	Historically the development of French Naturalism is easy to understand. It arose from the conscious reaction against Romanticism, against the lies and the bombast of Victor Hugo, Dumas, Sue; but the reaction has been so violent that literature is in danger of falling directly into the opposite extreme of telling new lies and, in

---

[32] *Le Naturalisme au théâtre*, *Les OEuvres complètes*, texte de l'édition Eugène Fasquelle, 50 vols (Paris: Bernouard, 1927–29), XLII, 15.

wiederum neue Lügen und statt des Schwulstes Flachheit zu gebären.	place of bombast, producing dullness.

Heinrich Hart attacks Zola's theory of the experimental novel – which is at best a metaphor, at worst a polemic over-statement – with a curious literal-mindedness. Not without a certain *Schadenfreude*, he invokes the authority of none other than Claude Bernard (whose *Introduction a l'étude de la médecine expérimentale* had prompted *Le Roman expérimental*) to support his view that an experimental novel is an impossibility: 'In art and literature personality is dominant. A work of art is a spontaneous spiritual creation and that has nothing to do with the verification of natural phenomena, in which we can have no creative role.' He argues *both* that the novel can never be an experiment in the scientific sense, *and* that such novels are, in any case, undesirable: 'Science seeks to abstract the general from the particular and express it in concepts; the novel, and, no less, literature on the whole, attempts to represent the general in the particular, and to incorporate it in forms.'[33]

In all this Heinrich Hart does not differ radically from the more traditional critic, Karl Hillebrand (the father of the Naturalist writer, Julius Brand). Writing on the subject of the new, scientific novel in the *Deutsche Rundschau* (1884) Hillebrand declares that whereas science seeks causal relationships, ignores individuality in order to discover the operation of general laws, art tries to reproduce life in its individuality, eliminates the abstract generality in order to understand better the particular, and eliminates chance in order to grasp the essential.[34]

Heinrich Hart's own appreciation of the traditions of French and German literature may appear limited, but he is right to insist that the theoretical views of any writer should be seen against the background of the formative tradition from which he comes. The similarity between the views of Heinrich Hart and Hillebrand is not accidental; it is the product of a literary tradition which, a generation earlier, had borne fruit in Otto Ludwig's theory of 'Poetic Realism', a form of art midway between Naturalism and Idealism, which was to recreate the world by purging it of irrelevance and making its essential unity more visible than in the real world; a kind of art which is not yet fantastic, but which owes more to the creative imagination than to observation and reason.[35] Like Ludwig – and of course Schiller – Heinrich Hart and

---

[33] *Kritische Waffengänge*, 2, pp. 51–3.
[34] 'Vom alten und vom neuen Roman', *Deutsche Rundschau*, 38 (1884), 425.
[35] Otto Ludwig, 'Poetischer Realismus', in *Gesammelte Werke*, edited by Adolf Stern and Erich Schmidt (Leipzig: Grunow, 1891), V, 458. It is interesting to note that Otto Brahm claimed to recognize in Ludwig a German forerunner of Zola; see Sigfrid Hoefert, 'Emile Zola dans la critique d'Otto Brahm', *Les Cahiers naturalistes*, 30 (1965), 150.

Hillebrand share the prejudice that Naturalism (and perhaps even Nature itself) is essentially base, and needs desperately to be refined by the artistic imagination.

Both these critics assert that there is a discrepancy between Zola's theory and practice, indeed that there must *a priori* be this discrepancy; nevertheless they do criticize parts of Zola's work as if there were no discrepancy, and it really were scientific. Where they do speak of a discrepancy, they do not go further and illuminate this with any appreciation of Zola's creative personality. Among Zola's more receptive German critics there is, however, an increasing tendency to recognize, as Henry James did, that Zola 'reasons less powerfully than he represents';[36] they begin to see in him a strong imaginative personality, and to admire him for this (though without always clearly saying so).[37] That is to say Zola's German followers come to adopt a view – 'a work of art is a personality, an individuality' – that is as much a part of Zola's personal conviction as his more famous Naturalist doctrine of a work of art as a corner of nature, but which, in a flush of enthusiasm for science, he rather played down in his reflections on the experimental novel.[38] One of the reasons for this inconsistency in Zola's theory lies in his very personality: his enormous reserves of creative energy, which consistently well up in descriptive spectacle throughout his novels, unchecked by the inhibitions of a critical intellect, and which lend to his descriptions a vitality which puts them beyond reach of the well-known criticism of Lukács.[39] As Thomas Mann recognised, some of these personal qualities were shared by the man who worked most energetically as his German proselyte, Michael Georg Conrad.[40] In his newly-founded *Die Gesellschaft*, Conrad defended Zola's theory of the experimental novel, but the tone in which he wrote of Zola effectively converts the theoretical ideal of scientific objectivity into the moral quality of fearless personal integrity:

Zola ist die personifizierte Aufrichtigkeit, der Freimut à outrance. Nicht zufrieden mit	Zola is integrity personified, he represents the extreme of outspokenness. Not

---

[36] Henry James, 'The Art of Fiction' (1884), in *Partial Portraits* (London: Macmillan, 1919), p. 397.
[37] See Winthrop H. Root, *German Criticism of Zola, 1875–1893* (New York: Columbia U.P., 1931).
[38] See F. Doucet, *L'esthétique de Zola et son application à la critique* (Paris: Nizet, 1930), p. 91.
[39] See the essay 'Zum hundertsten Geburtstag Zolas' in 'Balzac und der französische Realismus' in Georg Lukács, *Werke*, edited by Franz Benseler (Neuwied and Berlin: Luchterhand, 1964–), VI, *Probleme des Realismus III* (1965), 510–21.
[40] Thomas Mann, 'Dem Andenken Michael Georg Conrads' (1930) in *Rede und Antwort, Gesammelte Werke in Einzelbänden, Frankfurter Ausgabe*, edited by Peter de Mendelssohn (Frankfurt a.M.: S. Fischer, 1984), pp. 567–69.

den tausend Schwierigkeiten	content with the thousand
der delikatesten sachlichen	difficulties of the most
Probleme, tritt sein	delicate technical problems,
ungestümer Reformdrang	his violent desire for reform
auch an die empfindlichsten	also leads he him to tackle
Personalfragen heran.	the most sensitive personal
Er kennt nur ein Heiliges	problems. He recognizes
und Unverletzliches: die	only one thing as sacred
Wahrheit.[41]	and inviolable: the truth.

In 1886 Georg Brandes, the Danish critic (a figure who exerted an immense influence on the development of German literature at the end of the nineteenth century), published in the *Deutsche Rundschau* an important essay in which he intelligently clarified the position of those who admired the personal rather than the scientific elements in Zola's works. Unlike Heinrich Hart, Brandes did not claim to perceive a discrepancy between theory and practice, but seized on the word 'temperament' in Zola's famous definition of the work of art: 'un coin de la nature vu à travers un tempérament', and made this, the personal contribution of the individual creative artist, the focus of critical attention. His analysis of Zola's writings leads to the first diagnosis of Zola's 'romantic' temperament; Brandes draws attention to the French novelist's love of the epic, the grandiose, the monumental, his simplification of characters to make them representatives of various social groups, his use of symbols, his taste for personification. The idea of Zola, the Naturalist, as an impersonal, scientific, objective observer and recorder of external reality, hindered in his aims only by a minimal 'temperament', is seriously undermined:

Die Frage ist... ob nicht das, was	The question is... whether
jetzt Temperament genannt wird,	that which is now called
ganz wie das, was vorher der	temperament, just like
Geschmack, spater die Phantasie	what was once called
genannt wurde, läutert und	taste, later imagination,
beschneidet, vergrößert und	does not refine and
verschönert?... Die Antwort muß	condense, magnify and
lauten: daß auch nicht der	beautify?... The answer must
Naturalismus jener Umbildung	be that Naturalism too
der Wirklichkeit entgehen	cannot avoid that
kann, die sich aus dem Wesen	re-shaping of reality which is
der Kunst ergibt.[42]	an essential feature of art.

---

[41] 'Zola und Daudet', *Die Gesellschaft*, 1 (1885), 747f.
[42] 'Emil Zola', *Deutsche Rundschau*, 54 (1888), 30.

The consequence of this change of emphasis was to hasten the transformation of what had been generally (and sometimes distrustfully) regarded as a stringently realist credo into a sanction for the completely subjective interpretation of nature. A subsequent chapter will show how this transformation is mirrored in the theoretical writings of Arno Holz, which date from the time when German Naturalism was beginning to stress observation less, and individual imagination very much more. While this transformation was not of course confined to the German literary scene – in France it was to lead to the radical interiority of some of the great writers of early modernism[43] – it was particularly welcome in Germany as a continuation of the literary tradition which set a higher value on inwardness than social observation. Whereas in other European countries this new emphasis on the imagination was a post-Naturalist trend, in Germany, it is especially important to note, the Naturalist movement did not really get under way as a creative literary movement, did not begin to produce works of literature that are in the slightest degree memorable, until after the theoretical insistence on the observed realities of the social world had been somewhat diluted. In Germany even Naturalism, far from being stricter than elsewhere, displays that tendency to dissociation from the social world which has been shown to be a recurrent characteristic in the literature of that country.[44]

To reach a full understanding of German Naturalism it is essential to realize that the ambiguities and contradictions of the movement cannot conveniently be reduced to the inevitable discrepancy between impossibly rigorous theoretical demands and the limitations of any artistic medium, between 'Nature' and 'Art', but that the ambiguities represent a genuine reluctance to embrace fully certain new views even though these were found intellectually attractive. One of the characteristics of the German Naturalist movement which is least widely appreciated is that this dilemma is resolved in the way which might be felt to have been, in the then prevailing circumstances, the less likely way: it was resolved in favour of the artist rather than the scientist. Even Bölsche's *Die naturwissenschaftlichen Grundlagen der Poesie*, which was expressly presented as an apology for the scientific approach in art, leaves an opening for an artistic resolution. In a way which distantly recalls Nietzsche's admiration of the strong and healthy, his replacement of a transcendental deity with the concept of the Superman, Bölsche proclaims a new object for essentially imaginative idealization

---

[43] *See* Proust, *A la recherche du temps perdu*, IV, *Le Côté de Guermantes*, ii (Paris: Nouvelle revue française, 1920), 20. Cf. René König, *Die naturalistische Ästhetik in Frankreich und ihre Auflösung* (Borna and Leipzig: Noske, 1931), pp. 189f.
[44] See J. P. Stern, *Re-interpretations* (London: Thames and Hudson, 1964).

(which was soon to find a champion in Hauptmann's character Alfred Loth):

Wir haben gebrochen mit der Metaphysik...das Ideal geben wir doch nicht auf. Wenn es nicht mehr der Abglanz des Göttlichen sein darf, so ist ihm darum nicht benommen, die Blüte des Irdischen zu sein, die tiefste, reinste Summe, die der Mensch ziehen kann aus allem, was er sieht.... Wenn er den Blick schweifen läßt über diese ganze Erde, über sein ganzes Geisterreich, sieht er im Grunde all' dieser wechselnden Formen ein einziges großes Prinzip, nach dem alles strebt, alles ringt: das gesicherte Gleichmaß, die fest in beiden Schaalen schwebende Wage, den Zustand des Normalen, die Gesundheit.	We have broken with metaphysics...but we are not renouncing ideals. If our ideal may no longer be the reflection of the divine, then there is no reason why it should not be the fullness of the earthly, the purest and profoundest sum of all that man can see.... When he casts his eyes over this whole earth, over his entire spiritual realm, he sees at the root of all these changing forms one single great principle, which all is striving to secure: equilibrium, the exactly balanced scales, the state of normality, health.

While this new 'realist ideal' may not be created by the imagination of the artist, the artist has nevertheless the special function of bringing it into the open.[45] Wolfgang Kirchbach's reflections on the same theme lead to a similar conclusion, in which a religious or metaphysical need is more clearly accepted: the purpose of literature, according to this argument, is to endow an apparently mechanical and senseless world with value and beauty, and so counteract the contemporary tendency to cynicism and nihilism.[46]

We shall encounter this same attitude in Gerhart Hauptmann's *Das Friedensfest*, in which an old-fashioned idealist (and an artist), Wilhelm Scholz, is favourably contrasted with a cynical, modern intellectual, his brother, Robert; and in the drama, *Marianne*, by Carl Hauptmann (a pupil and friend of the biologist, Ernst Haeckel, and a writer deeply involved in the scientific and religious discussions of the day). In this play of 1894 the romanticism, which was only implicit in the theoretical works to which I have referred, becomes explicit; *Marianne* dwells very much on the distinction between the artist, with his sense of wonder and

---

[45] *Die naturwissenschaftlichen Grundlagen der Poesie* (Leipzig: Reißner), 1887, pp. 69, 73.
[46] 'Was kann die Dichtung für die moderne Welt noch bedeuten?', pp. 31–32.

the philistine, and on the duty of the gifted individual to cultivate his own imaginative potentiality regardless of others; such special-pleading is a common feature of the literature of this period.

Up to about 1887, and notwithstanding the reservations I have already made, Zola was undoubtedly the writer who exerted the most powerful influence on the German Naturalists. Among the most obvious consequences of this was a concentration on the novel rather than the drama; this trend was also helped by the tolerance of publishers like W. Friedrich of Leipzig (the theatre-directors offered much greater resistance). These years were therefore one of the few periods in German literature when the urban novel was among the most favoured genres – although the specifically Naturalist examples are rather undistinguished: Conrad's cycle, *Was die Isar rauscht*, (1888) Max Kretzer's *Die Betrogenen* (1882) and *Die Verkommenen*, Alberti's *Riesen und Zwerge*, Bleibtreu's *Größenwahn* (1888). But in Berlin things had been happening which were soon to change all this. A power-base was gradually being established, and in Ibsen a champion had been found who was to lead Naturalism into the theatre.

2
NATURALISM AND THE THEATRE: FROM HEINRICH HART TO OTTO BRAHM

The early period of German Naturalism was not rich in positive suggestions as to how the literature of the day should be revolutionised. There is a widespread awareness that an older reality has been called in question, and that old forms are therefore no longer viable; but there is very little agreement about how the new reality is to be handled. The emphasis placed on the contribution of the creative artist, for instance, is constantly being revised. From the theoretical writings of the time it is quite impossible to abstract a picture of the Naturalist drama about which there is any degree of conformity. Two important principles of dramaturgy did meet with substantial approval both of them anti-Aristotelian: the elevation of characterisation over action, and rejection of the doctrine of generic purity leading to a breaking-down of the distinction between the epic and dramatic genres; but even these did not pass entirely without contradiction. It is typical of this period of transition and its opposition to aesthetic rules that two attempts to formulate a literary credo, Eugen Wolff's 'Zehn Thesen' and Conrad Alberti's 'Die zwölf Artikel des Realismus', failed to attract a single endorsement other than that of their respective authors.[1]

Programmatic tracts of such a general nature are not among the most important or the most influential of the Naturalists' theoretical writings. By the time these two manifestoes had appeared the works of Ibsen were being performed in the theatres of Berlin, and the example of a successful practising dramatist was far more influential in determining the pattern to be followed by the new drama. The most important items in the mass of critical and theoretical works produced by the German Naturalists are those which are most directly concerned with specific topical issues, such as Otto Brahm's Ibsen-essay of 1886, which did so much to determine the Naturalists' view of Ibsen, and Heinrich Hart's essay in the *Kritische Waffengänge* of 1882, 'Das Deutsche Theater des Herrn L'Arronge', which outlined for the theatre of the age a policy which was actually put into practice, and whose fulfilment is one of the great achievements of the Naturalist movement in Germany.

---

[1] Wolff, *Deutsche Universitätszeitung*, 1 (1888), 1; Alberti, *Die Gesellschaft*, 5 (1889), 2–9.

On the strength of this essay and the Zola-essay discussed in the previous chapter, Heinrich Hart must be considered among the more important theorists of the German Naturalist movement. Like the Zola-essay, this particular work shares the moderately conservative attitude of the rest of the *Kritische Waffengänge*. There are no demands for literary revolution, but for 'idealised Realism'. Indeed the drama is singled out as the highest literary form in words which could almost have been written by Schiller in his most resolutely idealist mood: 'The theatre gives us access... to the pure world of ideas, free of trivialities and restrictions; it shows us Man in his essence, in the full range of his deeds and actions'.[2] Here the drama is valued for what has widely been regarded as the quality which distinguishes it in its Aristotelian form from the epic and lyric genres: its suitability for the creation of a complete, enclosed world, in which the part represents the whole by standing symbolically for it. This is an example of that same idealist tendency which lies behind the coolness of the Hart brothers towards the more radical scientific Naturalism proclaimed by many of their contemporaries. It also explains why they virtually disowned the later achievements of Otto Brahm in the staging of social drama, although he appears to have fulfilled so much of the programme outlined by Heinrich Hart in 1882. Heinrich Hart did, in fact, anticipate this and opposed the appointment of Brahm as the first director of the *Freie Bühne* in 1889, arguing that he was not enough of an idealist.[3]

In the first place, however, Brahm, the Harts, and the bulk of their contemporaries were agreed that the literature and, more especially, the theatre of the day were inadequate and trivial. They were agreed that the function of the theatre should be serious, even, in the broadest sense, didactic; it should be used to cultivate the spiritual qualities and the taste of the nation, and so to contribute to a revival of national greatness.[4] The theatre should not be simply a place of entertainment, nor should it be a place of moral instruction. (Once again Heinrich Hart makes clear his reservations about the *pièce à thèse*; although his distinction between a work with a moral purpose, which he condemns, and a work with a moral effect, which he does not, is not a very helpful one.) Broadly speaking then, Heinrich Hart subscribes to that view of the work of art which we began to explore in the previous chapter: he regards it as the product of a higher perception and spiritual application, because of which the artist has the privilege of observing and lending expression to the whole of life, free from moral or aesthetic

---

[2] *Kritische Waffengänge*, 4 (1882), 20.
[3] 'Literarische Erinnerungen', *Ges. Werke*, edited by Julius Hart, 4 vols (Berlin: Fleischel, 1907), III, 71.
[4] *Kritische Waffengänge*, 4 (1882), 6.

limitations; but at the same time the artist has a duty to extend the consciousness and self awareness of his fellow men.[5]

Consequently the most important factor in judging the work of a theatre is, in Heinrich Hart's view, its repertoire. While accepting the need for a strong classic and foreign element – he mentions Shakespeare, Calderon, Lessing, Schiller, Goethe, and the newly popular Kleist – his interest is clearly in the development of the contemporary German drama. He is not enthusiastic about the historical drama, and insists that the past can only have a role in as far as it is still meaningful to the present – an insistence reflected in plays such as Hauptmann's *Florian Geyer* and in Bleibtreu's privileging of the period since the French Revolution.[6] The theatre must treat specifically modern problems and ideas if it is to become a popular national institution, a *Volksbühne*, which stands in a living relationship to the entire nation and which unites all sections of the community; it should be democratic in character; it should not cultivate an exclusive intellectual literature, nor should it, by relying too heavily on contemporary French drama, appeal to just one section of the community, even though that section, the bourgeoisie, may well be capable of providing full houses. The ideal repertoire should engage the interest of the whole people and should show, writes Heinrich Hart, anticipating the themes subsequently to be treated by the Naturalist dramatists, serious intellectual struggles, social conflicts, and the lighter and darker scenes of family life.[7] The democratic impulse, reflected in the recommendation that the price of an ordinary seat should be kept low, is very precariously balanced with a certain intellectual arrogance, which is recognizably a symptom of resentment against the contemporary theatrical set-up. The theatre, Heinrich Hart argues, cannot begin to have its proper effect and influence in the community until it has won back the intelligentsia, the 'geistige Aristokratie' – a phrase which is to occur increasingly in the writings of the Naturalists. The conclusion of the essay, that the impulse for a real National Theatre must arise from the initiative of enthusiastic writers, is an important idea, and might be considered the first tentative call for the establishment of the *Freie Bühne*; it also suggests who, in Heinrich Hart's opinion, constitute the 'Aristocracy of the Spirit'.

The policy outlined in 'Das Deutsche Theater des Herrn L'Arronge' is, in all respects, a strong plea for the rights of the creative artist; it is a plea for drama rather than theatre as it then existed; it is a criticism of the rights assumed by theatre administrators, star-performers,

---

[5] *Kritische Waffengänge*, 4 (1882), 14.
[6] *Revolution der Literatur*, edited by Johannes J. Braakenburg, Deutsche Texte, 23 (Tübingen: Niemeyer, 1973; reprint of 3rd edition, Leipzig: W. Friedrich, 1887), p. 22.
[7] *Kritische Waffengänge*, 4 (1882), 24f.

and the box-office. The desire of the Naturalists gradually 'to get rid of "theatre" from the theatre'[8] anticipates that renewal of the literary basis to the theatre shortly to find expression in the European Arts-theatre movement.[9] It represents the wish of the writer and his ally, the serious literary critic, to acquire some influence on the style of theatrical production. Heinrich Hart complains that actors tended to regard the dramatist as an intruder in their kingdom.[10] Eventually Gerhart Hauptmann did come to have this influence; he worked very closely with Brahm, and later with Max Reinhardt, and his contributions to the productions of various plays have been highly praised.[11] Brahm and his friend Paul Schlenther made the same sort of breakthrough; after starting their careers as literary critics they became, in the 1890s, the directors of the two most important German-speaking theatres, the *Deutsches Theater* in Berlin and the *Burgtheater* in Vienna.

For Heinrich Hart the text, the literary artist's creation, is what really matters.[12] It is important that the text should be communicated clearly, and so he demands, and Brahm subsequently makes, increased use of the preliminary reading rehearsal, the 'Leseprobe'. All the elements of the production should be co-ordinated in the interest of artistic unity – the lesson of the Meiningen company; decorations should not contradict the knowledge of the more cultured members of the audience, but should not attract attention for themselves; above all the individual actor should learn to restrain the declamatory style, and seek only naturalness in speech and movement.[13] An urgent need is felt for an actors' school, to function in close association with the National Theatre; such a school was subsequently to be founded by Emanuel Reicher, an actor intimately associated with Brahm, and directly involved in the successes of Hauptmann and Ibsen.

Heinrich Hart had no illusions that he was proposing a popular policy. On the contrary, he took an idealistic relish in the aesthetic leadership he associated with a model theatre: 'May L'Arronge have the moral strength to bring about a better understanding in the public, even if this means forcibly imposing it.'[14] L'Arronge did not have such moral strength, and it was only in its early years that his theatre provided the

---

[8] Arno Holz, 'Die Evolution des Dramas', *Das Werk von Arno Holz*, edited by Hans W. Fischer, 10 vols (Berlin: Dietz Nachfolger, 1924–25) X, 214.

[9] Erika Fischer-Lichte, *Kurze Geschichte des deutschen Theaters* (Tübingen and Basel: Francke, 1993), pp. 236–37.

[10] *Kritische Waffengänge*, 4 (1882), 41f.

[11] See Julius Bab, 'Gerhart Hauptmann als Regisseur', *Gerhart Hauptmann Jahrbuch*, Neue Folge, 1 (1948), 148–53.

[12] *Kritische Waffengänge*, 4 (1882), 17.

[13] *Kritische Waffengänge*, 4 (1882), 48; 51.

[14] *Kritische Waffengänge*, 4 (1882), 35.

Naturalists with any sort of satisfaction. His personal régime at the *Deutsches Theater* (of which he had become the proprietor) was no more than an interlude in its history between the visits of the Meiningen company in the 1870s, and the tenure of Otto Brahm, who took over as director in 1894 and proceeded to make it the centre of the modern movement.[15]

Otto Brahm was born in Hamburg in 1856, the son of a Jewish merchant. From an early age he had both journalistic ambitions and an interest in the theatre. On the strength of an essay he wrote on Paul Lindau, Julius Rodenberg, the editor of the *Deutsche Rundschau*, encouraged Brahm to study, and he went to the University of Berlin in 1876. A year later he moved for a short while to Heidelberg, where he met his lifelong friend, Paul Schlenther. The style of Professor Kuno Fischer did not appeal to Brahm, who already had a pronounced dislike of rhetoric, and the two young men soon returned to Berlin, where Brahm became a protégé of the literary historian, Wilhelm Scherer. Scherer subsequently recommended Brahm to Erich Schmidt, with whom he began work on his doctoral dissertation, 'Das deutsche Ritterdrama', which was presented in Jena, in 1879. In 1881 Brahm joined the *Vossische Zeitung* as junior theatre-critic; Theodor Fontane was his senior colleague with responsibility for reviewing the productions of the *Königliches Schauspielhaus*, which left Brahm to cover both the visits of the Meiningen company (1882, 1887) and, from 1883, the *Deutsches Theater*. He was dismissed from this post in 1885 because of a dispute arising out of his criticisms of the *Wallnertheater* and then worked as theatre-critic for the weekly *Die Nation* until the foundation of the *Freie Bühne*.[16]

Brahm shared Heinrich Hart's expressed admiration for the sober, restrained, realistic style of theatre, which had been associated with the city of his birth since the time of Lessing, and which was practised in the 1880s by Adolf Ernst's company at the *Thalia Theater*. His whole disposition, his distaste for external pomp and declamatory pathos and his reluctance to compromise, made him just the man to force through the kind of policy which Heinrich Hart had envisaged and which Brahm had himself approved in a piece he wrote welcoming L'Arronge's new theatre.[17] Brahm himself had over a decade to wait before he became director of this same theatre, and by this time the enthusiasms and tastes of his former allies were being re-directed, but

---

[15] Alfred Dreifuß, *Deutsches Theater in Berlin, Schumannstraße 13: Deichmann, L'Arronge, Brahm, Reinhard, Hilpert: 5 Kapitel aus der Geschichte einer Schauspielbühne* ([East] Berlin: Henschel, 1983).

[16] See Horst Claus, *The Theatre Director Otto Brahm*, Theatre and Dramatic Studies, 10 (*Ann Arbor, Michigan*: UMI Research Press, 1981), pp. 13–14.

[17] *Kritische Schriften*, edited by Paul Schlenther, 2 vols (Berlin: S. Fischer, 1913–15), I, 30–36.

his own dedication was undiminished; in the meantime he clearly established himself as the leading critic of his generation.

As a critic, Brahm is distinguished from his fellow-agitators by an ability to do more than just polemicise. While the *Kritische Waffengänge* contain masterpieces in the art of demolition, the Harts have little to put in place of Heinrich Kruse and Paul Lindau. In 1882 Heinrich Hart declared that the promising dramatists of the day were Wilbrandt, Anzengruber, Fitger, and Wildenbruch. From about 1884 Brahm began to devote himself increasingly – and effectively – to Ibsen, Anzengruber, and Hauptmann; he discovered *Vor Sonnenaufgang* (at about the same time as Fontane) after Bleibtreu had rejected Hauptmann's play when it had been submitted for publication in *Die Gesellschaft*.[18]

Brahm's first significant contribution to the development of Naturalism in Germany was the part he played in the campaign on behalf of Ibsen, which led to the Norwegian dramatist replacing Zola as the writer most admired by the younger generation. I believe that the breakthrough of Ibsen represents an important turning-point in German Naturalism and, before going on to consider Brahm's other achievements, I wish to establish the date of this as precisely as possible. *Pillars of Society* and *A Doll's House* reached the German theatre at a fairly early date (1878 and 1880), in fact only one year after they had each been completed.[19] Yet this early success of Ibsen's social dramas was something of a false start. In 1881 Karl Frenzel, the influential theatre critic of the *Nationalzeitung*, was already writing of it as a thing of the past: 'A short while ago [Ibsen's] drama, *Pillars of Society* had a firm place in the repertoire of many German theatres.'[20] Until 1887 Ibsen's social dramas seem to have been virtually absent from the German stage.

Brahm and Schlenther together saw *Pillars of Society* when it was performed in Berlin in 1878, but their accounts of how they responded to the play are rather different. Looking back in 1904, Brahm declared that he was immediately won over by Ibsen: 'From that moment onwards we were dedicated to the new art of realism and our aesthetic life had acquired its new content.'[21] Schlenther recalls, however, that Brahm was rather cool about this play, and decidedly critical of *A Doll's House*, when it appeared two years later.[22] We can, I believe, accept Schlenther's assertion that it was only in 1884, when he came across *Ghosts*, that

---

[18] See M. G. Conrad, *Von Emil Zola bis Gerhart Hauptmann: Erinnerungen zur Geschichte der Moderne*, Leipzig: Seemann Nachf. (1902), p. 80.

[19] *Ibsen auf der deutschen Bühne: Texte zur Rezeption*, edited by Wilhelm Friese, Deutsche Texte 38 (Tübingen: Niemeyer, 1976), p. 141.

[20] *Deutsche Rundschau*, 26 (1881), 308.

[21] *Kritische Schriften*, I, 447.

[22] 'Otto Brahm', *Theater im neunzehnten Jahrhundert*, edited by Hans Knudsen (Berlin: Gesellschaft für Theatergeschichte, 1930), p. 78.

Brahm began the long and loyal campaign on behalf of Ibsen, which lasted right up to the end of his career, as director of the *Lessingtheater*, for Brahm's work during the period before 1884 shows no marked interest in the Naturalist social drama with which he was to become so closely associated. Apart from his doctoral dissertation and his well-known study of Kleist, which appeared in 1884, his longer works include an article for the *Deutsches Montagsblatt* (1880), entitled 'Goethe und Berlin', in which he puts forward moderate views similar to those of the Hart brothers; here he urges his contemporaries to hold fast to the idealising tradition in German literature, 'which finds poetry not in the prosaic reproduction of everyday reality but strives to capture the heightened image of pure reality in classical form'.[23] There is a similar anti-naturalist bias behind Brahm's admiration of Paul Heyse, about whom he wrote an essay for *Westermanns Monatshefte*; and behind his early, unfavourable, criticisms of the work of Zola.[24] But in the present context the most interesting piece of criticism Brahm wrote in these years is an essay on Keller, which appeared in the *Deutsche Rundschau* of 1882. This essay concludes with a direct comparison between Keller's *Das Sinngedicht* and *A Doll's House*, which surely confirms Schlenther's statement that Brahm was, at this time, unenthusiastic about the work of Ibsen. Here again Brahm's views resemble those expressed in the *Kritische Waffengänge* for his criticism reflects the same reaction against the tendentious social drama of his own day:

Wieviel bitterer und heftiger ist die Satire des Norwegers als die des Schweizers, wieviel ernster ist er in seinem letzten Akt der Gefahr verfallen, an Stelle der Dichtung die pure unpoetische Tendenz vorzutragen... für uns handelt es sich nicht, um das soziale Problem als solches, sondern um seine poetische Realisierung, und im Bereiche der Kunst ist es zweifellos Gottfrled Keller gewesen. der die vollendetere Schöpfung gegeben hat.[25]	How much more bitter and violent is the satire of the Norwegian than that of the Swiss, and in his last act how much more seriously has he fallen into the danger of replacing poetry with pure, unpoetic tendentiousness... for us it is not a question of the social problem as such, but its poetic realisation; and on an artistic level it is undoubtedly Gottfried Keller who has produced the greater work.

---

[23] Quoted from Schlenther, 'Otto Brahm', p. 67.
[24] Cf. S. Hoefert, 'Emile Zola dans la critique d'Otto Brahm', *Les Cahiers naturalistes*, 30 (1965), 145–52.
[25] *Kritische Schriften*, II, 192.

In discussing the reception of Zola by the early German Naturalists, I drew attention to one issue over which the younger writers were unanimous: the question of *bienséance*. Even among those writers who have reservations about Zola's scientific approach there is an insistence on his right to complete freedom in the choice of subject matter. In the early years of German Naturalism there is a strong desire to get literature out of the 'salon'. Many writers therefore turned to the seamier side of city life for their new material, among them the novelists mentioned in the preceding chapter and a number of lyric poets, including Arno Holz. The effect of this was to give the Naturalist movement its slightly unsavoury reputation: 'When people talk about naturalism or verism they are usually thinking about subject matter, and mostly about a particular sort of subject matter, the most material matter.'[26]

Brahm was another for whom progress in art meant the extension of its boundaries to include material previously excluded: literary history, he claimed, shows 'how Art acquires the art of absorbing more and more of nature'.[27] Boldness in introducing new material was thus one of the features of Kleist's work which Brahm singled out for praise in his early study of that writer: 'He strives to extend the boundaries of representation and, like Faust, to colonise for art territories which before him were inaccessible to it';[28] and he praises the same tendency in the work of Anzengruber. In his first season as director of the *Freie Bühne* Brahm presented, out of a total of ten plays, three (Ibsen's *Ghosts*, Anzengruber's *Das vierte Gebot*, and Arthur Fitger's *Von Gottes Gnaden*) which had previously had censorship problems; the remaining seven included *Vor Sonnenaufgang*, *Die Familie Selicke*, and Tolstoy's *The Power of Darkness*, which all contained the sort of material regarded as highly offensive by the audiences of 1889–90.

To a generation of writers with the sort of attitudes I have been outlining Zola clearly had more to offer than Ibsen; and I believe that this explains why his success in the early 1880s was more spectacular. Perceiving just how little Ibsen had to offer, one recent critic reflects:

> There were...some things which the German Naturalists, no matter how hard they tried to fit Ibsen into the framework of their own literary philosophies or prejudices, were unable to find in his work. Most conspicuously absent were any traces of 'Großstadtpoesie', and 'Armeleutepoesie' or other strongly proletarian sympathy, any real

---

[26] Leo Berg, *Der Naturalismus* (Munich: Poessel, 1892), p. 23.

[27] 'Der Naturalismus und das Theater' (1891), in Otto Brahm, *Theater-Dramatiker-Schauspieler*, edited by Hugo Fetting (Berlin: Henschel, 1961), p. 404.

[28] *Heinrich von Kleist* (Berlin: Allgemeiner Verein für deutsche Literatur, 1884), p. 206; and 'Der Naturalismus und das Theater', p. 404.

approach to 'konsequenter Naturalismus' in the dialogue. Indeed Ibsen's world was in its class framework so predominantly bourgeois, in its intellectual pretensions so persistently aristocratic, and in its speech habits so deficient in raw dialect, that one even wonders how he escaped their censure.[29]

The explanation is, I believe, the relatively simple one, that the philosophies and prejudices of the German Naturalists were not fixed and unchanging; that Ibsen's dramas did not, in fact, appeal at once, largely because of the attitudes to which I have been drawing attention; but that round about 1887 a change was taking place in German Naturalism which was to make the movement very much more sympathetic to Ibsen (and, incidentally, to the work of the Goncourts) and rather less enthusiastic about Zola.[30] One of the results of this is that the German Naturalist drama soon comes to rely less on shocks and sensations; another is that, dialogue apart, the dramas of the 1890s are enacted in a world very similar to Ibsen's world, as it is described above. Among few exceptions *Die Weber* is the most notable; *Einsame Menschen* is more typical of the work being done at this time.

One possible objection to this hypothesis might be that Brahm's interest in Ibsen is unquestionably established with his review of *Ghosts* in 1884, and that quite a substantial campaign preceded the first performance of this play. But then *Ghosts* quite clearly is the sort of play which would have appealed to those among the Naturalists who were calling for new and challenging material; it is scarcely surprising that their enthusiasm should have been kindled by, and for a time have been concentrated upon, this particular play. The search for new material is most probably what attracted Brahm to Ibsen and to Naturalism in the first place, but he soon became reconciled to the other main impulse behind this literary trend: the social-critical impulse, 'to expose the wounds of a suffering society and to heal them'.[31] His earlier dislike of tendentious literature soon waned and he came to be an advocate of the

---

[29] J. W. McFarlane, 'Hauptmann, Ibsen and the concept of Naturalism', in *Hauptmann: Centenary Lectures* edited by K. G. Knight and F. Norman (London: University of London, Institute of Germanic Studies, 1964) pp. 31-60 (p. 50).
[30] Cf. Kurt Wais, 'Zur Auswirkung des französischen naturalistischen Romans in Deutschland', in *An den Grenzen der Nationalliteraturen* (Berlin: de Gruyter, 1958), pp. 215-33. Wais draws attention to three characteristics in the work of the Goncourts which distinguish it from Zola's, and to which the Germans became increasingly sympathetic: the Goncourts drew their material from the world of the bourgeoisie, not the proletariat, their achievement lay less in the field of concrete, visual description than in psychological perception; they adopted a consciously refined literary style; in all this they resemble Ibsen more closely than Zola.
[31] 'Der Naturalismus und das Theater', p. 403.

social drama. This development is already in evidence in his Ibsen-essay of 1886, where he is disposed to interpret Ibsen predominantly as a social-realist; indeed, his essay was one of the most influential works to propagate this view of the Norwegian dramatist.[32]

Brahm sees the basis of Ibsen's social criticism in his individualism. In his work he finds a consistent emphasis on independence and strength of character:

[Ibsen] glaubt leidenschaftlich an das Recht der starken Persönlichkeit, des Einzelnen gegenüber der Gemeinschaft... er hat ein tiefes Mißtrauen gegen das Recht jener Ansprüche, welche der Staat an die Bürger, die Gesellschaft an ihre Mitglieder stellt, auf Kosten der stolzen und freien Entwicklung der Persönlichkeit. Er glaubt an sein Talent, ein Mensch zu sein; und er zweifelt an seinem Talent, ein tätiger Staatsbürger und eine Stütze der Gesellschaft zu sein. Er blickt in eine ferne Zukunft, welche den Bestand der Welt erschüttern, Staaten zerbrechen und vielleicht gar die Idee des Staates selbst antasten wird; aber vor der gegenwärtigen politischen Bewegung in seiner Heimat zieht er sich mit vornehmer Scheu zurück.[33]	Ibsen believes passionately in the right of the strong personality, in the right of the individual as opposed to society... he has a profound mistrust of the right of those demands which the state makes of its citizens, society of its members, at the expense of the free and proud development of the personality. He believes in his talent to be an individual; and he is rather dubious about his talent to be a solid citizen and a pillar of society. His eyes are fixed on a distant future which will shake up the world, destroy states, and perhaps call in question the very idea of the state; but he turns away with aristocratic reserve from the present political activity in his own country.

This emphasis on a non-political individualism is an important foretaste of the development of German Naturalism in the 1890s; so also is Brahm's reference to *An Enemy of the People*, for here he begins to convert an individualist ethic into a piece of special-pleading for the 'outstanding' individual, for 'the rights of noble individuals, of lonely independent spirits, who have taken up an advanced position in the service of emerging new truths'.[34] Here we already have the underlying thesis of such plays as *Einsame Menschen*, Dehmel's *Der Mitmensch*,

---

[32] David E. R. George, *Henrik Ibsen in Deutschland: Rezeption und Revision* (Göttingen: Vandenhoeck und Ruprecht), 1968, pp. 34f.

[33] 'Henrik Ibsen', *Deutsche Rundschau*, 49 (1886), 193–220 (p. 193). Reprinted in *Ibsen auf der deutschen Bühne*, pp. 19–55.

[34] 'Henrik Ibsen', p. 216.

Carl Hauptmann's *Marianne*, and Flaischlen's *Martin Lehnhardt*. In the history of German Naturalism this individualist slant to the interpretation of Ibsen is more significant than the tendency to regard him as a social dramatist in a more general sense. In 1889 this ideal of the free development of the individual personality will be extended by Halbe to the sphere of artistic creation:

Wer Ibsen wirklich erfaßt hat, [sollte] vor dem Recht der Individualität, vor dem freien, schrankenlosen Sichausleben der Persönlichkeit... als dem obersten Gebot im sozialen und Gesellschaftsleben ebensowohl wie in Literatur und Kunst in Demut sein Haupt beugen,	Whoever has fully understood Ibsen, ought to bow his head humbly before the right of individuality, before the free, unrestrained assertion of the personality... as the highest law, not only in social life, but also in literature and art,

With this a synthesis has been achieved between the German interpretations of Ibsen and Zola, between aesthetic and ethical individualism; for the unrestricted development of the personality here means the free activity of the artistic imagination. Where such an attitude is combined with a denunciation of the scientific attitude, the signs are that a Naturalism based on the principle of exact observation has run its course.[35]

Otto Brahm's agitation on behalf of Ibsen, which culminated in the essay of 1886, had its reward in a single performance (the police would permit no more) of *Ghosts* at the *Residenztheater* in Berlin on January 9, 1887. The previous year had seen two private performances of this play, one at the Meiningen Court Theatre on December 22, and one in Augsburg on April 14, and both these performances no doubt had some influence in securing the Berlin production. The performance at the Municipal Theatre in Augsburg was arranged by a number of young writers from Munich, including Ludwig Fulda, Max Bernstein, and Felix Philippi, and was described as a dress rehearsal for invited guests in order to circumvent the censorship. It was an example of the kind of initiative demanded by Heinrich Hart, and, as such, an anticipation of the *Freie Bühne* idea. The subsequent performance of *Ghosts* in the capital was all that was needed to encourage this sort of initiative, to unite the young writers in a common purpose. In the words of Otto Brahm: 'The route was signposted and the goal set; it was now a question of marching ahead and crushing any obstacles.'[36] From now on the novel

---

[35] Max Halbe, 'Berliner Brief', *Die Gesellschaft*, 5 (1889), 1183.
[36] *Kritische Schriften*, I, 465.

began to give way to the drama as the most favoured literary genre; Gerhart Hauptmann wrote that the 1887 performance of *Ghosts* in Berlin showed him the resurrection of the theatre.[37] Munich came rapidly to be supplanted by the theatre capital, Berlin, as the centre of literary activity. Here an Ibsen-community was formed, and made its presence felt as a *claque* at the first performances of his plays.[38] These now followed in swift succession: *An Enemy of the People* and *Rosmersholm* in 1887; *The Wild Duck, Lady Inger*, and a revival of *A Doll's House* in 1888; *The Lady from the Sea* and a revival of *Pillars of Society*, as well as a further single performance of *Ghosts* in 1889. March 5, 6 and 7 of 1889 saw the performance in Berlin of three different plays by Ibsen.

The confidence generated among the Naturalists by the feeling that they were really on the point of breaking through led them to take matters more firmly into their own hands. By 1889 their circle of influence was large enough to support a regular programme of private performances and, modelling themselves on Antoine's Parisian *Théâtre Libre*, they formed the *Freie Bühne*. The original proposal came from Theodor Wolff and Maxmilian Harden, and the founder-members included the Hart brothers, Schlenther, and the publisher, Samuel Fischer, but the most important individual was Brahm, who was elected leader, and given almost dictatorial powers. His exercise of these powers soon led to a great deal of friction among the active members of the society, but Brahm was a difficult man to dislodge; his achievement is his justification.

The society was designed to be an exclusive organization, run by the avant-garde for that section of the public with a serious interest in literature. Even where the project did not gain sympathy, it did succeed in gaining support, and by the end of the first season the *Freie Bühne* had a membership of over 1,000, which included theatre-directors (Blumenthal, Lautenburg, L'Arronge) and critics (Landau, Frenzel, Lindau) who might have been expected to regard such a society with suspicion, if not downright hostility.[39] Because he now had a firm base, Brahm was able to put into practice the anti-popular policy which he and the Harts had advocated, and so to revolutionise the theatre from above. He was also more than a little fortunate in the nature of the literary style he supported, for where enthusiasm might not quite have filled his theatre, sensation and controversy helped out. The first play he presented was *Ghosts*, still banned from public performance; but his real *succès de scandale*, and at the same time his theatre's major contribution

---

[37] Diary entry for 18.12.1897, Gerhart Hauptmann, *Die Kunst des Dramas: Über Schauspiel und Theater*, edited by Martin Machatzke (Berlin and Frankfurt a.M.: Propyläen, 1963), p. 196.
[38] Cf. Halbe, 'Berliner Brief', p. 1183.
[39] Cf. Gernot Schley, *Die Freie Bühne in Berlin* (Berlin: Haude und Spener, 1967), p. 15.

to the development of the German drama, came with the notorious première of *Vor Sonnenaufgang* in the *Lessingtheater* on October 28, 1889.

The Naturalist theatre in Germany was built on the twin pillars of Ibsen and Hauptmann (Brahm was strangely unsympathetic to Strindberg and Wedekind). By 1889 the success of the former had been secured; the purpose of the *Freie Bühne* was to smooth the passage of just such a native dramatist as Hauptmann, whose *Vor Sonnenaufgang* had, as we noted, been turned down even by *Die Gesellschaft*. When his third drama, *Einsame Menschen*, was taken into the repertory of the public theatre, and his next available play, *Kollege Crampton*, was given its première at the *Deutsches Theater*, the *Freie Bühne* had served its purpose.[40] After 1891 the society was resurrected only in special circumstances: to present *Miss Julie* in 1892 (one of Brahm's rare Strindberg productions), and in 1893, to present two plays threatened with censorship by the Berlin president of police, *Die Weber*, and *Dämmerung*, a work by Naturalism's leading woman dramatist, Else Bernstein (who wrote under the name Ernst Rosmer). After 1894 the direction of the *Freie Bühne* was taken over first by Schlenther and then by Ludwig Fulda. It continued to be a forum for experimental drama, but on a much smaller scale, moving with the times away from its original Naturalist programme.[41]

One effect of the success of this particular private venture was imitation. The *Volksbühnen*, which will be discussed at some length in a later chapter, were the most important and most enduring extension of the *Freie Bühne* idea, though their purpose was rather different, and their audiences came from a different section of the community. The *Verein Deutsche Bühne* was founded in direct rivalry to the *Freie Bühne* and with a great deal of personal animosity towards Brahm by Alberti and Bleibtreu. It gained the support of the Hart brothers, but its policy of concentrating on German authors met with no success. Halbe's *Intimes Theater* and the various literary societies, the most notable of which was Walter Harlan's *Litterarische Gesellschaft* in Leipzig, were intended,

---

[40] *Einsame Menschen* opened at the *Deutsches Theater* on March 21, 1891. It was not the first play by Hauptmann to be performed in the commercial theatre, though it was the first to be accepted before its private performance. *Vor Sonnenaufgang* had been taken up by an opportunist director shortly after its noisy première, but the planned four-week run was curtailed after two weeks because of lack of public interest; see Conrad Alberti, 'Die Freie Bühne', *Die Gesellschaft*, 6 (1890), 1104–12 (p. 1112). For a different view of the purpose of the *Freie Bühne* see Michael Hays, *The Public and Performance: Essays in the History of French and German Theater*, Theatre and Dramatic Studies, 6 (Ann Arbor, Michigan: UMI Research Press, 1974), pp. 142–44. Hays, however, misreads the evidence, seriously understates the resistance which the naturalist dramatists faced in the 1880s, and attributes too much to the naked personal ambition of Brahm, disregarding the intellectual coherence and consistency – over almost three decades – of his project as critic, organiser, and director.

[41] See Peter Sprengel, *Gerhart Hauptmann: Epoche – Werk – Wirkung* (Munich: Beck, 1984), pp. 49–50.

without rivalry, to achieve the same purpose as the original *Freie Bühne*, that is to provide a modern repertoire for a select audience of enthusiasts, free from commercial pressures, and to give to the serious young writer the encouragement of seeing his work performed, even if only in an amateur production.

The success of the *Freie Bühne* was such that Brahm was able to do much more than had originally been planned. In 1894 he began the first of two five-year leases of the *Deutsches Theater* from L'Arronge, who had decided that the time had come for him to step down. Still relying principally on Hauptmann and Ibsen, Brahm rapidly established himself as the undisputed leader in the theatre of the German-speaking world, until the emergence of his pupil, Max Reinhardt. That he was able to do so without abandoning his ascetic, anti-popular, and anti-theatrical style, is a clear enough indication of his personal greatness as a director, for the Naturalist impulse alone would never have sustained Brahm's theatres, the *Freie Bühne*, the *Deutsches Theater*, and finally the *Lessingtheater*, for over two decades. As we have seen, this impulse was already flagging when Brahm took over at the *Deutsches Theater*. The flexibility of the policy which Brahm, as editor, outlined in the introduction to the first number of the periodical, *Freie Bühne für modernes Leben*, showed a keen awareness of the way the wind was blowing:

Dem Naturalismus Freund, wollen wir eine gute Strecke Weges mit ihm schreiten, allein es soll uns nicht erstaunen, wenn im Verlauf der Wanderschaft, an einem Punkt, den wir heute noch nicht überschauen, die Straße plötzlich sich biegt und überraschende Blicke in Kunst und Leben sich auftun.	As a friend of the Naturalist movement we will go along with it a good way, but we must not be surprised if, in the course of the journey, at a point which is not yet in sight, the route takes a sudden turning, and astounding views into art and life are opened up.

But Brahm was less ready than many of his contemporaries to explore the first turning. In 1891 he was still speaking out for a Naturalism of social observation and criticism; his production of *Die Weber* in 1893 was designed to bring out just that element of social criticism which Julius Hart sought, in his review, to play down, by subordinating it to what he called pure art and pure humanity.[42] He was

---

[42] Quoted from Gerhart Hauptmann, *Die Weber*, *Dichtung und Wirklichkeit*, edited by Hans Schwab-Felisch (Frankfurt a.M. and Berlin: Ullstein, 1963), p. 195. For detailed comments on Brahm's production of *Die Weber*, see H. Henze, *Otto Brahm und das deutsche Theater in Berlin* (Berlin: Mittler, 1930), p. 22.

not very receptive to the 'impressionism' and 'décadence' developed in the 1890s by writers such as Hermann Bahr, whose work he described as 'parfümiertes Ekel'.[43]

As editor of the periodical, *Freie Bühne*, Brahm had rather less success than as theatrical director of the organization. Already on the defensive when the periodical was founded, Brahm did not here acquire the dictatorial powers he was granted in the theatre. Discontent with his policies led to a revolt in the first year of the periodical's life, and Bahr, Bierbaum, Paul Ernst, Holz, Liliencron, and Schlaf publicly dissociated themselves from Brahm. More important, Samuel Fischer, the publisher, had rather different ambitions for his periodical than Brahm, and so Brahm also had to go, to be followed in rapid succession by Bölsche, Julius Hart, and Bierbaum, until Fischer found in Oskar Bie a rather more pliant editor. The *Neue deutsche Rundschau*, as the periodical became known in 1894 (in 1904 *Die neue Rundschau*), very soon left its programmatic origins behind to become Germany's leading literary periodical. This is a rare example of such a transformation, and the credit is Fischer's.[44] But this is pre-eminently a publisher's achievement, and as such has little to do with the literary movement, Naturalism.

In the theatre Brahm did have sufficient power, independence, and obstinacy to hold out much longer. In his ten seasons at the *Deutsches Theater* he never performed works by Strindberg, Wedekind, or the increasingly fashionable Oscar Wilde; he did not perform anything by Maeterlinck until his ninth season. Heinrich Hart, who had declared in 1890 that the time was ripe for a retreat from Naturalism and a return to the verse-drama, compares Brahm's activity in the theatre unfavourably with the development of Fischer's periodical: 'The richer the development of the journal, the more impoverished was the manner in which the theatre dragged out its existence'.[45] In fairness it should be pointed out that Brahm did introduce Schnitzler and, rather less typically perhaps, Hofmannsthal to the German theatre; but in an atmosphere of increasing criticism he continued to build his repertoire around Ibsen and Hauptmann, performing all of the latter's plays as they became available, and vigorously defending his contractual agreement against the predatory moves of Reinhardt.[46] Brahm's last great productions were the cycle of Ibsen's dramas from *The League of Youth* to *When we dead awaken* given at the *Lessingtheater*.

---

[43] Cf. W. Grothe, 'Die neue Rundschau', *Börsenblatt für den deutschen Buchhandel*, 17 (1962), p. 2186.
[44] See Grothe, 'Die neue Rundschau', p. 2176.
[45] 'Literarische Erinnerungen', *Ges. Werke*, III, 73.
[46] See Claus, *The Theatre Director Otto Brahm*, p. 117.

The achievement of Otto Brahm in the German theatre of the 1890s resembles very closely the achievement of the late George Devine in the English theatre of the 1950s; he gave a completely new impetus to the German theatre by renewing its contact with the literature of the day and restoring it as a forum for public debate;[47] he gave to a new generation of writers encouragement and confidence; he gave to the Naturalist movement its theatres, its successes, its public controversies; he gave it a new school of actors, Else Lehmann, Rosa Bertens, Rudolf Rittner, Oscar Sauer, Albert Bassermann, and above all he gave his own services as a director. It was perhaps inevitable that this impetus should eventually lead to a point beyond which Brahm could not, or would not, himself go; it was, perhaps, inevitable that 'Theatre' should reassert itself, and that the restraint of Brahm should give way to the rather more ambiguous splendour of Reinhardt, for Brahm's success was, in a sense, a tour de force. Hauptmann was a dramatist to whose work the sober style cultivated by Brahm was eminently suited, and it is arguable that his unofficial position as Brahm's resident dramatist is one of the reasons for the discipline of his best plays, and for the relatively long duration of his Naturalism; but from *Hanneles Himmelfahrt* to *Die Ratten* even Hauptmann was straining at the leash, alternately accepting and ignoring the implications of Brahm's methods. The demise of Hauptmann the dramatist after 1912 is probably not unconnected with the death of Otto Brahm.[48]

---

[47] Fischer-Lichte, *Kurze Geschichte des deutschen Theaters*, pp. 238–43.
[48] See *Der Briefwechsel Arthur Schnitzler-Otto Brahm*, edited by Oskar Seidlin, Deutsche Texte, 35 (Tübingen: Niemeyer, 1975), p. xxi.

3
NATURALISM IN THEORY: ARNO HOLZ

In the foregoing account of the rise of Naturalism in Germany I have placed a great deal of emphasis on the success of Ibsen after 1887 and Gerhart Hauptmann after 1889. There is no doubt that these are the most important events of the period under discussion. So far I have virtually overlooked the role of Arno Holz who, as a theorist and practising dramatist, is most closely associated with the style known in literary history as 'konsequenter Naturalismus' (consistent Naturalism). Hauptmann dedicated *Vor Sonnenaufgang*, in its first edition, to 'Bjarne P. Holmsen [the pseudonym used by Holz and Schlaf], the most consistent realist, author of *Papa Hamlet*', and stated that the work of Holz and Schlaf had exercised a decisive influence on him. Subsequently, though, he became distinctly hostile towards Holz (he re-dedicated *Vor Sonnenaufgang* in its second edition to Brahm and Schlenther) and denied that his influence had ever been decisive. This later view is probably a more accurate one. Even before the publication of *Papa Hamlet*, in January 1889, Hauptmann was himself already attempting to reproduce accurately everyday speech in his works; *Fasching* (*Siegfried*, 1887) and *Bahnwärter Thiel* (*Die Gesellschaft*, 1888) had already been published, and *Vor Sonnenaufgang* had been completed. *Papa Hamlet* marked a step beyond Hauptmann in terms of realization; but the difference is one of degree rather than kind.

An examination of the work of Holz is nevertheless indispensable to an account of Naturalism in Germany. His aesthetic writings and, even more so, the works written in collaboration with Johannes Schlaf, occupy a central position as representative works of this period. An unprejudiced examination of them can tell us a great deal about the real quality of German Naturalism. I say unprejudiced because the importance of these works does not reside, as has often been argued, in their rigid adherence to extreme principles of verism. The picture of Holz as a single-minded defender and exponent of an extreme doctrine is not a convincing one. The length, the detail, and the triviality of his arguments with his critics are symptoms of anything but supreme self-confidence. Behind the apparent certainty, even arrogance, of his statements there lurk all the uncertainties and contradictions of an age in ferment. His theoretical writings occupy over 700 pages of his collected works, and they form a vast and confusing edifice. I propose to consider them, and his creative writings, only relatively briefly, and only in so far as they are relevant to the work of the Naturalist period.

Arno Holz, like many of his contemporaries, began his literary career as an admirer and imitator of one of those established figures who soon became anathema to his generation. His early poems *Klinginsherz* (1883) and *Deutsche Weisen* (1884) owe a lot to the lyric of Geibel, in whose honour Holz edited an anthology, *Emanuel Geibel: Ein Gedenkbuch* (1884). In 1885 he first became associated with the Naturalist movement through his contributions to the lyric anthology, *Moderne Dichtercharaktere*, and in the following year he was widely acclaimed as the leading Naturalist poet for his *Buch der Zeit: Lieder eines Modernen*. In these early works he displays a greater facility than most of his contemporaries, but, except in the 'Phantasus' poems of the *Buch der Zeit*, there is little attempt at formal innovation. As I have suggested in the previous chapter, the literary revolution for the Holz of these years amounts to rejecting the heritage of German romanticism and finding new material for his poetry:

> Ich lache, wollt' ihr blöden Blicks
> verjährten Tand modern staffieren
> und himmelbläulich phantasieren
> vom Waldgnom und vom Wassernix.[1]

Like other young writers Holz found his new material in the city and in the struggle of the oppressed proletariat. He also came to share the general feeling of solidarity with the banned Social Democratic Party. In poems such as 'An die "obern Zehntausend"' and 'Ecce Homo' he gave direct enough expression to the aspirations of the working-classes to win for the *Buch der Zeit* the lasting admiration of the Marxist critic, Franz Mehring.

In 1885 Holz made a clean break with socialism – he was the first of the Naturalists to do so – and henceforward he began to indulge in aesthetic speculation and formal experiment of a kind which inevitably lost him the sympathy of his former admirers. Among the Naturalists Holz was the writer who always possessed the greatest formal awareness, and he soon came to hold the view that the revolution of the early 1880s would remain insubstantial unless it became a stylistic revolution: 'the development of any art depends in the first place on the development of its method'.[2] Heinrich Hart was also beginning to think along these same lines at about this time:

> What counts most in literature is not the matter, but the manner. The choice of modern subjects, the depiction of contemporary political conflicts, the exploitation of the 'burning' issues of the day, can by

---

[1] Arno Holz, *Das Werk*, edited by Hans. W. Fischer, 10 vols (Berlin: Dietz Nachfolger, 1924–25), X, *Die neue Wortkunst* (1925), 13.
[2] Holz, *Das Werk*, X, 190.

themselves arouse the interest of large sections of the public, but this success will be a success for today only, if all the writer can offer is new material.[3]

Springing, as it does, from his consciousness of form, Holz's Naturalism is much more literary than that of his contemporaries. Like a younger and, let it be said, much greater poet, who at an early stage in his career attained a remarkable facility in the lyric genre, Holz soon found himself in the predicament of the epigone, and unable to write poetry. In their dissatisfaction with a language seemingly deprived of meaning and force by the weight of traditional usage, Holz and Hofmannsthal have much in common; and they both write about their problems in an attempt to overcome them; Holz theorizes, he says, to improve his practice.[4] His aesthetic writings, therefore, are free of the nationalism of the Harts, and the moralism of the socially-committed Naturalists.

As his point of departure Holz takes the theory of Zola, concentrating in particular upon his famous definition of the work of art as 'a corner of nature seen through a temperament'. In a previous chapter we noted that by 1888 there was a tendency among German critics of Zola to admire him for his creative personality rather than for the scientific accuracy of his work or his originality as a theorist. Holz was familiar with Brandes' important Zola-essay, and shared this particular tendency:

nicht die Funkelnagelneuheit seiner 'Ideen' war es, nicht die mehr als zweifelhafte Tiefe seiner 'Wahrheiten', die Zola auch als Theoretiker so hoch über den trivialen Haufen emporragen ließ, sondern die wunderbare Wärme seiner Überzeugung, das Pathetische seiner Perioden, das ganze Machtvolle seiner Persönlichkeit, das, wie seinen übrigen Werken, so auch seinen kritischen Schriften zur Folie dient.[5]	What made Zola, as a theorist, stand out so far above the common herd was not the originality of his 'ideas', nor the more than dubious profundity of his 'truths', but the wonderful warmth of his conviction, the pathos of his sentences, the whole power of his personality, which acts as a foil to his critical writings as it does to his other works.

Holz does not feel it necessary to point out any discrepancy between Zola's theory and his practice but, like Brandes, he accepts that the concept 'temperament' can adequately – was actually intended

---
[3] 'Die realistische Bewegung', *Kritisches Jahrbuch*, 1 (1889), 51.
[4] Holz, *Das Werk*, X, 105.
[5] Holz, *Das Werk*, X, 59.

to – embrace such things as taste and imagination; he therefore describes Zola's definition as a trivial commonplace. Although Zola's theories are not free of ambiguity, the concept 'temperament' was much narrower than Holz implies and almost certainly did not, so far as he was concerned, include these things. For Zola his definition of a work of art is part of a meaningful realist credo, and while he was always a respecter of the strong artistic personality he was never prepared to see it entirely free of restraint. It is certainly arguable that in the case of Zola (as, I believe, in the case of Hauptmann) the discipline of Naturalism had a beneficial effect on an over-exuberant imagination; that the quality of his works derives from a certain balance that is achieved between two conflicting aspects of his character.[6] The tradition in which Zola wrote – the tradition of Balzac, Stendhal, and the French Realists – accepts that there is a substantial external reality, as distinct from our subjective image of it, and Zola's theory demands that the artist should not lose touch with this reality: 'There comes a day when one no longer has the strength to play the role of creator. Then, when works are too personal, one goes on inevitably repeating oneself. Reality, on the other hand, is a good mother, who continues to nourish her children with fresh food.'[7]

The impression given by Holz's theory is that he is less confident about the existence of such a reality and therefore resistant to the confinement of novelistic practice by the principle of fidelity to the given facts of nature, which is implicit in the theory of the experimental novel. This is entirely characteristic of the German tradition in which he stands. As his theory develops Holz insists with greater explicitness on the artist's freedom to chose his point of departure, while reorienting criticism to techniques of representation; as Henry James asserts in a similar context: 'We must grant the artist his subject, his idea, his donnée: our criticism is applied only to what he makes of it.'[8] Specifically Holz displays an increasingly monistic tendency to identify nature with its reflection in the mind of the individual, or with the sensation it arouses in him. He will thus ask: 'Is the feeling aroused in me by a sunset not a process of nature?', and go on to argue that even music re-creates nature by recreating such sensations.[9] Views like this make it very difficult to define exactly what Holz means by 'Nature' in his oft quoted statement: 'Art has the tendency to become Nature again. It becomes Nature in so far as this is permitted by the prevalent conditions of

---

[6] Cf. J. H. Matthews, *Les deux Zola; science et personnalité dans l'expression* (Geneva: Droz and Paris: Minard, 1957), pp. 91–93.

[7] *Mes Haines*, p. 86.

[8] Henry James, 'The Art of Fiction' (1884), in *Partial Portraits* (London: Macmillan, 1919), pp. 394–95. See also Mark Seltzer, *Henry James and the Art of Power* (Ithaca and London: Cornell University Press, 1984), pp. 16–17.

[9] Holz, *Das Werk*, X, 139.

imitation and their exploitation.' One could say that by nature Holz means the whole of the spiritual, social, and physical world, including the world of imagination and dreams, in so far as it is ever experienced by any single individual or artist.[10] This would certainly mean that Holz was right when, in 1898, he reassured his critics that he had never advocated the confinement of mimetic realism, and had never sought to restrict the freedom of artistic individuality in the slightest degree.[11] But it also virtually deprives Holz's 'artistic law' of any programmatic (naturalist) meaning; and so an apparent demand for realistic literature becomes a sanction for complete subjectivity.

In this rather cursory comparison of the theories of Holz and Zola I have sought to bring out the most consistent line in Holz's argument, the monistic line, according to which the 'temperament' is already regarded as a part of nature. I must, however, concede that Holz's theory is not remarkable for its consistency; and the inconsistency derives from a lack of clarity on the part of Holz about what he is trying to achieve. On the one hand, Holz's theory does amount to a programmatic demand for Naturalism, which is what his contemporaries took it for; on the other hand, it aspires to be a scientific aesthetic, and purports to reveal a law applicable to all art, whatever its particular style.[12] The balance shifts from the prescriptive to the descriptive as German Naturalism stresses observation less and imagination more. One is therefore tempted to conclude that Holz set out to introduce into his country a modern, realist style of literature, only to find that, by the time he had evolved his theories, no one wanted to be a realist any more. He, and certain of his contemporaries, therefore spent the 1890s unsaying (or denying that they had ever said) much of what is implicit in their theoretical writings of the previous decade. This judgement is a little unjust, for the process is not that conscious a process, and the earlier writings are open to development in a number of possible directions. It is certainly not true, as Rasch and others have asserted, that the essay of 1891 quite unambiguously defines artistic activity as the exact reproduction of a physically perceivable object; nor do I accept that Holz's work can be conveniently divided into three periods, each characterized by a different view of nature; or that the later theoretical writings can be dismissed as an obstinate hanging on to his 'law' of art once it had been formulated.[13] When Holz claimed that he had never demanded that a

---

[10] Wilhelm Emrich, 'Arno Holz und die moderne Kunst', in *Protest und Verheißung*: Studien zur klassischen und modernen Dichtung (Frankfurt a.M. and Bonn: Athenäum, 1960), pp. 155–68 (p. 165).
[11] Holz, *Das Werk*, X, 522.
[12] See Rob Burns, *The Quest for Modernity: The Place of Arno Holz in Modern German Literature* (Frankfurt a.M. and Bern: Peter Lang, 1981), p. 51.
[13] Cf. W. Rasch, 'Zur dramatischen Dichtung des jungen Gerhart Hauptmann', in

work of art should be an exact imitation of nature, then, strictly speaking, his claim was just. Nevertheless he had dismissed as an *unsound* dogma the view, attributed to Taine, that the essence of art does *not* consist in the exact imitation of nature;[14] intentional or not, the implication behind these words is reasonably clear: art does consist in the exact imitation of nature.

The same contradiction is often present when Holz speaks of his theory as a law. In his *Die Kunst: Ihr Wesen und ihre Gesetze* (1891) he supports the deterministic view that all phenomena are subject to certain immutable laws and he sees his task as an aesthetician not in the laying down, but in the discovery of the laws of art; as he puts it in a letter of 1892: 'We are not legislators, but discoverers of laws.'[15] He therefore claims that his aesthetic law, like the law of gravity, necessarily governs anything which comes within its sphere of influence: a Japanese idol just as much as a modern French statue, a painting by Böcklin just as much as one by Menzel.[16] Nevertheless Holz does adopt the role of proselyte in stylistic matters; in the same essay, *Die Kunst: Ihr Wesen und ihre Gesetze*, he claims that his basic law of art can provide the artist with a method of attaining the truth; and elsewhere he speaks of his duty to teach others to apply this law.[17]

I have suggested that the contradictions in Holz's theories arise because of the developments taking place in German Naturalism at the time these theories were being worked out. As a result of these developments style is re-established as a means of expression rather than a means of precise and accurate reportage. But, curiously, the very search for accuracy and objectivity has a great deal to do with this change. I have already indicated that Holz's theory develops in an unexpected direction, and I believe that this is much more evidently true of the literary style, the *Sekundenstil* which he and Schlaf employed.

Heinrich Hart gives an impression of what was most probably Holz's original intention in developing this style:

Er entwickelte seine Ansicht am Beispiel eines vom Baume fallenden Blattes. Die alte	He used the example of a leaf falling from a tree to explain his ideas. The

---

Festschrift für F. R. Schröder (Heidelberg: Winter, 1959), p. 245; Helmut Praschek, 'Das Verhältnis von Kunsttheorie und Kunstschaffen im Bereich der deutschen naturalistischen Dramatik', (unpublished doctoral thesis, University of Greifswald, 1957), p. 17.

[14] Holz, *Das Werk*, X, 53; see also p. 364.

[15] Quoted from Dieter Schickling, *Interpretationen und Studien zur Entwicklung und geistesgeschichtlichen Stellung des Werkes von Arno Holz* (doctoral thesis, University of Tübingen, Tübingen, 1965), p. 72.

[16] Holz, *Das Werk*, X, 159.

[17] Holz, *Das Werk*, X, 96; cf. Schickling, *Interpretationen und Studien*, p. 67; and Holz, *Briefe: Eine Auswahl*, edited by Anita Holz and Max Wagner (Munich: Piper, 1949), p. 266.

Kunst hat von dem fallenden Blatt weiter nichts zu melden gewußt, als daß es im Wirbel sich drehend zu Boden sinkt. Die neue Kunst schildert diesen Vorgang von Sekunde zu Sekunde; sie schildert, wie das Blatt, jetzt auf dieser Seite vom Licht beglänzt, rötlich aufleuchtet, auf der andern schattengrau erscheint, in der nächsten Sekunde ist die Sache umgekehrt, sie schildert, wie das Blatt erst senkrecht fällt, dann zur Seite getrieben wird, dann wieder lotrecht sinkt, sie schildert – ja, der Himmel weiß, was sie sonst noch zu berichten hat.[18]	old kind of art could only say of the failing leaf that it sinks to the ground in a spiralling motion. The new art describes this process second by second; it describes how the leaf, illuminated on one side, appears red, on the other a shadowy grey, and how, a second later, this is reversed; it describes how the leaf first falls vertically, then is blown to one side, then falls vertically again, it describes – heaven knows what else it has to report.

Lamprecht, writing more sympathetically of Naturalist poetry, describes its distinctive qualities as intensity and precision: 'Such intense observation of the intimate details of the world of appearances is something absolutely original.'[19] Holz himself, when speaking of the potentiality of the new style emphasizes similar characteristics:

Was die alte Kunst mit ihren primitiveren Mitteln, an die wir nicht mehr glauben, die uns keine Illusion mehr geben, schon einmal getan, diese neue Kunst mit ihren komplizierteren Mitteln, hinter denen wir mal wieder bis auf weiteres noch nicht so die Fäden sehen, wird es noch einmal leisten: den ganzen Menschen von neuem geben![20]	What the old kind of art once did, with its more primitive means, in which we no longer have any faith, and which no longer provide any illusion, this new art, with its more complex means, through which we cannot yet see, will achieve once again: it will reveal the whole man anew!

In view of the scientific background to Naturalism this emphasis on accuracy, precision, and complexity is not surprising; it did not,

---
[18] 'Literarische Erinnerungen', *Gesammelte Werke*, edited by Julius Hart, 4 vols (Berlin E. Fleischel, 1907), III, 69.
[19] Karl Lamprecht, *Deutsche Geschichte*, 14 vols (Berlin: Gaertner, 1895–1909), 1er Ergänzungsband (1902), p. 212.
[20] Holz, *Das Werk*, X, 215.

however, feature quite so exclusively in the theory of Zola, who chose also to emphasize the opposite virtues of simplicity and amplitude, vigour and even crudity; and, of course, these qualities are fully reflected in the novels of Zola, as those German critics who praised his epic breadth and grandeur were well aware.

Furthermore it is not self-evident that the precision advocated by Holz is at all likely to lead to works of art that are, in any sense, more 'objective' than the work of Zola. I should like to illustrate this by comparing a short passage from Holz's and Schlaf's *Ein Tod*, with a piece of English prose, written with a degree of precision at least equal to that of Holz and Schlaf.

Der erste Sonnenstrahl blitzte jetzt goldig uber die Dächer weg in das Zimmer. Er legte einen hellen Schein auf die dunkelblaue Tapete uber dem Bett und zeichnete die Fensterkreuze schief gegen die Wand. Die Bücherrücken auf dem Regal funkelten, die Gläser und Flaschen auf dem Tisch fingen an zu flinkern. Die Arabesken des blanken Bronzerahmens um die kleine Photographie auf dem Tisch mitten zwischen dem weißen, auseinandergezerrten Verbandzeug und dem Geschirre glitzerten. Auf den Dächern draußen lärmten wie toll die Spatzen. Unten auf dem Hofe unterhielten sich ganz laut ein paar Frauen. 'Donnerwetter! Ist das eine wüste Wirtschaft hier!' Jens, der zum Sofa ging, war uber ein Paar Stiefel gestolpert, die mitten im Zimmer auf dem verschobenen, staubigen Teppich lagen. 'Mir ist ganz öd im Schädel!' Schwer hatte er sich wieder auf das knackende Sofa	The first ray of golden sunlight shone over the rooftops into the room. It cast a bright gleam on the dark blue wall paper and inscribed the slanting shadow of the window frame on the opposite wall. The backs of the books on the shelves glistened, the glasses and bottles on the table began to sparkle. The arabesques of the shiny bronze frame around the small photograph on the table, between the unwrapped white bandages and the dishes, glittered. On the roofs outside the sparrows were chirping madly. Down below in the yard a few women were chatting loudly. 'Good Lord! What a mess!' Jens, who was going to the sofa, had stumbled over a pair of boots which were lying in the middle of the room on the crooked, dusty carpet. 'I feel all washed up!' He had sunk back heavily on the creaking sofa.

sinken lassen. Olaf hatte nicht geantwortet. Jens reckte sich. 'Übrigens... Es war eine schneidige Mensur!' 'Ja! Sehr korrekt!' 'Ja! Sehr ehrenhaft! – Fur" beide!' 'Eversen ist ins Ausland, nicht wahr?' 'Wahrscheinlich!' Jens betrachtete nachdenklich die beiden blitzenden Pistolenläufe über dem Sofa. 'Wenn sie nun kommen?' 'Hm.' 'Ae!' Jens gähnte nervös. Wo bleibt denn dieser alte – Ohrwurm?!' 'Wann können sie denn hier sein?' Olaf hatte sich vom Bett in die Höhe gerichtet. 'Ich denke, nach sechs?' 'Hm!'	Olaf had not replied. Jens stretched himself 'By the way... It was a first-rate duel!' 'Yes! Very correct!' 'Yes! Very honourable! – For both!' 'Eversen has gone abroad, hasn't he?' 'Probably!' Jens looked thoughtfully at the two gleaming pistol barrels above the sofa. – 'What do we do when they come?' 'Hm.' 'Ae!' Jens gave a nervous yawn. 'Whatever's keeping that – Old woman?!' 'When can they get here by?' Olaf had got up from the bed. 'I should say after six?' 'Hm!'

I shut the closet door and went out of the bedroom, holding my handkerchief ready for more doorknobs. The door next the linen closet, the locked door, had to be the bathroom. I shook it but it went on being locked. The key for this ought to be kept on the top shelf of the linen closet but it wasn't. I tried my knife blade, but that was too thin. I went back to the bedroom and got a flat nail file off the dresser. That worked. I opened the bathroom door. A man's sand-coloured pyjamas were tossed over a painted hamper. A pair of heelless green slippers lay on the floor. There was a safety razor on the edge of the washbowl and a tube of cream with the cap off. The bathroom window was shut, and there was a pungent smell in the air that was not quite like any other smell.

Three empty shells lay bright and coppery on the nile green tiles of the bathroom floor, and there was a nice clean hole in the frosted pane of the window. To the left and a little above the window were two scarred places in the plaster where the white showed behind the paint and where something, such as a bullet, had gone in.

The shower curtain was green and white oiled silk and it hung on shiny chromium rings and it was drawn across the shower opening. I slid it aside, the rings making a thin scraping noise, which for some reason sounded indecently loud.

I felt my neck creak a little as I bent down. He was there all right – there wasn't anywhere else for him to be. He was huddled in the corner under the two shining faucets, and water dripped slowly on his chest from the chromium showerhead. [From The Lady in the Lake, copyright © 1944 by Raymond Chandler (Hamish Hamilton, London).]

The most obvious difference between the extracts is that Chandler's is clearly structured towards a point of provisional closure. It is also a first-person narrative, and we see in both structure and style a reflection of the narrator's character. The precision is the precision of a trained observer, the detective, coolly, and detachedly taking in all the details, because any one of them – at the time of the investigation he does not know which – may later prove to be a vital clue. But the time of the narration is not the time of the investigation; so the narrator does know what eventually turned out to be significant and what did not, but it is not in his interest as a story-teller to reveal this.[21] He can best create suspense by giving the details without relating them to a whole; this is the same kind of suspense as the cinema creates by showing a scene in a series of close-ups, and keeping the audience waiting, not knowing what the next frame might bring (but suspecting that sooner or later it will be something nasty). The suspense arises largely from the audience's tendency to draw inferences from what it is shown, and, what is part of the same thing, a desire to fit all the pieces together, and so get some kind of grasp over the whole.

It is not entirely frivolous to compare the style of Holz and Schlaf with that of Chandler for their descriptions have much in common with his, and can, above all, create a similar kind of suspense. Holz and Schlaf do not tell us what any chance observer would see, they describe with a more than ordinary precision; and by bringing us so close to objects they deprive us of reassuring familiarity. The objects in this room are seen only in their immediate context – the books on the shelf, the glasses, the bottles, and the photograph on the table, the boots on the carpet – and we need to read very attentively, or to keep looking back in the text, if we are to understand the disposition of objects about the room as a whole. The dialogue of the latter half of the passage is similarly fragmented. The narrator does not distil it into a completely meaningful conversation; he does not discriminate between the incidental noises, and the articulated thoughts, but reports everything as it comes. In ordinary conversation the listener does discriminate, and eliminates the noises, unless they really are very obtrusive. By putting them down on paper, where we are not accustomed to seeing them recorded, Holz and Schlaf draw a disproportionate amount of attention to them, making conversation seem difficult, the familiar seem

---

[21] Cf. Gérard Genette, *Figures III*, (Paris: Éditions du Seuil), 1972, pp. 214–15.

strange. The price of over-close scrutiny is a frightening loss of grasp. Hofmannsthal makes a similar point with a nice analogy:

> Mein Geist zwang mich, alles... in einer unheimlichen Nähe zu sehen so wie ich einmal in einem Vergrößerungsglas ein Stück von der Haut meines kleinen Fingers gesehen hatte, das einem Blachfeld mit Furchen und Höhlen glich, so ging es mir nun mit den Menschen und ihren Handlungen.[22]

> My mind forced me to see everything in mysterious close-up; just as when I had once observed a section of the skin of my little finger through a magnifying glass, which looked like a ploughed field with furrows and hollows, so it was now with people and their actions.

In the passage by Chandler the narrator is carefully and consciously building up excitement; he is *unwilling* to order his material in such a way that the reader can survey it in a relaxed manner; Holz and Schlaf present their story through the eyes of a narrator who is, it seems, *unable* to put things in their place, or to differentiate between the significant and the insignificant. All he can do is register everything he sees, and in so doing register his own incomprehension, as Hofmannsthal does by the use of parataxis in the first few strophes of the 'Ballade des äußeren Lebens':

> Und Kinder wachsen auf mit tiefen Augen,
> Die von nichts wissen, wachsen auf und sterben,
> Und alle Menschen gehen ihre Wege.
>
> Und süße Früchte werden aus den herben
> Und fallen nachts wie tote Vögel nieder
> Und liegen wenig Tage und verderben.

The hostility which was evident in the account of this style by Heinrich Hart, which I quoted above, is not just a personal matter; it is the hostility of the idealist who likes to see a pattern in things or, if none is apparent, likes to see a spiritual effort made to impose one. The *Sekundenstil* irritates the reader by depriving him of the possibility of a synthesising overview and leaving him only with the disintegrated fragments of existence; this irritation is accurately summed up by Hofmannsthal in his essay 'Der Dichter und diese Zeit' (1907).[23] It is a

---
[22] 'Ein Brief' (1902), in *Gesammelte Werke in Einzelausgaben*, edited by Herbert Steiner, 15 vols (Stockholm and Frankfurt a.M.: S. Fischer Verlag, 1945–59), *Prosa II* (1951), 14.
[23] *Prosa II*, 287.

style which expresses, though it does not state explicitly, a sense of loss and anxiety in an atomised world, and it is not therefore surprising that the early prose of Kafka has been seen to have its roots in Naturalism.[24]

In developing the precise style of 'konsequenter Naturalismus' in literature Holz was probably motivated by the veristic intention common to many of his contemporaries, but this intention is irrelevant, for the quality of this style makes it more appropriate to a decidedly subjective kind of work, or one that is realistic only in the sense that it shows how certain people experience reality. In the context of German literature, with its distaste for actualities and for the presentation of the external social world, it would indeed have been remarkable if the *Sekundenstil* had been employed principally as a means of registering visible realities, rather than the response of individuals to them. Despite their claim to have created in *Papa Hamlet* a work of complete originality, Holz and Schlaf are most definitely still within an established tradition. This emerges very clearly in the early part of Holz's essay, *Die Kunst: Ihr Wesen und ihre Gesetze*, where Holz includes a short extract from an autobiographical novel, 'Goldene Zeiten', on which he had been working. He draws attention to one sentence which gave him particular satisfaction, because it seemed to exclude the momentary temperament of himself, the writer: 'In Holland mußten die Paradiesvögel entschieden schöner pfeifen und die Johannisbrotbäume noch viel, viel wilder wachsen.'[25] This exotic evocation of Holland, with birds of paradise singing and carob trees growing luxuriantly, is manifestly not a piece of objective description; and Holz's pleasure must have derived from his rendering of the mood of boyish enthusiasm and naivety, that is to say his elimination of direct author-intervention by the use of free indirect speech. The novel, then, if it had been completed, could have taken its place among those nineteenth-century German works by writers from Grillparzer to Keyserling which, according to Richard Brinkann, tend increasingly to present a subjective view in a basically objective manner.[26] Holz rarely discussed such technicalities as free indirect speech in his theoretical writings, but a comment by Schlaf shows that he did, for a time, turn his mind to its possibilities:

| Holz war damals dahin gekommen, dem Zolaschen Satze 'Un chef d'oeuvre est | Holz had reached the point of comparing Zola's sentence 'A work of art |

---

[24] See Jörg Thalmann, *Wege zu Kafka Eine Interpretation des Amerikaromans* (Frauenfeld and Stuttgart: Huber, 1966), pp. 70–93.
[25] Holz, *Das Werk*, X, 45.
[26] *Wirklichkeit und Illusion* (Tübingen: Niemeyer, 1957), pp. 321ff. Brinkmann's book might be said to continue the process I have been discussing, for he too, redefines 'realism' in such a way as to make it an essentially subjective style.

un coin de la Nature vu à	is a corner of nature seen
travers un tempérament' den	through a temperament',
anderen gegenüberzustellen:	with the sentence: A
Ein Kunstwerk ist ein Stück	work of art is a piece of
Leben, angesehen nicht	life seen not through the
durch das Temperament des	temperament of the artist,
Künstlers, sondern aller der	but of all the people he
Personen, die er geben will.[27]	wishes to present.

This brings us to the principal contribution which Holz makes in the collaboration with Schlaf. The latter's sketch, *Ein Dachstubenidyll*, which provided the basis for *Papa Hamlet*, is a completely unremarkable little story which covers the short and miserable life of the child of an unemployed actor and his wife.[28] Holz seized on the fact that one of the main characters in the story was an actor, interwove into the narrative quotations from a role with which the actor, Thienwiebel, might have identified himself, and so produced a story with considerable satirical bite, centred on the illusory relationship of Thienwiebel to the world around him. The interruption of Thienwiebel's bombastic monologues with brief, restrained descriptive passages cuts the protagonist down to size, by enabling the reader to judge that his view of things is hopelessly incongruous:

Armes kleines Menschenkind!	'Poor little mortal! What evil
Welch böser Stern verdammte	star condemned you to this
dich in dieses Elend!' Das	misery!' The poor little
arme kleine Menschenkind	mortal kicked at him and
zappelte ihn an und lachte.	laughed. 'But stay! Stay!
'Aber still! Still! Ich will alles	I will venture all!... I will
einsetzen!... Ich werde dem	defy destiny; I will wrest
Schicksal die Stirn bieten;	from it the acknowledgement
ich werde ihm abtrotzen, daß	that some day you may take
du in dieser Welt dereinst	up a place in the world meet
jene Stellung einnimmst, die	for someone of your
deinen Talenten gebührt... Ja!	talents... Yes! Thus
So macht Gewissen Feige aus	conscience does make
uns allen...' Seine Stimme	cowards of us all...' His
bebte, seine Schlafrocktroddeln	voice trembled, behind him
hinter ihm, die er sich	his dressing-gown tassles,
zuzubinden vergessen	which he had forgotten
hatte, zitterten.[29]	to tie up, were shaking.

---

[27] Quoted from Holz, X, 336.
[28] Reprinted in Arno Holz and Johannes Schlaf, *Papa Hamlet. Ein Tod*, edited by Fritz Martini (Stuttgart Reclam, 1968), pp. 83–102.
[29] Bjarne P. Holmsen, *Papa Hamlet* (Leipzig: Reißner, 1889), pp. 34f.

The distance between narrator and character gives the sketch a satirical dimension. An illusory view of the world is ironically rejected. A critical realism informs the work, giving it a satisfying hardness, rare in a literary movement which is, on the whole, over-indulgent to the whims and irresponsibilities of the artist. Thienwiebel's escapism is, nonetheless, made understandable. It is only by adopting a role that he is able to attain any sort of mastery, and this an illusory one, over the world in which he lives. In the extract from *Ein Tod* which I discussed above the only flash of actual conversation is where the two characters speak of the duel, for the duel is a convention in which they each have roles they understand; the rest of the time they spend talking past each other in a painfully embarrassed way. Among Hauptmann's characters, Robert Scholz needs to adopt the role of a hard-bitten cynic, and Johannes Vockerat that of a moral pioneer, in order to find the strength to survive. The sense of exposure and isolation in an incomprehensible and therefore hostile world is responsible for these various forms of escapism. This is the only kind of resistance offered by the weak character; without his role Thienwiebel can only wander around aimlessly while the world seems to disintegrate about him. It is at this point that the satirical perspective of the story, depending as it does on the firm distinction between subject and object, becomes blurred, and the narrator rather clumsily invites us to identify with the main character: 'The great Thienwiebel was not so wrong: his whole household was the abstract and brief chronicle of the times.'[30]

In the second story of the *Papa Hamlet* collection, *Der erste Schultag*, the satirical element is less important and the narrative perspective, despite the variable focalisation, more consistent.[31] Here free indirect speech is exploited more consistently, the dominant perspective being that of the young Jonathan, a boy experiencing a very full and very frightening first day at school. His experience includes a violent verbal assault on one of his fellow-pupils by the sadistic *Rektor*, severe intimidation at the hands of the school bully, and the terrifying discovery when he flees to an aged friend that the latter is sitting dead in his chair. More evidently and more sensationally than in *Papa Hamlet* Holz (who claimed sole authorship of this story) is concerned to create an impression of terror and to encourage the reader to share it by objectivizing it; but he still preserves some of the irony of *Papa Hamlet* by adopting the viewpoint of so obviously limited a character (although a touch of

---

[30] *Papa Hamlet*, p. 72
[31] See Roy Pascal, 'Arno Holz, *Der erste Schultag*: The Prose-style of Naturalism', in *'Erfahrung und Überlieferung': Festschrift for C.P. Magill*, edited by Hinrich Siefken and Alan Robinson (Cardiff The University of Wales Press, 1974), pp. 151–65 (p. 159), and Rob. Burns, *The Quest for Modernity*, p. 92.

sentimentality rather softens this irony). *Ein Tod*, the third of these sketches, is free of any trace of critical irony. Here the writer, and this time it was almost certainly Schlaf alone, concentrates, as I have already begun to demonstrate, on re-creating an attitude of mind, in this case a sense of being hopelessly trapped. For all its apparent precision the information conveyed by the narrator's words actually amounts to very little; their purpose is to create atmospheric intensity, and so empathy, by impressionistic means.[32] Dialogue combines with silences and pauses, descriptive passages alternate with fragments of dialogue to give expression to the predicament of characters waiting (the characteristic symbol of dependence in German Naturalist literature), watching over their dying companion, seemingly imprisoned in a dark, cheerless and silent room, cut off from the outside world, whose light and noise only penetrate as a series of fragmentary impressions of the inaccessible:

Draußen krähte wieder der Hahn. Ein leiser Windstoß strich am Fenster vorbei. In der Nachbarschaft kräuselte sich aus einem Schornstein ein feiner, weißer Rauch in das mattblaue, eckige Stück Himmel über den Hinterhäusern.[33]	Outside the cock crew again. A gentle puff of wind passed the window. Near by a thin column of white smoke wound out of a chimney into the dull blue corner of sky above the backs of the houses.

This discussion of the prose sketches of Holz and Schlaf provides a convenient point at which to make a brief mention of Hauptmann's *Bahnwärter Thiel*, for it too is a work in which the point-of-view technique is used to considerable effect. As in *Papa Hamlet* and *Der erste Schultag* the point of view adopted is the obviously relative one of a limited character, whose own delusions contribute to his personal tragedy. The story is one which Hauptmann takes up again in his drama *Fuhrmann Henschel*, that of a man unable to reconcile the spiritual and the sensual aspects of his personality, represented by his first and second wives, and failing in his attempt to order his life in such a way that they are kept strictly apart. He devotes the hours he has to spend in the lonely silence of the countryside to the memory of his dead wife, Minna, and tries to contain the more physical Lene in the home environment. But just as the train disturbs the peace of the countryside, breaking into his dreams of

---
[32] Cf. Dieter Kafitz, *Johannes Schlaf – Weltanschauliche Totalität und Wirklichkeitsblindheit: Ein Beitrag zur Neubestimmung des Naturalismus-Begriffs und zur Herleitung totalitärer Denkformen*, (Tübingen: Niemeyer, 1992), pp. 56–57, p. 237.
[33] *Papa Hamlet*, p. 170

Minna, and demanding his attention as crossing-keeper, so Lene insists on coming out to his workplace, and defiling ground which Thiel regards as sacred:

Es war ihm plötzlich eingefallen, daß ja nun Lene des öfteren herauskommen würde, um den Acker zu bestellen, wodurch dann die hergebrachte Lebensweise in bedenkliche Schwankungen geraten mußte. Und jäh verwandelte sich seine Freude über den Besitz des Ackers in Widerwillen.... Er wußte kaum warum, aber die Aussicht, Lene ganze Tage lang bei sich im Dienst zu haben, wurde ihm, so sehr er auch versuchte, sich damit zu versöhnen, immer unerträglicher. Es kam ihm vor, als habe er etwas ihm Wertes zu verteidigen, als versuchte jemand sein Heiligstes anzutasten (VI, 50f).	It had suddenly occurred to him that Lene would frequently be coming out to see to the land, which was bound to disturb his customary way of life considerably. And at once his joy in the possession of this land turned into revulsion. He scarcely knew why, but the prospect of having Lene with him at work for whole days became more and more unbearable, however much he tried to reconcile himself to it. It was as if he had something valuable to defend, as if someone were trying to encroach on that which was most sacred to him.

A vague parallel is thus established in the mind of Thiel – and in the structure of the story – between Lene and the train, which becomes most evident in the description of Lene at work: 'After the woman had hastily devoured a thick crust of bread, she threw her jacket and scarf away and began to dig with the speed and stamina of a machine' (VI, 56). While on a rational level Lene is guilty only of negligence in allowing young Tobias to play on the railway-line, in Thiel's mind she is part of those forces which are hostile to his first wife, Minna, and her child, and is therefore directly responsible for Tobias' death. In this way the symbolic meaning of the story is skilfully integrated in the psychological motivation of the central character. However to integrate it in the psychology of this character is to render it suspect; yet there is no explicit statement of suspicion and no irony in the actual narrative; the story-teller identifies himself completely with the symbolism.

The tendency away from critical realism which is evident here, and which we noted in Holz's and Schlaf's sketches, is taken a stage further in their drama, *Die Familie Selicke* (1890). Here again it was Schlaf who provided the material for the work, from another prose sketch of his, *Mainacht*, but in the present context Holz's contribution is more significant than would appear from Schlaf's subsequent claim that it consisted of no more than his share in a few lines on the first seven pages of Act I and the last three pages of Act III. It was on the suggestion of Holz that Schlaf altered the play by bringing in the character 'der olle Kopelke', who had already appeared in the sketch *Die papierne Passion* (1887–88; published 1892); and it is precisely on the pages which Schlaf mentions that Kopelke appears. He is a character who is open to the same hostile treatment as Thienwiebel received in *Papa Hamlet*. By profession a cobbler, Kopelke is also an old quack who offers advice and assistance to the family of the dying child, Linchen Selicke. He is evidently not motivated by anything but the impulse of a good-natured old man to help this wretched family, but he cannot help basking in the illusion of status that his role gives him, as the following passage rather subtly suggests:

FRAU SELICKE.... Und... na ja, wenn wir Sie nicht noch hatten... KOPELKE. *leichthin.* Jo!... na!... Wissen Se: det kommt jo bei mir nich so druf an!... Ick... nu ja! Se wissen ja! Ick bin man sozusagen 'n janz eenfacher Mann... Abber det kann'k Ihn' versichern: jeholfen hab 'k schon manchen!... Jott! Ick kennt jo wat bei verdienen! Wat meen'n Se woll! Abber sehn Se... will 'k denn? Ick... nu ja! Ick bin nu mal so! *Eifrig.* Wissen Se? de Hauptsach' is jetz': man immer scheen warm halten! det Ibrije, verstehn Se, det Ibrije jibt sick denn janz von alleene!... man bloß nich immer so ville mang der Natur fuschen, sag ick!...³⁴	FRAU SELICKE.... And... well, if we hadn't still got you... KOPELKE. *casually.* Yes!... well! You know! I'm just an ordinary sort of man... But I can tell you, I've helped lots of people in my time! Heavens! I could earn a lot like that! Don't you reckon? But you see... do I want to? Me... ah well! That's what I'm like! *Eagerly.* You know what? The main thing now is just keep her nice and warm! You see the rest will take care of itself!... what I say is, you don't want to keep mucking about with nature!

Kopelke resembles Thienwiebel in that he too is in an illusory relationship with reality, but his illusions are not criticized from a rational standpoint, and are not shown as socially harmful; they are smiled on

---

³⁴ *Die Familie Selicke* (Berlin: Issleib, 1890²), p. 14.

tolerantly and indulgently. In this respect *Die Familie Selicke* anticipates Hauptmann's comedy, *Kollege Crampton*.

In its basic situation *Die Familie Selicke* closely resembles the *Papa Hamlet* sketches; once again the authors choose a subject which expresses the complete helplessness of the individual in the face of his environment. The play was criticized by Carl Spitteler (one of its more sympathetic critics) for the monotony engendered by the lack of progress between the first and second acts, both of which open with the family waiting despairingly for the homecoming of Selicke.[35] The situation throughout most of the first act of *Das Friedensfest* is exactly the same; but Hauptmann's play is superior in its execution, its atmosphere is tenser. There is nothing wrong with the conception of *Die Familie Selicke* at this point. This state of nervous and anxious waiting need not be a dull and monotonous experience for reader or audience, for it is an artistically adequate expression of the predicament of the characters involved; and the message of the play is that the predicament of a family sitting at home, waiting, impotent, dependent, and imprisoned, can be a predicament of wide representative significance and interest.

If the play is looked at in this way the fate of Toni Selicke becomes more poignant, and its social implications more evident. She is the only character who is offered any chance of escape, the possibility of marriage to the *Kandidat*, Wendt, and retreat from the loathsome city to a comfortable country parsonage (this particular nuance is recognizably a contribution of Schlaf[36]). Indirectly, but no less effectively for that, critical light is cast on the institution of marriage in a society where woman is tied to the family, and where it is thus debased to a means of escape. The situation does not, however, permit Toni to make a free choice; with the death of her younger sister, Linchen, she feels an obligation to stay with her parents, and keep the home together. The objection that this is an unlikely decision in the circumstances cannot be sustained; it is a very likely decision because it is shown to be hardly a conscious decision at all, and certainly not an exemplary moral one. It is one of those deeds 'performed without thought, without choice, perhaps even without love', an example of what Lionel Trilling has described as the 'morality of inertia'.[37] In the case of Toni Selicke the implied causes are both social and ideological, but they are interiorised to such a degree that it is simply inconceivable to her that she should now leave her

---

[35] Carl Spitteler, 'Die Familie Selicke' (1890), in *Gesammelte Werke*, 10 vols, edited by Gottfried Bohnenblust and others (Zürich: Artemis, 1945–58), IX (1950), 331–39 (p. 338).
[36] Cf. the first act of Schlaf's play *Meister Oelze* (1894); see also below, p. 69.
[37] Cf. Lionel Trilling, 'The morality of inertia', in *A Gathering of Fugitives* (London: Secker and Warburg, 1957), pp. 31–40.

parents.[38] She does not therefore think about her position, and does not explicitly announce a decision, but simply reverts to the polite form as she speaks to Wendt of his impending departure: 'Sie müssen ja um elf – fort'.[39] She cannot really explain her change of mind, but can only appeal for Wendt's understanding, and strengthen herself with the brave rationalisation that they would not have been happy anyway.

Holz and Schlaf are capable of revealing complex psychological motivation through very ordinary sounding language. At the same time their drama is based on a subtle analysis of social and, especially, family structures in Wilhelmine Germany.[40] Within its limited range their writing can reach a high analytical level. In *Die Familie Selicke*, however, this level is not sustained. Holz' and Schlaf's play suffers – like Hauptmann's *Vor Sonnenaufgang* – from a certain lack of structural and stylistic consistency, without being an obviously inconsistent play, for it has another, lesser, sort of consistency – a sentimental appeal – running right through it. The play, if we consider its impact as a whole, does not confine itself to the analysis of an experience of isolation and the unmasking of false consciousness, it forcefully invites its audience to spare some sympathy for a family cut off by poverty from the happiness (and especially the Christmas festivities) of the world outside. In the final scene Wendt emerges as a *raisonneur* to voice this sentimental appeal in the most obvious and banal way, by drawing attention to the sacrifice made by Toni, and declaring that this has renewed his belief that life is, despite all its misery, worthwhile: 'Life is serious! Deadly serious! ... But now I see that it is also beautiful! And do you know why, my dear Toni? Because there are people like you!'[41]

By being reduced to objects of sentimental sympathy the characters are made remote, their predicament less disturbing; and this distance is increased by the conventional nature of certain aspects of the play. Among the characters the two sons, Walter and Albert, are quite finely drawn and differentiated, but the nagging mother, the drunken father, and the sceptical *Kandidat* are from stock. The action moves very slowly, but it is structured in an unoriginal way; the acts all have a strong theatrical ending, and in the last act an artificial tension is created by the announcement that Wendt's train is due to leave in two hours,

---

[38] Helmut Scheuer, 'Arno Holz/Johannes Schlaf: *Die Familie Selicke*', in *Interpretationen: Dramen des Naturalismus* (Stuttgart: Reclam, 1988), pp. 67–106 (pp. 100–101).
[39] *Die Familie Selicke*, p. 80.
[40] See Dieter Kafitz, 'Struktur und Menschenbild naturalistischer Dramatik' *Zeitschrift für deutsche Philologie*, 97 (1978), 225–55 and Klaus Müller-Salget, 'Autorität und Familie im naturalistischen Drama', *Zeitschrift für deutsche Philologie*, 103 (1984), 502–19.
[41] *Die Familie Selicke*, p. 89.

and therefore Toni must hurry and decide whether she is to marry him or not. To conclude, all the characters assemble to form a tableau in the conventional manner (Kopelke having conveniently returned), and they hear Wendt make the comforting announcement that he will return.[42]

It cannot be stated too strongly that the major failings of *Die Familie Selicke* are not failings of the *Sekundenstil*. *Ein Tod* shows that Holz and Schlaf could use this style without any directly sentimental appeal and without such manifest concessions to traditional literary forms. As it is, these weaknesses are a reminder that, even in what are regarded as their most extreme moments, the German Naturalists can be very uncertain and timid.

---

[42] *Die Familie Selicke*, p. 94. Cf. Wolfgang Kayser, 'Zur Dramaturgie des naturalistischen Schauspiels', in *Die Vortragsreise: Studien zur Literatur* (Bern: Francke, 1958), pp. 214-31 (pp. 222-24).

4
NATURALISM AND SOCIALISM

In my examination of the early prose writings of Holz and Schlaf I suggested that the achievement of the style which the two writers employed was to give direct expression to the anxiety experienced in the face of a world which can be understood in precise, scientific detail, but whose overall purpose or shape cannot be comprehended. This style involved the accurate reproduction of everyday speech, and the precise inventory of physical detail; in his early theory Holz rationalized this into the doctrine of mimetic naturalism. But as Holz turned his attention to the more evidently personal genre, the lyric, it became increasingly apparent that he felt the need of this newly-won precision to express his own individual and unique sensations; he began to make the same demands on language as were made by Rilke in *Das Stundenbuch*:

> Ich glaube an alles noch nie Gesagte.
> Ich will meine frömmsten Gefühle befrein.

Holz's success in doing this is rather less evident than Rilke's, but however foolish his claims to have restored the 'natural value' of words, however eccentric his theories of rhythm and diction, however grotesque his *Mittelachsenverse*, there is about all these experiments a tenacious consistency of purpose: they are all part of a protest against the crushing weight of tradition, against what Holz describes as the 'tyranny' of Goethe and Heine over subsequent lyric poetry. As such, I believe they have a parallel in the various protests of Ibsen and his young German followers against the 'tyranny' of the past in the ethical sphere. The preoccupation of German Naturalist theorists with the precision of language is not just an indication of their concern over the distortion of nature by art, but it is part and parcel of an individualism which influences their outlook over the widest area. The early Naturalist manifestoes abound with statements like the following one from Hermann Conradi's introduction to the anthology, *Moderne Dichtercharaktere*: 'unrestrained, unconditional cultivation of their artistic individuality is the watch-word of these rebels and innovators', or Bleibtreu's demand: 'As an absolute priority subjectivity must be released, in order to put an end to ossifying convention'.[1] I draw attention to this attitude because

---

[1] Hermann Conradi, 'Unser Credo', *Moderne Dichtercharaktere*, edited by Wilhelm Arent (Leipzig: W. Friedrich, 1885), p. iii; Bleibtreu, 'Andere Zeiten, andere Lieder!', *Die Gesellschaft*,

in this chapter I propose to examine the political history of the Naturalist movement, the flirtation with, and subsequent estrangement from, socialism; and I wish to emphasize that this latter development is no more surprising than the socialism itself.

Most of the writers associated with the Naturalist movement in Germany were born around 1860. They grew up during the years of Germany's delayed industrial revolution, in that period of intense commercial activity which saw the Buddenbrooks displaced by the Hagenströms. As young men of university age they came from the provinces to the rapidly growing cities, with their drab proletarian quarters, and their grim barrack-like tenements ('Mietskasernen'). To Berlin, the great literary centre, came the Hart brothers from Westphalia, Arno Holz from East Prussia, Johannes Schlaf from Halle, Max Dreyer from Pomerania, and from Silesia, by way of Zurich, the brothers Carl and Gerhart Hauptmann. Young, idealistic, and not particularly wealthy, the natural alliance for these writers was with the underprivileged, with the people who found themselves on the fringes of society (the waitress is a favourite figure in the novels of the 1880s). These newcomers soon perceived that they were in a society whose higher ranks were indifferent, if not hostile, to the less fortunate. Max Halbe writes of his early experiences of university life in Munich: 'I saw a large number of my fellow-students behaving in a crude, even barbaric way, and at the same time cultivating an exclusiveness which shut out every vestige of harsh reality'.[2] This critical judgement by an outsider is a common experience in this period, and is reflected in the form so closely associated with the German Naturalist drama: the play opening with a tense or 'ripe' situation, which is then set in motion by a newcomer, the 'Bote aus der Fremde'.

If their natural ally was the proletariat, the young writers' natural enemy was the bourgeoisie, that section of the community which read the family journal, *Die Gartenlaube*, and went to plays by Paul Lindau and Charlotte Birch-Pfeiffer, and whose taste and influence are attacked by the Hart brothers in the *Kritische Waffengänge*. This attack was taken up by many others and so, for a time at least, the Naturalists looked to the working-classes and to socialism to bring about a cultural revival – if only by destroying the bourgeoisie.[3]

One of the principal factors which directed the attention of the young Naturalist writers to the working-classes was the anti-Socialist legislation, imposed by Bismarck in 1878, which singled out Social Democracy as the enemy of the established order. In the first place this encouraged the tendency to regard the proletariat as an oppressed and

---

1 (1885), 892.

[2] *Scholle und Schicksal* (Munich: Knorr and Hirth, 1933), p. 280.

[3] Conrad Alberti, 'Die Bourgeoisie und die Kunst', *Die Gesellschaft*, 4 (1888), 840.

persecuted underdog, and so fostered a certain sentimental sympathy among the Naturalists; the early resistance among some of them to the ideas of Nietzsche is symptomatic of this attitude: 'Friedrich Nietzsche decisively rejects compassion, whereas Schopenhauer regards compassion as love, love as compassion. It was to be this kind of compassion which later dictated my Weavers,' wrote Gerhart Hauptmann in that part of his autobiography which covers these years (VII, 1079).[4] Of more direct importance was the inhibiting effect this legislation had on political activities and, after 1886, trades unions; this meant that the energies of the more articulate members of the working-classes were directed into organizations which were – or claimed to be – primarily cultural organizations: educational societies and discussion clubs. Writers such as the Hart brothers, Wilhelm Bölsche, and Bruno Wille thus came into contact with a kind of socialism which seemed to correspond to every middle-class intellectual's dream: 'Never have I come across a more passionate striving for knowledge, a more fervent hunger for education and culture than among those comrades who participated in the social struggles of the eighties and the nineties,' wrote Heinrich Hart.[5] In these years of close collaboration they gained, and helped to cultivate, the impression that immediate economic improvement and eventual political power were rather minor issues in comparison with the ultimate cultural purpose of socialism.

One development from the discussion clubs of the 1880s gave the Naturalists particular, and justifiable, satisfaction: the foundation of the *Volksbühnen*. The 1880s had seen a number of proposals (including one by Heinrich Hart) for the foundation of a 'People's Theatre'. In certain instances this had meant the revival of traditional popular festivals, but this was not the aim of the members of the Berlin discussion-club, the *Alte Tante*, who approached Bruno Wille in 1890. Their interest stimulated by contact with the Naturalist writers, they proposed that the club should join the *Freie Bühne*, and send members to its performances. Instead, Wille proposed that they should form their own organization, the *Freie Volksbühne*, and an appeal for support was published in the *Berliner Volksblatt* of 23 March 1890. The political situation of the time excluded any possible argument about how the society's aims should be defined; it was to be a cultural and educational enterprise: 'The aim of the Freie Volksbühne... is to have an educational influence on its public – an elite section of the people – and through this public to have

---

[4] Cf. Bruno Wille, 'Erinnerungen an Gerhart Hauptmann und seine Dichtergeneration', in *Mit Gerhart Hauptmann: Erinnerungen und Bekenntnisse aus seinem Freundeskreis*, edited by W. Heynen (Berlin: Stilke, 1922), pp. 83–116 (p. 98).
[5] H. Hart, 'Literarische Erinnerungen', *Gesammelte Werke*, edited by Julius Hart, 4 vols (Berlin: E. Fleischel, 1907), III, 78.

an impact on an even wider circle'. Wille vigorously defended the *Freie Volksbühne* against the charge (from right-wing opponents) that it was a front-organization for essentially political activity, insisting that the enterprise would not be taken over for party-political purposes, and quoting in support the proposed repertoire which included plays by Ibsen, Hauptmann, Zola, Gogol, Tolstoy, Ludwig, and Büchner.[6] The constitution resembled that of the *Freie Bühne* in its distinction between active and passive members; élite or not, the body of the membership was to have no direct influence on repertoire or policy: 'The Society consists of a leading group and its members. The leadership selects the plays to be performed and the actors. The members pay a quarterly subscription which entitles them to a theatre seat for three performances.'[7]

The choice of works to be performed was placed in the hands of a committee consisting of a chairman, a treasurer, a secretary and six members. Bruno Wille became the first chairman, with Karl Wildberger as treasurer, and Julius Türk as secretary; the other committee-members were Kurt Baake, Otto Brahm, Wilhelm Bölsche, Julius Hart, Conrad Schmidt, and Richard Baginski. The response from the working-class public, who were effectively excluded from the commercial theatre by the high cost of tickets, was considerable, and by the end of its first year the *Freie Volksbühne* had a membership of 1,873.

All this suggests that the 1880s were a period of fruitful and harmonious collaboration between the Naturalist movement and the organized working classes, which is superficially true. But there were special reasons why collaboration was so easy, and after 1890, when the anti-Socialist laws were allowed to lapse, these reasons no longer obtained. The effect of these laws within the Social Democratic Party had been to encourage centralization, to close the ranks, and discourage public controversy. Internal disputes, such as criticisms of the Gotha Programme of 1875, were left in abeyance; and because of the restrictions on the Party as a whole the parliamentary party in the *Reichstag* was able to establish itself as the official voice of the Party leadership. The Party actually came through the period with an immensely increased voting strength: 437,158 when the laws were imposed, and 1,427,298 in 1890, when Bismarck failed to have them extended further. This was an impressive achievement, and many contemporaries were duly impressed; Fontane wrote in a letter to James Morris:

---

[6] See Siegfried Nestriepke, *Geschichte der Volksbühne Berlins, 1890–1914* (Berlin: Volksbühnen Verlags- und Vertriebsgesellschaft, 1930) for a full history of the *Volksbühnen* during this period.

[7] Quoted from Nestriepke, *Geschichte der Volksbühne*, p. 11.

Alles Interesse ruht beim vierten Stand. Die neue bessere Welt fängt erst beim vierten Stand an. Man würde das sagen, auch wenn es sich bloß um Bestrebungen, um Anläufe handelte. So liegt es nicht. Das, was die Arbeiter denken, sprechen, schreiben, hat das Denken, Sprechen und Schreiben der altregierenden Klassen tatsächlich überholt. Alles ist viel echter, wahrer, lebensnäher, voller. Sie, die Arbeiter, packen alles neu an, haben nicht bloß neue Ziele, sondern auch neue Wege.[8]	All that is interesting now resides with the working class.... The new, better world begins with the working class. One would say this even if it were only a question of aspirations and beginnings. But it is not so. What the workers think, say, write, has really outdated the thinking, speaking, and writing of the ruling classes. Everything is more genuine, more vigorous. The working classes attack everything in a new way; not only are their ends new, but also their means.

There can, I think, be little doubt that the success of the socialist movement during these years contributed to the optimistic – often naively optimistic – belief of certain of the Naturalists in the benefits to be achieved by social reorganization. This found expression in the early lyric of Holz and Karl Henckell, and in the Utopianism of many young men, including a group with whom Gerhart Hauptmann was associated, who undertook a colonial enterprise, the *Ikarierbund* (which is referred to by Loth in *Vor Sonnenaufgang*) after the model of Étienne Cabet. It was in connection with this enterprise that Hauptmann was called as a witness in the *Breslau* treason trial of 1887.[9]

However naturally it arose, this alliance with socialism was a very insecure arrangement; even at the time when it was at its strongest there were clear signs that it was not destined to last, for the writers made all sorts of reservations, sometimes about socialism, sometimes about politics in general. Max Kretzer is a writer usually associated with the Naturalist movement; yet his novel *Die beiden Genossen* (1880) is a decidedly conservative work. It is, in fact, a defence of older values against the assault of organized socialism. It shows a conflict between the somewhat naive Utopianism of Schorn, and the radical communism

---

[8] 22.02.1896; *Werke, Schriften und Briefe*, edited by Walter Keitel und Helmuth Nürnberger, 20 vols (Munich: Hanser, 1962–94), Abt. IV, *Briefe*, edited by Otto Drude and others, 5 vols, IV (1982), 539. Cf. Käthe Kollwitz: 'Das eigentliche Motiv, warum ich... zur Darstellung fast nur das Arbeiterleben wählte, war, weil die aus dieser Sphäre gewählten Motive mir einfach und bedingungslos das gaben, was ich als schön empfand'; *Aus meinem Leben* (Munich: List, 1957), p. 50.

[9] See Heinrich Lux, 'Der Breslauer Sozialistenprozeß: Auch eine Hauptmann-Erinnerung', in *Mit Gerhart Hauptmann*, ed. Heynen, pp. 69–82; and A. Ziegelschmidt, 'Gerhart Hauptmanns Ikarier', *Germanic Review*, 13 (1938), 32–39.

of Raßmann (which, for good measure, is associated with such ideas as divorce and free love), and proclaims that changes in economic conditions need to be brought about peacefully and legally. Like Kretzer, few of the Naturalists really made a radical break with their origins; they tended to cling to the traditional middle-class values of the small provincial towns from which they came, where, as Schlaf declared, 'the old romantic-idealist Germany, with its stricter, in the last analysis patriarchal and religious attitudes, had been longest, most warmly and most faithfully preserved'.[10] This provincialism was, of course, bound to clash with the international character of the socialist movement.

Equally at odds with socialism was the ambivalent attitude of the Naturalists towards Bismarck. Despite their criticism of his social policy, and despite their solidarity with the Social Democrats, there were many among the Naturalists who admired the Chancellor as a great personality, a great individual, and even some who regarded him as an exponent of 'naturalism' in politics.[11] His supporters included the novelist and editor, Michael Georg Conrad, the poet, Karl Henckell, the dramatist, Max Halbe, and, from the fringe of the Naturalist movement, one of his most ardent supporters, Maximilian Harden. Such an attitude clearly went hand in hand with the attitude adopted increasingly in the latter part of the 1880s towards the work and personality of Zola and Ibsen; not surprisingly it was accompanied during these same years by a growing interest in the ideas of Nietzsche. (The reception of Nietzsche, like the German reception of Zola and Ibsen, was decisively influenced by George Brandes.)[12]

These few years saw some attempts to reconcile the general individualist trend with the ideas of Marx. Gerhart Hauptmann's *Vor Sonnenaufgang* perhaps owes some of its ambiguity to an attempt to do just this; Alfred Loth, a Social Democrat, who shares much of the Naturalists' philosophy, is presented as both an altruist and an egoist, and is unaware of any conflict: 'My struggle is a struggle for the happiness of the human race; if I am to be happy, then all my fellow men must be happy first' (I, 47). At the end of the play he sees his own position as unproblematical: for him his defection from Helene is consistent with both his struggle for the general good and his refusal to become a traitor to himself. Whether he intended it or not, Hauptmann's

---

[10] 'Die Freie Bühne und die Entstehung des naturalistischen Dramas', *Der Greif*, 1 (1914), i, 404.

[11] See Helmut Scheuer, 'Zwischen Sozialismus und Individualismus – Zwischen Marx und Nietzsche', in *Naturalismus: Bürgerliche Dichtung und soziales Engagement*, edited by Helmut Scheuer (Stuttgart: Kohlhammer, 1974), pp. 150–74 (pp. 161, 172n).

[12] For comments on the growth of Nietzsche's influence at this time, see M. Boulby, 'Optimism and Pessimism in German Naturalist Writers' (doctoral thesis, Leeds, 1951), pp. 534–41.

play contains an implicit criticism that Loth's theoretically consistent behaviour is not adequate in the face of real human problems, but it is worth noting that a number of critics sympathetic to Naturalism failed to see this, among them Gustav Landauer, who praised the 'healthy disinterest' of Loth's behaviour. (Brandes, by the way, condemned what he described as Loth's shallow theories of philanthropy, and recommended the study of Nietzsche.)[13] Another attempt to reconcile socialism and individualism can be seen in Heinrich Hart's essay of 1890, 'Die Moderne':

Nur scheinbar zielt der Sozialismus auf Uniformierung, auf eine noch drückendere Einzwängung in ein Staatsganzes. Sein Zweck ist es, das Individuum von der Sorge um das tägliche Brod zu entlasten, ihm seinen Lebensunterhalt unbedingt zu sichern, durch eine gleichmäßige und gerechte Verteilung von Arbeit und Arbeitsertrag, die materielle Arbeit selbst aber zu erleichtern und zu vermindern. Auf diese Weise kann es erreicht werden, daß der Mensch Zeit und Kraft gewinnt, sich in höherem Maße als heute der Ausbildung alles dessen zu widmen, was ihn wahrhaft erst zum Menschen macht.[14]	Socialism only appears to aim at uniformity, at a more oppressive subordination of the individual to the state. Its purpose is to free the individual from concern for his daily bread, to guarantee his subsistence unconditionally by a just and equitable division of labour and profit, and to ease the burden of physical work. In this way a man will have more time and energy to devote to the cultivation of what really makes him a man.

The theories of the young Marx on social alienation are here combined with an attitude towards the state which is reminiscent of Nietzsche: 'There is nothing of greater cultural importance than the preparation and generation of genius. Even the state, despite its barbaric origins and its authoritarian gestures, is only a means to this end'.[15]

---

[13] Gustav Landauer, 'Gerhart Hauptmann', *Die Neue Zeit*, 10 (1891–2), 615f. See also Felix A. Voigt, 'Die Aufnahme von *Vor Sonnenaufgang*', in *Hauptmann Studien* (Breslau: Maruschke and Berendt, 1936), pp. 63–85.
[14] *Der Kunstwart*, 4 (1890–91), 149. Cf. Bruno Wille, *Philosophie der Befreiung durch das reine Mittel* (Berlin: S. Fischer, 1894), pp. 298–99.
[15] Fragment, February, 1871; original version of the preface to *Die Geburt der Tragödie*, 'Vorwort an Richard Wagner', *Werke*, Kritische Gesamtausgabe edited by Giorgio Colli und Mazzino Montinari, 30 vols (Berlin and New York: de Gruyter, 1967–78), III/iii (1978), 371.

However, these are not words which show Nietzsche at his most prophetic or at his most independent. Indeed they are sufficiently typical of the this period to have been echoed by Paul Heyse: 'the aim of the statesman must be...to educate the public sense of justice in such a way that as many free individuals as possible can live in harmony together, and each can independently...devote himself to timeless tasks'.[16] Heinrich Hart's individualism, then, is essentially a continuation of Heyse's attitude, interrupted by a socialist interlude; it is not the startling new insight he himself claims.

During the 1880s such reservations were allowed to pass because, as I have suggested, the Social Democrats were in a tight corner; they had no reason to look for a quarrel with those who supported them, however ambiguous this support may have been; and even if they had wanted to quarrel, they were not favourably placed to do so, for they had very restricted means of publicity, and, as yet, no Franz Mehring, who could attack the young writers where it hurt them most, through criticism of their literary works. But by 1890 a quarrel was brewing. Throughout the period of the anti-socialist legislation the parliamentary party had followed a policy of restraint and moderation, rejecting anarchism and violence, and carefully not provoking any further repressive measures.[17] This policy, which had been sporadically criticized by younger socialists, came under heavy fire in 1890 and 1891 from a group, known as *die Jungen*, which included Bruno Wille and Paul Ernst, and a number of intellectuals closely associated with the Naturalist writers. The aims of the rebels were confused: the most articulate were hostile to the idea of the State as such, held individualistic or anarchistic views, and were critical of the increasingly centralized organization of the Social Democratic Party. At the same time there was a great deal of resentment between the local party leaders – many of them young men who had risen very quickly in the hierarchy – and the older, more experienced, and more cautious national leaders, who wished to reassert their authority in the new situation, and who were particularly anxious that radical minority views should not be allowed to jeopardize this new situation. The whole weight of the Party leadership was thrown against the revolutionary intellectuals; August Bebel addressed meetings in their strongholds, Dresden, Magdeburg, and Berlin, and Bebel again led the attack at the Erfurt congress in November 1891, which resulted in the withdrawal of Bruno Wille and his followers from the Social Democratic

---

[16] Quoted from Hermand, 'Zur Literatur der Gründerzeit', *Deutsche Vierteljahrsschrift für Literaturwissenschaft und Geistesgeschichte*, 41 (1967), 202–31 (p. 208).

[17] See Gerhard A. Ritter, 'Die Arbeiterbewegung im wilheminischen Reich: Die Sozialdemokratische Partei und die Freien Gewerkschaften', *Studien zur europäischen Geschichte aus dem Friedrich-Meinecke Institut der Freien Universität Berlin*, 3 (Berlin: Colloquium Verlag, 1959).

Party, and the formation of the Independent Socialists, the *Verein unabhängiger Sozialisten*.[18]

Less than a year later the same quarrel was re-enacted in the context of the *Freie Volksbühne*, for it soon became evident to the orthodox Socialists that the leadership of this organization was virtually in the hands of the 'independents', who were strongly backed up by such less politically-minded intellectuals as Brahm, Bölsche, the Hart brothers, Fritz Mauthner, Halbe, and Richard Dehmel.[19] A dispute arose between Julius Türk and Bruno Wille over the expense involved in the use of the *Lessingtheater*, but it soon became apparent that the real issue was the more fundamental one of who should control the society and how it should be run. The explanation of a later Marxist critic is that the influence of the 'independents' continued in the *Freie Volksbühne* and prevented this organization from becoming an instrument in the struggle for the emancipation of the proletariat.[20] The effect of this influence on the repertoire was not significant – at least not significant enough to warrant a clear change in policy after the 'independents' had withdrawn – but clearly a great deal of bitterness had been generated by a rather exclusive, undemocratic attitude on the part of the writers. In a very stormy general meeting on 12 October 1892, Paul Dupont (a trades union representative) demanded a greater number of workers on the committee, and questioned the need for any intellectuals at all. When he was elected deputy chairman, and Bruno Wille was replaced as chairman by the leading Socialist critic, Franz Mehring (who had not hitherto belonged to the society), some two or three hundred members, led by Wille and including most of the writers, walked out.

Mehring reorganized the society on more democratic lines, attacking the paternalism of his predecessors and encouraging the active participation of the rank-and-file members. His proclaimed principle was:

| daß unser Verein nur dann leben kann, wenn die Mitglieder nicht die Gegenstände einer noch so wohlgemeinten Erziehungskunst | that our society can only prosper if the members are not treated as objects of a pedagogic exercise, however well-meaning, |

---

[18] See Hans Manfred Bock, 'Die Literaten- und Studenten-Revolte' der Jungen in der SPD um 1980', *Das Argument*, 63 (1971), 22–41 (pp. 26–27).

[19] There are two accounts which examine in detail the connection between the political and the cultural quarrels: Manfred Brauneck, *Literatur und Öffentlichkeit im ausgehenden 19. Jahrhundert: Studien zur Rezeption des naturalistischen Theaters in Deutschland* (Stuttgart: Metzler, 1974), pp. 20–49; and Herbert Scherer, *Bürgerlich-oppositionelle Literaten und sozialdemokratische Arbeiterbewegung nach 1890* (Stuttgart: Metzler, 1974), pp. 79–137.

[20] Hans Koch, in Franz Mehring, *Gesammelte Schriften*, edited by Thomas Höhle, Hans Koch, and Josef Schleifstein, 15 vols (Berlin: Dietz, 1960–63), XII, 327.

sind, sondern als freie Männer und Frauen, prüfend und wählend, erobernd und erwerbend, und sei es noch manchmal tastend und irrend, sich die Geistesschätze der Weltliteratur zu eigen machen.[21]	but as independent men and women, who by examination and selection, by effort and application, and despite occasional errors and uncertainties, are getting to grips with the treasures of world literature.

Under Mehring the repertoire continued to consist of classical and contemporary plays with social–historical content, such as Lessing's *Emilia Galotti*, Schiller's *Kabale und Liebe*, Goethe's *Egmont*, and Ibsen's *Pillars of Society*; plays by Naturalist writers were not excluded, but the performance of *Dantons Tod*, planned by Wille, was cancelled thanks to Mehring's negative appraisal of Büchner's play. An arrangement with Oskar Blumenthal, the director of the *Lessingtheater*, enabled the *Freie Volksbühne* to present a programme of popular and well-performed plays from the repertoire of the commercial theatre, and by 1895 it had a membership of 7,600, principally wage-earners. During this year the society, which was being increasingly harassed by the authorities, who wished to class it as a political organization, went into voluntary dissolution.

Wille and his friends reacted to the events of October 1892, by forming a rival organization, the *Neue Freie Volksbühne*, an avowedly 'non-political' organization, with an individualist emphasis, 'which requires personalities at its head and not representatives of some majority or other'.[22] Their appeal for members, published in *Vorwärts* and *Der Sozialist*, complained that the original pedagogic and artistic aims of the *Freie Volksbühne* had become subordinated to political ends, and emphasized that the members of the *Neue Freie Volksbühne* should be regarded as pupils in a process of popular education. Accordingly the constitution did not even grant them the right to elect the committee – the founders, who included Bölsche, Julius Hart, Otto Erich Hartleben, Adalbert von Hanstein, Ernst von Wolzogen, George Ledebour and Gustav Landauer, formed a self-perpetuating oligarchy whose proposals could be rejected only by a two-thirds majority of the membership. It is hardly surprising that this new organization failed to arouse the confidence of the working class in the way the older *Freie Volksbühne* was able to do; and with a smaller membership it could not afford to present performances of a comparable standard to those at the *Lessingtheater*. *Die Weber*, which the *Neue Freie Volksbühne* was able to perform before its rival, boosted membership to about 2,000, but in 1895 it numbered scarcely 1,000.

---

[21] Quoted from Nestriepke, *Geschichte der Volksbühne*, pp. 98, 85.
[22] Nestriepke, *Geschichte der Volksbühne*, p. 68.

The foundation of the *Volksbühnen*, and through them the popularization of the theatre, must be considered one of the most substantial achievements of the German Naturalist movement, but the subsequent history of these institutions, their re-amalgamation in Berlin, their extension to the provinces, in short, their emergence as an important, enduring, and occasionally influential feature on the German theatrical scene, need not concern us further in these pages. My purpose in discussing this controversy, and the struggle between the two opposing factions within the Social Democratic Party, *die Alten* and *die Jungen*, which triggered it off, was to show how two rapid blows brought to a sudden end the Naturalists' attempts to align themselves with a political tendency for which they had some sympathy, leaving the way clear for the increasingly fashionable cult of individualism.

There was a further unsuccessful attempt by Edgar Steiger, an early historian of the Naturalist drama, and the editor of the socialist literary journal, *Die neue Welt*, to align Naturalism and socialism.[23] This led to a heated debate about Naturalism at the party congress of 1896 in Gotha, but the events of 1891–92 had effectively put an end to the political aspirations of the Naturalists. This is reflected in the introductory article to the fourth volume of the *Freie Bühne* (1893), which runs:

kraftvolle Individualitaten der Zeit, die direkt nichts mit irgendeiner politischen Partei zu tun haben, erheben ihre Stimme unnachsichtig vor den öffentlichen Schäden unserer Kultur und suchen Wege zur Besserung auch aus einer Reformierung der Geister, nicht bloß aus Besserung der Verhaltnisse heraus. Solche Stimmen zu sammeln – zumal wo sich der Kritik ein positives, aufbauendes Element beimischt errachten wir nach wie vor für unsere wesentliche Aufgabe.	energetic modern individuals, who have no connection with any political party, unsparingly denounce the manifest ills of our culture, and are seeking ways of improvement by spiritual reform, not just by the improvement of material conditions. We continue to regard it as our fundamental task to provide a forum for such voices – especially when the criticism contains a positive, constructive element.

The socialists for their part could not reconcile themselves to the pessimism of their Naturalist contemporaries, to their 'faithlessness' to the belief that improvement in social conditions can bring about a real

---

[23] See Brauneck, *Literatur und Öffentlichkeit*, pp. 104–12; Scherer, *Bürgerlich-oppositionelle Literaten*, pp. 142–53; and Vernon L. Lidtke, 'Naturalism and Socialism in Germany', *The American Historical Review*, 79 (1974), 14–37 (pp. 33–34).

and enduring improvement to the lot of mankind, and that the political activity of socialism was already furthering this process.[24] Then, as in the course of subsequent debates about the concept 'socialist realism', pessimism and tragedy were not compatible with a Utopianist ideology. Mehring's diagnosis of the principal shortcoming of Naturalism has become very familiar from twentieth-century Marxist criticism:

Es ist ein Verdienst des heutigen Naturalismus, daß er den Mut und die Wahrheitsliebe gehabt hat, das Vergehende zu schildern, wie es ist... Aber die ganze Gesellschaft ist nicht verfallen, und das Schicksal des Naturalismus hängt davon ab, ob er den zweiten Teil seines Weges vollenden, ob er den höheren Mut und die höhere Wahrheitsliebe finden wird, auch das Entstehende zu schildern, wie es werden wird und täglich schon wird.[25]	It is to the credit of contemporary Naturalism that it has had the courage and the integrity to describe decaying phenomena as they are. But the whole of society has not decayed, and the fate of Naturalism depends on whether it can fulfil the second part of its task, on whether it will summon up the greater courage and the greater integrity to describe nascent phenomena as they will be, and as they are already emerging.

After the breach had taken place the tendency among the socialists was to dismiss the earlier political activity of the Naturalist writers as opportunism. Mehring, with his customary delicacy, calls them

Bourgeoisknaben, die sich... an die Socialdemokratische Partei heranzuwerfen versuchen, und wenn ihnen hier keine Extrawurst gebraten wird, sich durch die straffe Disziplin der Arbeiterklasse in ihrer 'genialen Individualität' bedroht fühlen und sich zu 'höheren Gesichtspunkten entwickeln', das heißt reumutig zu dem alten Troge der kapitalistischen Schlagworte zurückkehren.[26]	Bourgeois youths, who... attempted to throw themselves at the Social Democratic Party, and when they did not get special treatment here, felt that their 'brilliant individuality' was endangered by the strict discipline of the working class, and so 'developed more elevated points of view', that is to say... they contritely returned to feed from the trough of capitalist slogans.

---

[24] See Dietger Pforte, 'Die deutsche Sozialdemokratie und die Naturalisten', in *Naturalismus*, ed. Scheuer, pp. 175–205 (pp. 181–91).
[25] 'Der heutige Naturalismus' (1892), *Gesammelte Schriften*, XI, 133.
[26] 'Hanna Jagert' (1893), *Gesammelte Schriften*, XI, 372.

Nor were such views confined to those as directly involved as Mehring. In 1896 Arno Holz, who had been one of the first of the Naturalists to turn his back on socialist ideas, and Paul Ernst, who by then had also retreated from his Marxist position, collaborated on a satirical comedy, *Sozialaristokraten*, in which Wille (Gehrke) is presented as a turncoat politician who moves from an extreme left-wing to an extreme right-wing position, merely to satisfy his desire for public recognition.[27]

The authors of *Sozialaristokraten*, however, do rather less justice than even Mehring to a dilemma which Wille shared with many of his contemporaries. Certainly there is much that is comic in the spectacle of the clumsy Wille being outmanoeuvred by the more skilful and nimble professionals, Bebel and Mehring, and reacting with resentful denunciations of party-politics and demagogy; but what Wille and his contemporaries were attempting was something which within their intellectual tradition was very difficult. Instead of retreating from the struggles of industrial society to indulge in the private, inward speculation so valued by many German artists, they attempted to engage themselves in social and political activity; when others settled in communities such as Worpswede they remained in Berlin. But all the time they were conscious – perhaps over-conscious – of the effort involved, the risks to themselves and the integrity of their own personalities. This is evident in all their reservations about socialism, in their attempts to reconcile Marx with Nietzsche, in their admiration of Ibsen, especially his *Enemy of the People*, in their – essentially defensive – anti-democratic organization of the *Volksbühnen*, and, most catastrophically, in their incompetence at political infighting, their unresisting collapse before the first serious political attack.

In Gerhart Hauptmann's case this dilemma is reflected in that indecision which is so characteristic of many of his works, and was to be characteristic of many of his public actions. A number of studies develop hints in his autobiography to explain Hauptmann's professed inability to come down firmly on either side in social and political conflicts. Hans Mayer explains this as an imprint left by Hauptmann's early familiarity with two distinct social groups and the conflicting loyalties which thus arose; the irreconcilables, he argues, do not derive from insoluble social conflicts, but from conflicts within the poet himself, expressed in the following comment on the dramatic genre: 'Dramatic art is erected, so to speak, on productive scepticism; it brings into conflict characters, of whom each is fully justified in his opinions and his behaviour. But which behaviour and which opinion is correct?'

---

[27] See Helmut Scheuer, *Arno Holz im literarischen Leben des ausgehenden 19. Jahrhunderts (1883–1896): Eine biographische Studie* (Munich: Winkler, 1971), p. 182.

(VI, 698).[28] W. G. A. Shepherd draws extensively on Hauptmann's *Das Abenteuer meiner Jugend*, to give a fuller psychological picture of the dramatist. He has no difficulty in tracing in Hauptmann's account of his life an insecurity which amounts to persecution mania on the one hand, and, on the other, compensatory delusions of grandeur, which are reflected in the movement and counter-movement of his works between an introspective and an expansive mood, between individualism and social-consciousness.[29] These particular studies, enlightening though they often are, have a certain limitation which will be apparent in the present context: Hauptmann's personal psychological constitution may well seem to explain his dilemma, but this should not blind us to the fact that this is very much the dilemma of his generation. Franz Servaes sums it up in words which could well have come from any of a number of the Berlin Naturalists:

> to find oneself, without retreating into isolation – to unite with others, without losing oneself: that is the problem which every creative artist has to solve privately, and which will then have to be solved again in the community at large 'to be a comrade and a hermit', as Bruno Wille has put it.[30]

It is this problem, the preoccupation of the artist with his own difficulties over the question of social involvement, which provides the political dimension of many of the plays of the Naturalist period. In works like Georg Hirschfeld's *Die Mütter* and Gerhart Hauptmann's *Einsame Menschen* the hero is a tortured individual who is asked to give up his own comfort and his own security for the sake of others. But the breadth of this issue is restricted by the widespread tendency of the Naturalists to concentrate on the drama of the artist, and to make general problems, like the inhibiting effect of middle-class upbringing on progressive ideas, or the rights of the individual within a programme of socialization, into special cases in which the hero is (or is said to be) a more than ordinary man who merits extraordinary consideration. It is not difficult to find some sympathy for Mehring's tendency to dismiss the problems treated in plays like *Einsame Menschen* as the problems of a small literary coterie. At the same time one senses that special-pleading of this kind, and in this quantity, is the symptom of a bad conscience. Whether it is because socialism had indeed had some effect on them, or because they were far too conservative by nature to embrace a truly

---

[28] Cf. Hans Mayer, 'Gerhart Hauptmann und die Mitte', *Von Lessing bis Thomas Mann* (Pfullingen: Neske, 1959), pp. 33–55.
[29] W. G. A. Shepherd, 'Social Consciousness and Messianic Vision: A study in the problems of Gerhart Hauptmann's individualism' (doctoral thesis, Edinburgh, 1962).
[30] 'Nietzsche und der Sozialismus', *Freie Bühne*, 3 (1892), 205.

radical individualism, is not clear, but in their individualist phase the German Naturalists never created ruthlessly self-assertive individuals who act with anything like the self-confidence of Wedekind's Lulu. Hartleben's Hanna Jagert in the play of that title, Hirschfeld's Robert Frey (*Die Mütter*), and Hauptmann's Johannes Vockerat (*Einsame Menschen*) are weighed down and inhibited by feelings of indebtedness to their benefactors. For all their increasing scorn of the masses, the Naturalists' views never harden into the exclusive aestheticism of certain of their contemporaries; where the views expressed in Stefan George's *Die Blätter für die Kunst* were known, they were rejected.[31]

I have suggested that political activity was something about which the Naturalist writers always had certain reservations, and that this was the case even before the confrontations of 1891-92. The disputes of these years were the last straw, and accelerated the withdrawal – the literal withdrawal – of even the most politically dedicated among them. In Friedrichshagen, a relatively peaceful and rural suburb of Berlin, the one-time pioneers of the Naturalist movement assembled to form a community united in anarchist and mystical tendencies.[32] As for the more famous Worpswede community the sandy moors and heaths meant freedom from the increasing pressures and social demands of life in the industrial metropolis. In the 1890s Friedrichshagen, which provides the setting for Gerhart Hauptmann's *Einsame Menschen*, became a centre for the discussion of personal and ethical rather than more broadly social issues. In his autobiography Max Halbe tells us that the principal topic of conversation was the 'new morality', the relationship between the sexes, and the question of free love; numerous articles in the *Freie Bühne* confirm the growing interest in such issues.[33] The literature of the Friedrichshagen period was very much more introverted than that of the previous decade; it consisted largely of plays concerned with ethical problems and the psychological analysis of the inner life, of poems and prose-poems of a pantheistic character. Some of these works, Gerhart Hauptmann's *Die versunkene Glocke*, or his brother Carl's *Sonnenwanderer*, have very little recognizable connection with the early impulses behind the Naturalist movement. Otto Brahm, who continued to champion the realistic social drama, was criticized for the narrowness of his policy at the *Deutsches Theater*, as his former allies, led by the chameleon-like Hermann Bahr, proclaimed the passing of the naturalist movement, 'Die Überwindung des Naturalismus', and began to look

---

[31] Hans-Egon Hass, 'Zur Kunstanschauung Gerhart Hauptmanns', *Jahrhundertfeier für Gerhart Hauptmann, 15-21 November, 1962* (Cologne, 1962), pp. 29-35; see also Arno Holz's letter to Bölsche, 30.03.1903, *Briefe*, p. 141.
[32] See Scheuer, 'Zwischen Sozialismus und Individualismus', pp. 163-65.
[33] *Jahrhundertwende: Geschichte meines Lebens 1893-1914* (Danzig: Kafermann, 1935), p. 39.

with admiration at foreign writers other than Ibsen: Huysmans, Bourget, Remy de Gourmont, Whitman, Maeterlinck, and Strindberg. And while not all of Bahr's contemporaries were wont to move on to the latest literary mode with the same rapidity as he, the traditional valuation of the inner life, and the old suspicion of the documentation of the social world meant that there was less resistance in Germany to the new 'impressionism' or 'Neu-Idealismus' than there had been to the innovations of the previous decade.

Much of the work of these years, even where it continues to be in a Naturalist vein, is tinged with a radical cultural pessimism; it is not just critical of particular social or historical manifestations, but tends towards the criticism of civilization as such. Looking back nostalgically to Friedrichshagen and his years of companionship with Wille, Bölsche wrote:

Von dieser Rekreation aus bin ich heute nicht nur der Weltstadt entfremdet, sondern ich meine auch, daß sie ein wahrer Kraken ist, der an unserem geistigen Leben saugt. Je höher die Etagen unter den Rauchmmel steigen, desto flächer wird die Gemütsbildung und desto mehr keucht jede Geistesäußerung vom Treppensteigen. Der Sinn geht verloren für die feinen Werte in Natur und Kunst, also gerade für das, worin die Entwicklung ansteigt.[34]	Thanks to this recreation I am now not simply alienated from the city, but I also believe that it really is a monster, which drains away our spiritual life. As the buildings rise higher into the smoke-laden sky, so our sensitivity becomes shallower, and all the stairs to be climbed leave us out of breath for spiritual utterances. We lose all sense of the finer values of nature and art, and so for the very source of progress.

Such an attitude was already implicit in Hauptmann's *Bahnwärter Thiel*, in which the train disturbs both the mystical inward life of Thiel and the peace of the countryside; but it becomes a dominant feature in the literature of the 1890s. In this respect the later works of German Naturalism diverge considerably from their European predecessors; there is nothing here to compare with Ibsen's biting condemnation of his narrow provincial homeland, nothing to compare with Zola's great urban novels and their exuberant depiction of a vast social panorama in all its concrete detail. The German Naturalists came positively to fear the city; Schlaf shares Bölsche's worry that urban growth will mean the extinction of all 'reliable values' – and among such values he includes racial values – which, he says, are the product of nature and the countryside,

---

[34] *Hinter der Weltstadt: Friedrichshagener Gedanken zur ästhetischen Kultur* (Leipzig: Diederichs, 1901), p. viii.

and he criticizes those of the Naturalist writers who allowed themselves to become reconciled to the city.³⁵ It is not easy to know at which writers his criticism was aimed. Certainly Gerhart Hauptmann and Max Halbe are second to none in their anti-urbanism, and in their dramas they rely increasingly on set responses to the concepts town and country. Of Hauptmann it has been said that he was never a real city-dweller, and that he was constantly in need of 'elemental contact with nature', in order to renew his spiritual powers.³⁶ (In one of his less successful stage-directions, at the beginning of Act II of *Vor Sonnenaufgang*, Hauptmann shows Alfred Loth, the visitor from the town, in just such 'elemental contact with nature'.)

One rather curious result of the constant recurrence of this anti-urban theme in the plays of this period was its effect on Rudolf Rittner, perhaps the greatest actor of the Naturalist school. His diaries show a sense of remorse at having left his native Silesia, and of guilt over the independence he achieved through success in society; and it is very likely that these feelings prompted his retirement in 1906, at the height of his powers. A diary entry written twelve years earlier runs:

Die Berliner Luft ist mir zu schlecht, moralisch schlecht und unrein, es liegt soviel moralischer Staub und Schmutz in der Luft, daß es mir oft den Atem verlegt, daß ich fühle, hier seelisch krank werden zu müssen. Ich möchte fort, in reinere Himmelsstriche, wo reines, edles Kunstschaffen gedeiht, dort möchte ich, losgelöst von allem Welt-und Großstadtschmutz, ganz der Kunst leben, so wie ich sie mir denke, der reinen, großen, ewigen Kunst, die ihre treuesten Jünger zu Halbögttern adelt. Hier in der Großstadt kann ich nicht für immer leben, das fühl ich klar, – hier geh ich zu Grunde.³⁷	The Berlin air is bad for me, morally bad and impure, there is so much moral filth in the atmosphere that it often takes my breath, so that I feel as if my soul must sicken. I should like to go somewhere else, under a cleaner sky, where pure and noble art can flourish; there, released from all the dirt of society and the metropolis, I should like to devote myself entirely to art, as I imagine it, pure, great, eternal art, which raises its most faithful disciples to demi-gods. I cannot always live here in the city, I feel that clearly, – here I shall be ruined.

---

³⁵ *Maurice Maeterlinck* (Berlin: Marquadt, 1906), pp. 20–22.
³⁶ C. F. W. Behl, *Gerhart Hauptmann: Überblick über sein Leben und Werk* (Würzburg: Holzner, 1956), p. 10.
³⁷ Quoted from Hans-Adolf Schultze, *Der Schauspieler Rudolf Rittner, (1869–1943), ein Wegbereiter Gerhart Hauptmanns auf dem Theater*, (doctoral thesis, Free University of Berlin, 1961), p. 117. See also Rittner's drama, *Narrenglanz* (1906).

It is very easy to see in all this nothing but the natural reaction of sensitive people to the very ugly effects of Germany's industrial revolution; but this is not all there is to be said, even on the subject of causation. The anti-urbanism of the German Naturalists is at the same time a continuation of the prejudice of a number of German writers – some of them great writers like Jean Paul, Gotthelf, and Stifter – who persistently warned against the town as a threat to the beauty of nature and the independence of man. It is, in part at least, a continuation of that tendency to idealize the peasant, which is characteristic of much nineteenth-century German literature, and which results in a view of the peasant as a timeless embodiment of Man, rather than the product of a particular social–historical situation.[38] The Naturalist writers do not, on the whole, consider town and country rationally, as two distinct modes of social existence, neither of which is inherently superior to the other; for them the country is not a milieu which can affect people's lives in much the same way as the town, but an absence of milieu, an unresisting natural environment, in which the real or pure character of an individual can freely unfold. Once again the attitude finds a naive echo in the longing of Rittner to retire to a Silesian farm where the pressures of society are not felt.[39]

This irrational response to social phenomena accords ill with a literary style which in many other respects owes much to rational social observation. To say that the sociologists provided the rational, sociological response and the poets a poetic one is to miss the point. Balzac found poetry in Paris, Dickens in London, and Döblin found it even in Berlin.

The political attitude embraced by the Naturalists in the 1890s – the advocacy of withdrawal from social involvement, the hostility to party politics, the appeal to man's spirituality for social improvement, the conservative emphasis on home and provincial roots, the slogans like 'Aristocracy of the Spirit', the cult of freedom and the open air – suggests (particularly to an observer from the second half of the twentieth century) an attitude at the opposite end of the political spectrum to the egalitarian socialism with which German Naturalism was associated in its infancy. I have been at pains to show that this was not a totally new attitude, and it had never been entirely rejected by many of the Naturalists, but it received a fresh impetus in 1890. A cause, or perhaps only a symptom, of this was Julius Langbehn's immensely successful book, *Rembrandt als Erzieher*.

One thing about Langbehn's book is certain: it was a bad book, and its success had nothing to do with its quality – that is unless one

---

[38] See Friedrich Sengle, 'Wünschbild Land und Schreckbild Stadt', *Studium Generale*, 16 (1963), 619–30.
[39] Quoted from Schultze, *Der Schauspieler Rudolf Rittner*, p. 134.

shares the view of Leo Berg: 'When you get poets like Bierbaum and Held, then a Langbehn belongs with them as a philosopher'[40] – but it was one of those books which appeal immediately because they bring together so much of what is vaguely in the air at a particular time. In a fascinating study of Cultural Pessimism Fritz Stern describes the atmosphere in which Langbehn's book was launched as follows:

> The decade of the 1890s was one of strife and unrest, when the cultural discontent which previously had been the complaint of a few artists and intellectuals became the faddish lament of the many. The revolt against modernity, the attack on civilization gathered force, hundreds of voices inveighed against all sorts of evils and repressions, and multitudes of people everywhere were repeating these imprecations. Nietzsche, ignored during his creative period, was suddenly read and admired, Ibsen was played and praised, Nordau's *Degeneration* vehemently debated. Everywhere... sprang up the cry for greater freedom, for self-expression, for more experience and less theorizing, for a fuller life, for the recognition of the tortured, self-torturing individual. The intensity of this awakening in Germany can be gauged by the instantaneous success of Langbehn's book'.[41]

The pages of the *Freie Bühne*, in which *Rembrandt als Erzieher* was favourably reviewed, are full of the sort of manifestations about which Stern is writing. The book could even number among its admirers the influential critic, Georg Brandes; in fact Theodor Fontane, who wrote a satirical review, 'Nante Strump als Erzieher', was one of very few to withhold approval.[42]

As an apostle of 'Germanic Individualism' Langbehn goes rather further than the Friedrichshagen circle in anticipating the violent irrationalism of the twentieth century, but not so far as to disguise a basic similarity in outlook and aspiration. *Einsame Menschen*, which was probably written too soon to have been directly influenced by *Langbehn's* book (but which is recognizably a product of the same period), draws attention by its very title to that isolation which Langbehn commends. The latter's insistence that political and social renewal can only arise from the private exertions of a few élite pioneers who are able to retreat from society, could well have come straight from Friedrichshagen:

| Der Weg von der heutigen | The way from today's |
| Majoritäts- zur künftigen | majority-rule to tomorrow's |

---
[40] *Der Übermensch in der modernen Literatur* (Paris, Leipzig, and Munich: Albert Langen, 1897), p. 213.
[41] *The Politics of Cultural Despair* (Berkeley: University of California Press, 1961), p. 97.
[42] This appeared anonymously in the journal *Deutschland*, 1 (1889–90), 493.

Minoritätsherrschaft führt, wenn er eingeschlagen werden soll, durch die Isolirung einzelner Deutscher; das heißt eine neue und feinere und wahrhaft selbständige Lebensrichtung wird sich zunächst abgesondert von und im Gegensatz zu der Masse des Volks entwickeln müssen.[43]	minority-rule leads, if it is to be taken, through the isolation of individual Germans; that is to say, a new, and more refined, and truly independent style of life has, in the first place, to be developed separately from and in opposition to the masses.

It is equally true that much of what Wille wrote in his *Philosophie der Befreiung durch das reine Mittel* would not have been out of place in Langbehn's book.[44] A coincidental confirmation of the striking similarity between the attitudes of Wille and Langbehn comes from Fritz Stern's study. In his researches Stern came across a contemporary play of which he remarks: 'between the type portrayed... in this play and Langbehn, whom [the authors] certainly did not have in mind, there was a strange resemblance'.[45] The play was Holz' and Ernst's *Sozialaristokraten*, and its main character was, as I have said, modelled very closely on Bruno Wille.

The political development of the German Naturalist writers from socialism to a supposedly non-political individualism is closely, but not obviously, related to the development of the literary movement, Naturalism, in Germany, and contributes significantly to one of the shortcomings of this movement, its lack of breadth when compared with European Naturalism. I do not wish to advance the view that the movement away from socialism is of itself a shortcoming, rather that in its early days Naturalism attempts to bring literature into society, the writers make contacts with politics and politicians, and in consequence a certain tension is generated, but this tension is never allowed to become a productive tension. Defeated over a specific issue, the response of the Naturalists was not to continue the fight on a political level, but to withdraw, and denounce politics from a safe distance, that is to slide back into the rather depressing old attitudes. *Die Weber* is the pinnacle of the Naturalists' achievement, and is a very fine social drama (although

---

[43] *Rembrandt als Erzieher*, 2nd edition (Leipzig: C. L. Hirschfeld, 1890), p. 280.

[44] There is a particularly close resemblance between Langbehn's comments on 'Majoritätsherrschaft' and Wille's on 'Parteiherrschaft'; both writers make similar references to Ibsen's Dr Stockmann, and both give Cologne Cathedral as an example of a positive mass achievement. Wille's work is, on the whole, coloured by a more personal resentment about the way he and his supporters (e.g. Gustav Landauer) had been treated by the Social Democrats.

[45] Fritz Stern, *The Politics of Cultural Despair*, p. 137. In the 1890s Moeller van den Bruck, a cultural pessimist of Langbehn's stamp, began his career – as an admirer of Johannes Schlaf. See his article in *Die Gesellschaft*, 13 (1897), iv, 154–62. Moeller occupies a place alongside Lagarde and Langbehn in Stern's study.

even in this it is something of an exception), but there is no Naturalist drama of this stature concerned with the issues of political priorities, choices, or means and ends. Gustav Landauer wrote in 1890:

> I wish our young authors would free themselves from the constraining bonds of the family; I wish they would go out into the street and among the public, so that if the power of fate is still to be effective then we will not simply be shown 'family-tragedies', but we will witness the effect of that power which, according to a famous statement, is the modern equivalent of fate: politics and society.[46]

Landauer's contemporaries, the Naturalist dramatists, did not respond; there is no Naturalist equivalent of Schiller's *Wallenstein*.

---

[46] 'Das neue soziale Drama', *Deutschland*, 1 (1890), 478. Landauer is, of course, referring to the words attributed by Goethe to Napoleon.

PART II
GERHART HAUPTMANN IN CONTEXT

5
VOR SONNENAUFGANG

The first performance of *Vor Sonnenaufgang* on 20 October, 1889, in Berlin's *Lessingtheater* marks the real breakthrough of the German Naturalist drama. This, the second production under the auspices of the recently-formed *Freie Bühne*, was one of the noisiest and most violent premières in the history of the German theatre. Gerhart Hauptmann's play had been published in the summer of 1889 by C. F. Conrad; sides had already been taken, and this first performance thus became a veritable trial of strength between the young Naturalists and the literary establishment.

Vor Sonnenaufgang, subtitled 'a social Drama', is set in Hauptmann's native Silesia. It opens with the arrival of Alfred Loth, a sociologist and a socialist, in the mining village of Witzdorf; he has come to investigate the conditions under which the local miners live and work. It so happens that two former friends of Loth now live in the district he is visiting. In the course of the play we learn that one of them, Hoffmann, has given up the ideals he shared with Loth in their student days, has married into a farming family recently enriched by the discovery of coal under their land (industrialization disturbing the peace of the countryside), and by a piece of sharp practice has secured a monopoly of the local retail coal trade. His views on social reform have been modified accordingly: 'I should be the last to be found wanting in sympathy for the poor, but if anything is to be done, then let it come from those in authority!' (I, 20). The other friend, Dr Schimmelpfennig, has reacted in a different way. He recognizes the corruption and injustice of the society in which he lives, but dismisses the possibility of effecting any root-and-branch change; as a doctor he confines himself to alleviating the most immediate suffering and making life as bearable as possible. Loth's active socialism represents a third response, and necessarily makes him an intruder in a way his friends are not. He threatens to break the enclosing circle which for Hoffmann and the landowners has meant freedom from the pressure of discontented workers, from outside public opinion, and from the assaults of their own consciences. The true significance of Loth's arrival is made abundantly clear in the brilliant opening scene in which he calls at the Krauses' house to look up his old friend, Hoffmann, and is greeted with a torrent of abuse from his friend's mother-in-law, who takes him for a beggar.

The dramatist, then, has skilfully placed Loth in the centre of a social conflict. On the one side are the landowners and their spokesman, Hoffmann, who attempts by bribery, by appealing to past friendship, by intimidation, to secure Loth's departure; on the other side are the miners, the servants, the labourer, Beibst, to whom Loth feels a social duty. The only character to change sides is Helene Krause, Hoffmann's sister-in-law. At the outset she is in an unnatural alliance with Hoffmann and her family; but she is a comparative newcomer, since she was educated at the Herrnhut convent, and still finds her family environment abhorrent. For Helene, as for Toni Selicke, the only escape from the family is through marriage; but Hoffmann, who would like to set up a *ménage à trois* with her, has discouraged any potential suitors from the immediate neighbourhood, and in the background is her cruel and moronic cousin, Wilhelm Kahl, to whom the family have betrothed her, and who is having an adulterous affair with her stepmother. Loth therefore has little difficulty in winning her over, both for himself and for his cause; and in the structure of the play Helene, as a disadvantaged woman, thus becomes the representative, if not the spokesman, of the various marginalised groups. To all of these it is Loth's duty to stay and complete his work; thus the curtain falls on Act I to Helene's desperate plea that he should not leave (I, 38).

This clear and straightforward structure is, however, complicated by the scope of Alfred Loth's optimism. Not only does he believe that man's social life can be improved by direct action, he also believes that the quality of the human race can be improved by prudent marriage.[1] Loth, who, like Hauptmann's friend Bölsche,[2] worships the immanent ideals of health, strength and normality, is not prepared to jeopardize future generations either by drinking himself, or by marrying into an unhealthy family. Alcoholism and intermarriage are said to have been significant causes in the degeneration of the families of the Witzdorf area, and the Krause family now contains two helpless dipsomaniacs,

---

[1] Loth was, to some extent, modelled on Hauptmann's friend, Alfred Ploetz, whose views on this subject are recorded in the article 'Alkohol und Nachkommenschaft', *Neue deutsche Rundschau*, 6 (1895), 1108–12. Ploetz's reaction to the play was that a type such as Loth is unsympathetic, but rather rare, that the situation was presented in an unnecessarily pessimistic light, but that so long as birth-control remains undeveloped Loth's behaviour would, in principle, be correct; see F. A. Voigt, 'Die Aufnahme von "Vor Sonnenaufgang"', *Hauptmann Studien*, p. 66. Hauptmann himself denied sharing Ploetz's (erroneous) views on hereditary alcoholism (VII, 1065), but the evidence of contemporaries suggests that he did; see Adalbert von Hanstein, *Das jüngste Deutschland*, 3rd edition (Leipzig: Voigtländer, 1905), p. 171, and Bruno Wille, 'Erinnerungen an Gerhart Hauptmann', in *Mit Gerhart Hauptmann: Erinnerungen und Bekenntnisse aus seinem Freundeskreis*, edited by W. Heynen (Berlin: Stilke, 1922), pp. 83–116 (p. 306).

[2] Cf. above, p. 24.

Helene's father and her sister, Marthe. Marthe's affliction has already caused the death of her first child; in the fifth act of the play her second is stillborn. In all consistency (which, in this case, has nothing to do with plausibility) Loth cannot marry Helene; he abandons her – and (to Hoffmann's great relief) his sociological investigation – and the play ends with her suicide. The 'hero' of the play therefore fails significantly in the individual tasks which face him; what are we to make of such a hero, and what are we to make of such a play?

The simplest answer, that the play is a critique of the mentality of the theoretical reformer, is I believe, too simple. An analysis based on this belief – and there have been a number – is likely to suggest that Hauptmann's first play is a better play than the *Vor Sonnenaufgang* one feels one has read. *Vor Sonnenaufgang* is a problematical play, and it is better that the problems it poses should be recognized, for they are crucial to the understanding of the transitional nature of the German drama of this period.

Josef Chapiro reports Hauptmann as once expressing strong reservations about the idea of formal closure: 'The ideal drama that I should like to write would be one with no dénouement and no conclusion. I have left many of my plays incomplete after one or two acts, because I could not make up my mind to force a conclusion upon them.'[3] Hauptmann omits to say that on a number of occasions he did just this; his first four plays suddenly accelerate in the last act, and come to an end with more or less violent deaths. Nor is this just true of Hauptmann's work; it happens also in Schlaf's *Meister Oelze* (1892), Max Halbe's *Jugend* (1893), Max Dreyer's *Winterschlaf* (1894), and Holz's and Schlaf's short story, *Papa Hamlet* (1889). But nowhere is the ending of a play more obviously forced than in *Vor Sonnenaufgang*.

From the outline I have given above it will be evident that *Vor Sonnenaufgang* is what has been called a 'drama of ripe situation', the form so often used by the German Naturalist dramatists, and derived directly from Ibsen.[4] Into the atmosphere of oppression and dormant tension suggested by such titles as *Stickluft*, *Winterschlaf* and *Tote Zeit*, there comes an outsider, 'der Bote aus der Fremde', who releases the latent conflict. By analogy with Zola, Halbe described this type of drama as an 'experimental drama'; the dramatist experiments by adding a further ingredient, or a catalyst, to a given mixture.[5] In demanding that a drama should consist, from beginning to end, of exposition (VI, 1037)

---

[3] Josef Chapiro, *Gespräche mit Gerhart Hauptmann* (Berlin: S. Fischer, 1932), p. 166.
[4] Richard M. Meyer, *Die deutsche Literatur des neunzehnten Jahrhunderts*, Das neunzehnte Jahrhundert in Deutschlands Entwicklung, vol. 3, edited by Paul Schlenther (Berlin: Bondi, 1900), p. 833.
[5] 'Berliner Brief', *Die Gesellschaft*, 5 (1889), 1180.

Hauptmann was almost certainly thinking of this kind of drama, which so frequently involves gradual revelation as further discoveries are made by the newcomer. This can lead to a kind of drama in which descriptions of conditions have rather more importance, inter-personal conflict expressed in dialogue form rather less importance, than in the classical drama, and in which individual scenes are not related by a closely-knit plot, but by a common theme, gradually amplified in a sequence of typical episodes.[6] Thus the earlier part of *Vor Sonnenaufgang* consists of the gradual uncovering of the social conditions in Witzdorf, as Loth makes his investigations, or explains what he has seen. Tension, conflict, drama, arise from the giving and receiving of information, from the way Loth reacts to what he discovers, and from the way the various characters respond to the challenge presented by the newcomer: the suspicious aggression of Frau Krause, the evasive façade of Hoffmann, Helene's desperate yearning for escape. This technique does not require that information be concealed from Loth.

However, in *Vor Sonnenaufgang* there is cultivated another, more superficial and more obviously theatrical kind of tension, which arises from the artificial extension of the question: Will Loth find out about the alcoholism in the Krause family? This begins to take effect from the dinner scene of Act I, when Loth states his convictions, and when Kahl nearly gives everything away by his tactless mutter that old Krause is pushing his luck (I, 35), which Loth does not hear. This tension is increased at the end of the act by Helene's plea that Loth should not depart, and it recurs with every successive attempt Helene makes to tell Loth about her father.

The latter part of the fourth and the whole of the fifth act differ from the rest of the play in that this second kind of suspense ceases to be an episodic feature; once obtained it is very carefully carried right through to the conclusion. Towards the end of Act IV, when the love scenes, which in many other respects are very moving, have reached the rather absurd point where Loth asks Helene whether her parents are healthy, and Helene anxiously asks: 'But what if they weren't – ?' (I, 80), their dialogue is interrupted by the screams of Frau Krause, announcing that Marthe is in labour. The act then comes to an end with Helene on her way to fetch the doctor. There now follows the first meeting between the old friends Schimmelpfennig and Loth, and so more delayed exposition, in which the doctor explains the extent of the degeneration among the local farming families. He just reaches a point which could have some bearing on the situation of Loth and Helene – and hastily leaves the room to attend to his patient. In the meanwhile the anxious Helene comes in, only herself to leave the room once the doctor returns. Schimmelpfennig

---

[6] See Peter Szondi, *Theorie des modernen Dramas*, 8th edition (Frankfurt a.M.: Suhrkamp, 1971; first published 1959), pp. 66, 70–71.

continues his revelations a little further, and again has to leave at the crucial moment; again Helene comes in, fearful lest Loth has already gone, and he promises her that they will leave together that night. From Schimmelpfennig's third entry what dominates the play is not a conflict of ideas, since the two men share the same views, nor is there any real personal struggle for Loth. What the dramatist now relies on to hold his audience's attention is the quite trivial question of whether Marthe Hoffmann's labour will last long enough for the doctor to say what he has to say, or whether he will be called away first to deliver the baby, so giving Helene an opportunity to leave with Loth as planned, and explain her situation to him herself. At this point during the first performance of the play a member of the audience, a certain Dr Kastan, stood up and impatiently offered Schimmelpfennig a pair of forceps – which he had had the foresight to bring into the theatre with him.[7]

After Loth's departure a similar kind of suspense is again contrived. The discussion between the two friends has made it reasonably clear that Helene's situation vis à vis Hoffmann resembles that of Emilia Galotti vis à vis the Prince towards the end of Lessing's play, and so the audience has every reason to fear that she will commit suicide. Any hope that this can be avoided must rest with Schimmelpfennig, who has promised to explain Loth's decision as best he can. A letter from Loth is therefore positively dangerous, unless it is left in Schimmelpfennig's hands; but, like Ibsen in *A Doll's House* – though to a quite different end – Hauptmann exploits this conventional device of melodrama to the full.[8] In the final scene Helene enters, looks round, and leaves in search of Loth without seeing his letter (she makes her exit by the conservatory door and must pass immediately behind the table on which the letter is lying); she returns by the same door and, when she hears her father approaching, makes to rush out again through the central door (upstage, middle) from where she sees the letter on the table (downstage, left), she reads it, and takes the step we have been dreading.

The 'love-interest' in the play, the Loth-Helene aspect, provides a forward-moving plot, conceived in terms of arrival-involvement-perception-departure on the part of Loth; or, to put it differently: a man called Loth goes to a place which, like the Berlin of Sudermann's nearly

---

[7] Cf. Szondi, *Theorie des modernen Dramas*, p. 67. Dr Kastan must have read the play very diligently, for Marthe's cries of pain, prescribed in the stage-directions (I, 86) were omitted for the first performance; see Paul Schlenther, *Wozu der Lärm? Genesis der Freien Bühne* (Berlin: S. Fischer, 1889), pp. 28f.

[8] In Ibsen's play melodramatic style and structure are dominant up to the moment in the final act when Nora herself decisively puts them aside, telling her husband to sit down at the table and talk seriously; the play thus contains its own critical reflection on theatricality; see Yves Chevrel, *Le Naturalisme* (Paris: Presses Universitaires de France, 1982), pp. 70–72.

contemporary play, *Sodoms Ende* (1891), more or less resembles Sodom, and departs rather hastily, leaving his wife or, in this case, the woman who might have been his wife in a rather unfortunate predicament.[9] Hauptmann thus uses the plot-structure of the 'well-made play' to round off *Vor Sonnenaufgang*, and in doing so destroys the formal unity of the work, which in other respects relies on the loose, expository style of epic theatre. The finality of Helene's death elevates an unmastered problem into an insoluble one, for its force is quite enough to nullify completely Loth's optimistic words: 'Live! Fight! Forward, ever forward' (I, 95). A more consistent drama might, a more consistently social drama would certainly, have left this issue open.

If in this formal respect, its reliance on a conventional plot-structure, on skilfully contrived suspense, and on strong closure, *Vor Sonnenaufgang* falls short of the theoretical ideals of Naturalism – though let us not forget that inconsistency of this order is a shortcoming by any standard – Hauptmann's first play is, in another respect, aggressively Naturalistic. Following the example of Ibsen's *Ghosts* and Tolstoy's *The Power of Darkness* – two plays which he knew and admired – Hauptmann joins in the attack on those who held that certain material was not suitable for the stage. And yet compared with Wedekind's *Frühlings Erwachen* – a startlingly modern play, written only one year later – the shock tactics of *Vor Sonnenaufgang* are rather dull and rather predictable. The reason is, no doubt, that Hauptmann *tells* a lot, but *shows* little, of various forms of immorality; in a synopsis of the play it is extraordinarily difficult to avoid the impression of parody. In fact, Hauptmann's play raises so many issues that it is hardly possible for him to treat any single one in depth, and it is only in his next three plays that he really begins to get to grips with these issues. The question of free will and determinism looms very large in *Das Friedensfest*; the conflict of individual freedom and the traditional demands of the middle-class family is the central theme of *Einsame Menschen*, and probably the most important theme in the German Naturalist drama as a whole; whilst *Die Weber* treats the problem of the relationship between the oppressed and resentful working classes and their exploiters, the problem which the sensitive Helene experiences most poignantly:

Wie sie einen immer anglotzen, so schrecklich finster. – als ob man geradezu was verbrochen hatte. – –	How they stare at you, so awful and grim – as if you'd committed some crime. – – In winter, when we've

---

[9] For a development of this idea so as to give a positive reading of Loth see W. A. Coupe, 'An ambiguous hero: In defence of Alfred Loth', *German Life and Letters*, 31 (1977–78), 13–22.

Im Winter, wenn wir manchmal Schlitten gefahren sind, und sie kommen dann in der Dunkelei in großen Trupps über die Berge, im Schneegestöber, und sie sollen ausweichen, da gehen sie vor den Pferden her und weichen nicht aus. Da nehmen die Bauern manchmal den Peitschenstiel, anders kommen sie nicht durch. Ach, und dann schimpfen sie hinterher. Hu! ich habe mich manchmal so entsetzlich geängstigt (I, 27).	been on our sleighs, and they're coming in the darkness in gangs over the mountains, through the snow, and they ought to get out of the way, they walk in front of the horses and won't stand to one side. Then the farmers sometimes use the handle of their whip, otherwise they wouldn't get past. Oh, and then they swear at you. Hu! I've sometimes been so dreadfully scared.

Vor Sonnenaufgang also treats, in passing, such topical subjects as the emancipation of women, the 'marriage lie', and the function of literature in the modern world.

In view of this density of texture the lack of clarity in Hauptmann's play is not very surprising. A further reason lies in the nature of the dramatist's talents; Hauptmann's characterizing impulse was such that it would almost always assert itself over his much weaker sense of a message, or his control of plot.[10] In this Hauptmann had considerable support from the dramatic theory of the Naturalist period; Arno Holz, for instance, writes: 'The law of the theatre requires not action, but the representation of characters.'[11] It is perfectly understandable that in the course of composition the interest of a dramatist whose strength is in characterization should fall to Helene. Her fate is still in doubt, whereas the remainder of the Krause household has already sunken unknowingly and unresistingly into dissipation and animality. Hoffmann is intelligent enough to know better, but intelligence allied with weakness of character has led him to the conviction that resistance is futile. His chief concern seems to be to anaesthetize any vestiges of the capacity to feel pain; hence his increasing reliance on tobacco and alcohol, and his attempts to seduce Helene. In the interests of theatrical suspense Loth is kept in ignorance of certain facts until the end of the play, which not only makes him appear a little obtuse, it also effectively excludes him from the sort of inner conflict which Helene is capable of experiencing.

---

[10] Cf. K. S. Guthke, *Gerhart Hauptmann: Weltbild im Werk* (Göttingen: Vandenhoeck und Ruprecht, 1961), p. 63. Cf. also the letter of James to Stanislaus Joyce, quoted by K. L. Tank, *Gerhart Hauptmann in Selbstzeugnissen und Bilddokumenten* (Hamburg: Rowohlt), 1959, p. 167.
[11] Holz, *Das Werk*, edited by Hans W. Fischer, 10 vols (Berlin: Dietz Nachfolger, 1924–25), X, 224; see also Hauptmann, *Sämtliche Werke*, VI, 1043.

Her knowledge is greater (quantitatively) than Loth's and her personality is more naive than Hoffmann's and so she is not disposed to resignation. At the crucial moment in the play, immediately after Loth has departed, it is Helene who enters to make the announcement that Marthe's second child has been stillborn; this confirmation of Loth's fears, at this point in the action, and by this character, can hardly mean anything but that Loth's course of action is the right one. Nevertheless, so much sympathy has by this time accrued to Helene, against an overall design which would suggest that Loth is, in principle, right, that the ultimate meaning of the play is obscured.

Whilst the drawing of the wide range of characters – and special mention should be made of Hoffmann – is this play's greatest virtue, the central character, Loth, is without depth. His psychology is flat, and we are left with the feeling that his motivation is inadequately explained. It is true that Hoffmann describes him to Helene as ruthless and inhuman, but Hoffmann is an interested party on more than one count. It is also true that Loth does utter certain rather crass clichés, such as 'I wouldn't trample on anyone, unless they wanted to make me become a traitor to myself' (I, 80); but if these words are to be seen as a sham rationalization, we need some more positive indication of the shortcoming they rationalize.[12] Moreover, the words are spoken before there is any question of departure – they are not offered as an excuse – and they are, to some extent, taken back by Loth's subsequent words, as he begins to reflect on his attraction to Helene:

es ist mir vielleicht nicht ganz so klar bewußt geworden wie jetzt, daß ich in meinem Streben etwas entsetzlich Ödes, gleichsam Maschinenmäßiges angenommen hatte. Kein Geist, kein Temperament, kein Leben, ja wer weiß, war noch Glauben in mir? Das alles kommt seit... seit heute wieder in mich gezogen. So merkwürdig voll, so ursprünglich, so fröhlich! (I, 92)	it has perhaps never been so clear to me as it is now that my activities have become terribly barren, almost mechanical. I was lacking in spirit, in energy, in life, and who knew if I still believed in it all? Since... since today all of this has welled up in me again. It is so wonderfully rich, so fresh, so joyful!

It does not seem likely that Hauptmann could have given Loth these words at this point if it had been his conscious intention to condemn him later as a cold doctrinaire and an automaton.

---

[12] The most persuasive argument advanced for this wholly negative interpretation of Loth's character is a literary rather than a psychological one: Cowen's comparison of the

A diary-entry of 1897 (VI, 1043) makes it clear that Hauptmann soon came to realize the problems attendant on treating a character such as Loth in a drama. And subsequently, in the conversations with Chapiro he argues that an absolutely consistent character, such as a fanatic, can have no place in a drama, because his behaviour is totally predictable:

> Characters who conform to a mould, who are, as it were, pre-formed, are not suitable for the theatre. Fanatics for instance, someone who thinks he possesses the absolute truth, can have only an episodic role in a drama. He will deprive the inner dialogue of all the suggestive power of the unexpected. For such a person everything is already decided.[13]

The catalytic function of the newly arrived character – to produce rather than to undergo a change – tends to make him a character of this kind; and it is, indeed, a precondition of the tension which informs the last act of *Vor Sonnenaufgang* that we can rely on Loth's response. The nearest such a character can come to the centre of the action is probably in one of the classic patterns of the 'Western': in a primitive, lawless community it takes a strong and disinterested individual to impose law and order, but once this is done there is no place in that community for the man who has subdued it; hence the final sequence shows the hero riding out, alone, into the sunset. Such a role demands emotional asceticism as well as physical courage, for emotional involvement distracts from the concentration which is necessary to complete the task. There is in *Vor Sonnenaufgang* just a hint of this problem when Loth shows how unimportant the friendship of Hoffmann is to him, or when he explains to Helene that his own personal happiness is a very distant prospect: 'I could, so to speak, only ever take the last place at table' (I, 47).

In *Winterschlaf* a play strongly influenced by *Vor Sonnenaufgang*, Max Dreyer avoids the ambiguities of Hauptmann's play by treating his newcomer in the way Hauptmann was later to suggest such figures should be treated. Hans Meincke, like Loth a socialist, a sociologist, and just released from gaol, is rescued from the snow by *Förster* Ahrens, in whose isolated home he remains for three days to recover – just long enough for the forester's daughter, Trude, to fall in love with him, and to acquire a longing to escape from her rather brutal fiancé and her restricted home environment to the wider outside world. Trude's evil old aunt stirs up the jealous fiancé, and provokes him into raping Trude, who gives up her plans to leave for Berlin, and commits suicide

---

virtuous Loth and the cynical Hoffman with Büchner's Robespierre and Danton; see Roy C. Cowen, *Der Naturalismus; Kommentar zu einer Epoche* (Munich: Winkler, 1973), pp. 162–63.
[13] *Gespräche mit Gerhart Hauptmann*, p. 164.

immediately after Hans' departure. There is no question of Hans' departure being seen as a defection, because, plausibly enough, he does not feel any emotional attachment to Trude; love is all on one side, and the young woman has, in fact, been at pains to conceal her feelings in order to secure her father's permission to leave for Berlin. Her 'unworthiness' is a purely subjective matter; Hans never knows of the rape, or her suicide, and there is no reason to believe that if he did he would have rejected her in the way Loth rejects Helene. We can therefore concentrate with undivided attention on the single issue, the question of self-determination and self-fulfilment regardless of gender differences, for which Hans emerges as the spokesman: 'No one – neither man nor woman – may suppress a vital force which lives within him.'[14]

In this simplified scheme there is no opposition between social altruism and the ideal of self-realization. When Hans reproaches Trude for her passivity he is criticizing her both for failing to fulfil herself and for failing to take up the 'great social task'. Toni Selicke's dilemma is avoided, for Trude has no duty to stay with her family. Hans shows some awareness of a potential problem in his account of his period of imprisonment: for the authorities he was an agitator, and was imprisoned as such, but the workers he had come to help suspected him of being an *agent provocateur*, and therefore ostracized him; but the tensions of this situation are not examined further. *Winterschlaf* is a simplified *pièce à thèse*, in which the situation is presented from one point of view; it is unquestionably a superiority of Hauptmann's play that it begins, at least implicitly, to illuminate the ambiguities of Loth's approach to social problems, and to suggest that Helene's perspective is worthy of consideration.

There is one indisputably great drama of this period which, it has often been suggested, may have influenced Hauptmann in the writing of *Vor Sonnenaufgang* – Ibsen's *The Wild Duck*. In Ibsen's play there is no doubt that Gregers Werle's intervention in the Ekdal family is misguided, and that he himself suffers from complex psychological problems which the dramatist, by skilful use of retrospective exposition, illuminates with immense subtlety.[15] Hauptmann's own comments on *Vor Sonnenaufgang* would seem to confirm the view that Loth is to be seen rather differently and rather more sympathetically. Writing shortly after the first performance, Hauptmann expressed some dissatisfaction with the actor who performed the role of Loth in a theatrical way which made him appear both naive and pretentious, whereas he was intended

---

[14] Max Dreyer, *Winterschlaf*, 3rd edition (Leipzig and Berlin: Georg Heinrich Meyer, 1904; first published 1894), p. 61.

[15] See Joan Carr, '"The Forest's Revenge": Subconscious motivation in "The Wild Duck"', *Modern Language Review*, 72 (1977), 845–56.

to be an intelligent and original character:

Alfred Loth redet nirgend zum Publikum. Er redet zu Hoffmann von Dingen, wie man sie nach einer langen Trennung notwendigerweise zur Sprache bringt... Er redet dann mit Helenen, einem guten naiven Kinde, und gibt ihr die ihm selbst alltäglichen Gedanken in einer leicht faßlichen Form, um sie ihr nahezulegen... Wie soll es anders als lächerlich wirken, wenn der Schauspieler mit gewollten Simplizitäten pratentiös austritt und sie wie Offenbarungen höchster Weisheit ins Parkett hinunterpredigt.¹⁶	Alfred Loth never addresses the audience directly. He speaks to Hoffmann of things which will necessarily come up after a long separation... And then he talks to Helene, a good, simple girl, and tells her what for him are commonplace ideas, in an easily comprehensible form in order to convince her. How can it be anything but laughable if the actor pretentiously enunciates deliberate simplifications and throws them down into the auditorium as if they were manifestations of the highest wisdom.

There is, however, another point in the play where a comparison with *The Wild Duck* is more illuminating. The discussion between Schimmelpfennig and Loth links the fifth act to the first, in which Hoffmann and Loth discussed different attitudes to social reform. Hoffmann's attitude is clearly a contemptible piece of hypocrisy; and even now, his wife in labour, he shows more concern about Loth's sociological investigation than does Loth himself. But Schimmelpfennig's attitude has a certain superficial attraction, in much the same way as Dr Relling's has in *The Wild Duck*; he is a bluff and good-natured man, with no illusions, dedicated to alleviating mortal pain: 'It's quite simple: mankind is in agony, and it is our job to drug them, and make their condition as bearable as possible' (I, 92). One might therefore expect him to be in

---

¹⁶ Gerhart Hauptmann, *Die Kunst des Dramas: Über Schauspiel und Theater*, edited by Martin Machatzke (Frankfurt a.M., Berlin, and Vienna: Propyläen, 1963), pp. 94–95. In the first performance the actor concerned was Theodor Brandt, but the same thing seems to have happened a year later when the *Freie Volksbühne* gave a performance with a different actor in the role; the critic of the *Berliner Volksblatt* (12. 11. 1890) wrote: 'Herr Hagemann is not a realistic actor... Herr Hagemann managed to step completely outside the boundaries of the work of art and speak directly to the public in an agitatorial manner as if he were standing on a platform, and he did not dispense with even the cheapest tricks'. It must, however, be conceded that Hauptmann's text is not as consistently anti-theatrical in its implications for performance as author and critic here claim; see John Osborne, 'Gerhart Hauptmanns "Vor Sonnenaufgang": Zwischen Tradition und Moderne', *Der Deutschunterricht*, 40 (1988), H. 2, 77–88 (pp. 86–87).

favour of the marriage of Loth and Helene, for this would certainly make Helene's life more bearable, but he is instrumental in preventing it, and we are led to believe that this is because of his convinced and dogmatic opposition to the institution of marriage as such. His suggestion that the companionship of Hoffmann might provide Helene with some consolation for the loss of Loth is quite consistent with his views on the function of medicine, but reveals the total inadequacy of his thinking, and his utter failure to understand Helene's character. Like Relling (and like Robert Scholz in Hauptmann's next play, *Das Friedensfest*) he responds to idealism with wounding mockery: 'You fellows keep getting involved up to the neck in things which you have in theory long rejected, what a lot of things you need to keep afloat, faith, hope, charity. For me that's all a load of rubbish' (I, 92); but in doing so he invites the answer which Gregers Werle gives Relling in the concluding lines of *The Wild Duck*: 'If you are right and I am wrong, life is no longer worth living.'

If *Vor Sonnenaufgang* has indeed been influenced by *The Wild Duck*, then, I believe, Hauptmann's play is to be seen as an idealist's attempt to rescue something from the jaws of Ibsen's grim pessimism. During his years in Zürich in the 1880s Hauptmann and his friends had shared the attitude which lays Loth open to Schimmelpfennig's mockery: 'What made those days, especially the days in Zurich, so spring-like, was our immanent belief. Shall I call it the old trinity, faith, hope, and charity? Yes, for we were filled with them' (VII, 1060). And in the play it is this attitude which makes Loth an optimist, who sees in medicine – as his comments on the work of Zola and Ibsen reveal – a means of *curing* mankind. This optimism enables Loth to change the situation he finds, to detach Helene from her alliance with the party of Hoffmann, to awaken her social conscience (her defence of the dismissed maid-servant), to break down the repressive defence-mechanisms she is in the process of building up (evidence of which is to be found in her description of the mine-workers), and to convert her from a limited reliance on alcohol to complete abstinence.

Loth is typical of Hauptmann's heroes in that he stands for exposure in both its senses: the exposure of unpalatable circumstances, and the complementary exposure of the self to suffering. Knowledge may bring suffering, but both are to be avoided only at great cost in terms of basic humanity. Hoffmann, for instance, remains human only in as much as he is still capable of suffering: 'That is what is tragic about the man, he suffers..., he suffers as much as he still can' (I, 93–4). It is Loth, the idealist, and not Schimmelpfennig, the cynic, who anticipates that his departure may be disastrous to Helene, for she too is an idealist. In the society in which she finds herself she, as a woman, does not have the same opportunities to change an evil world, and suicide is her only way of rejecting it. This suicide, unlike that of Johannes Vockerat in

Einsame Menschen, is not simply an act of despair at being left by someone she loves, but an assertion of all that is best in her, a refusal, comparable, as I have suggested, with that of Emilia Galotti, to sink slowly into a world of unfeeling and anonymity.

Without being fundamentally altered the play's idealist message is, as it were, transferred from Loth to Helene. Loth's 'immanent religion' is not in the end quite religious enough to provide a convincing motive for the course of action he takes. *Vor Sonnenaufgang* shows signs of a disenchantment with scientific rationalism, but this disenchantment is, as yet, not strong enough to have more than a negative influence, that is to say, to distract the author's interest from a character whose action is rationally thought out and to leave it, in consequence, on one who acts from an elemental impulse of horror.

6
DAS FRIEDENSFEST

Hauptmann's second play, *Das Friedensfest*, was first performed on 1 June 1890, bringing to an end the first season of the *Freie Bühne*. There was no repetition of the scandal which had accompanied the first performance of *Vor Sonnenaufgang*, but once again the dramatist had reason to be unhappy with the performance of his leading actor, the celebrated Josef Kainz, who arrived for the performance without having memorized his part.[1] Critical response to the play ranged from lukewarm to hostile, and it is only in recent years that it has come to be regarded as a key work in Hauptmann's *oeuvre*.

Das Friedensfest is a much more tautly constructed and firmly circumscribed work than its immediate predecessor. The broad social problem which lay in the background of *Vor Sonnenaufgang* is here abandoned in favour of greater concentration on the central issues of marriage and the family, and the interior struggles of the characters. Coherent argument between people of equal intelligence has a much larger role, as it does in the following play, *Einsame Menschen*; indeed, both plays illustrate the preference of the Naturalist dramatists for the middle-class, intellectual sphere, and they are, at the same time, the two of Hauptmann's plays in which the resemblance to Ibsen is most marked. *Ghosts* and *Rosmersholm* are the plays which most readily come to mind in this connection. Both had been performed in Berlin in 1887, and Hauptmann is known to have been present at the performance of *Ghosts*, at least. The superficial similarities between this latter play and *Das Friedensfest* are indeed considerable; the two plays share the same technique of analytical exposition, they reveal the tyranny of the past in hereditary disease, and they condemn the 'lie' of modern marriage. But, despite all this, they remain characteristically different, as two plays by Hauptmann and Ibsen inevitably are different. It is strange that Hauptmann should have said: 'Ibsen's plays point a certain vague moral' (VI, 1043), for without ever degenerating into the flat tendentiousness of many of his German imitators, Ibsen can convey with absolute clarity the rights and duties of a character such as Mrs Alving. It is no value

---

[1] Gerhart Hauptmann, 'Das zweite Vierteljahrhundert', *Die großen Beichten* (Berlin: Propyläen, 1966), p. 659. Hauptmann's complaints about Kainz are confirmed in Maximilian Harden's review, *Die Gegenwart*, 7 October 1890.

judgement to say that in *Das Friedensfest* Hauptmann does not, but gives a demonstration of determinism, of the loss and exposure of man in the world as he understands it; he explores the quality of his suffering, and considers the price it is necessary to pay to ensure survival.

The plot, the family-catastrophe of the subtitle, is based closely on an account of Frank Wedekind's homelife – so closely that Wedekind was deeply offended by what he considered to be a betrayal of confidence and made a riposte in a parody of Hauptmann in his early play, *Die junge Welt* (1889). The quarrel lasted many years, and left its traces in the prologue to *Erdgeist* (1896).[2] This plot is centred on an ill-conceived and unsuccessful attempt by Frau Buchner and her daughter, Ida, to bring about a reconciliation among the divided Scholz family. As a result, it is suggested, of an ill-advised marriage of convenience between Dr Scholz and a woman twenty-two years his junior and very much inferior to him in intellect and experience of life, the Scholzes are a family riven with strife and nervous disorder. As in the opening scene of *Vor Sonnenaufgang*, the atmosphere of the household in which the drama takes place is established brilliantly and quickly as Auguste (who must have seen her father waiting around outside the house) enters:

AUGUSTE, *in Hast und Bestürzung von draußen herein. Innen angelangt, schlägt sie die Glastür heftig ins Schloß und stemmt sich dagegen, wie um jemandem den Eintritt zu verwehren* (I, 106).	AUGUSTE, *enters from outside in haste and panic. Having got inside, she slams the glass door violently shut and leans against it as if to prevent someone from coming in.*

The culmination of the family quarrels was reached some six years before the play opens, when Wilhelm struck his father. The occasion of the blow was a visit by Wilhelm, during which he introduced a musician-friend into the house, his aim being to provide change and relaxation for his mother (I, 133), whose musical interests were not shared by her husband. Both Wilhelm and his father left the house on the same day, and have not subsequently been back. Robert, the elder brother, has taken a job which keeps him away from home, though he has been returning every Christmas; Auguste, the unmarried daughter, has remained with her mother.

In the intervening years Wilhelm has recovered a certain amount of equanimity through friendship with Frau Buchner and Ida, whom he now intends to marry. Frau Buchner, anxious to complete the cure of her prospective son-in-law, has persuaded the reluctant Wilhelm to

---

[2] See F. W. J. Heuser, 'Gerhart Hauptmann und Frank Wedekind', *Gerhart Hauptmann* (Tübingen: Niemeyer, 1961), pp. 226–46.

return home and celebrate Christmas with his mother. Quite by chance Dr Scholz, now aged and sick, has also decided to return, and so a happy coincidence sees the whole family reunited. The Buchners urge Wilhelm to take this opportunity of begging his father's forgiveness, and, in a silent scene of intense conflict, father and son are reconciled. It seems as if the Buchners have been successful beyond their original expectations when a state of harmony embraces the entire family; but they have underestimated their task; the old antagonisms destroy this superficial harmony; Robert and Wilhelm quarrel violently, the others take sides. Dr Scholz succumbs to a stroke. Robert, embittered, resolves to leave home once and for all. Frau Buchner regrets her interference, and departs in tears. Wilhelm decides that it is his duty to give up all ideas of marriage, but at the last moment the pessimism is muted as Ida, now almost in the position of the abandoned Helene Krause, persuades Wilhelm to have confidence in the power of love, and the final curtain falls as the two walk resolutely together into Dr Scholz's death chamber.

The subject of family-relationships and parental authority had provided the theme of a play much admired by the Naturalists, and performed four months earlier than *Das Friedensfest* by the *Freie Bühne* – Ludwig Anzengruber's *Das vierte Gebot*. Surprisingly, it is the earlier dramatist who is the more radical critic of social institutions, and the more clearly tendentious. Anzengruber argues that the fourth commandment (the fifth according to the reckoning of the reformed churches) has no absolute validity. The young pastor, Eduard Schön, follows it with confidence because his own parents have always acted with wisdom and understanding; but his advice to a young girl to marry a man of her father's choice brings disaster to herself, her parents, her child, and the man she loved. All those involved come to agree that insistence on filial duty was misplaced, and that each case must be decided on its merits; Eduard confides to his parents:

Ich hätte mich erst ganz genau mit den Verhältnissen vertraut machen sollen, und dann wäre es am Platz gewesen, ohne der Neigung irgendwie das Wort zu reden, dem Vater Hedwigs die geplante Verbindimg auf das eindringlichste...abzuraten... Ich dachte damals nur an euch und mich und ich war gewohnt, euch immer zu gehorchen.[3]	I should have enquired into all the circumstances first, and then it would have been proper, without speaking in favour of Hedwig's inclinations, to advise her father most strongly against the marriage... But at the time I only thought of you and me, and I was always accustomed to obey you.

---

[3] *Sämtliche Werke*, edited by Rudolf Latzke und Otto Rommel, 15 vols (Vienna and Leipzig: Anton Schroll, 1920–22), V, 226.

The moral is reinforced in the concluding scene of the play, in which the central character of the sub-plot, Martin Schalanther, now under sentence of death, gives the modified version of the commandment for which this play became famous: 'If you teach children at school: "Honour thy father and thy mother", then you should also tell their parents from the pulpit to behave accordingly'.[4]

Among other plays of the Naturalist period in which the father, the representative of the authority of the older generation, is called to account for the sufferings of the children are Ernst Rosmer (Else Bernstein)'s *Dämmerung* (1893) and Wilhelm Weigand's *Der Vater* (1894), but it is *Das Friedensfest* which takes up this theme with the greatest subtlety and the greatest force, and which, at the same time, anticipates most markedly the protests – and the topoi – of the Expressionist drama. Both in the 1890s and in the Expressionist period the conflict of fathers and sons is of particular importance in the field of education. Dr Scholz is described as having submitted his sons to a particularly brutal regime:

Volle zehn Stunden taglich hockten wir über Büchern... Wenn ich das Kerkerloch sehe, heutigen Tags noch... es stieß an sein Arbeitszimmer... Wenn wir in diesen Raum eintraten, da mochte die Sonne noch so hell zum Fenster reinscheinen, für uns war es dann Nacht (I, 131).	For ten whole hours a day we sat over books... When I see that prison, even today... it was next to his study... When we stepped into that room, no matter how brightly the sun was shining outside, for us it was night.

Unimaginative rationalism, the rigour of philological drill, the tyranny of systematic education (I, 126), are also severely criticized in *Der erste Schultag* by Holz and Schlaf, in Holz's and Jerschke's *Traumulus*, in Wedekind's *Frühlings Erwachen*, and, most notably perhaps, in Heinrich Mann's novel, *Professor Unrat*.

In *Das Friedensfest*, as in *Frühlings Erwachen*, it is the mother who intercedes on behalf of the children to offer something other than discipline and systematic knowledge. Three decades later, that is after the educational system of Germany has been subject to the criticisms of Julius Langbehn, Ellen Key, the *Jugendbewegung*, and numerous others, the same motif is taken up by the Expressionist, Arnolt Bronnen, in *Vatermord*. Here the father, symbolically named Fessel, wishes to make his son become a lawyer, despite the boy's own longing for the career of

---

[4] *Sämtliche Werke*, V, 235.

a farmer, in the free, open-air atmosphere of the countryside. For the father education means breaking his son's will, and imposing his own, as expressed in the paradoxical demand:

> Er soll nur in den Himmel wachsen!
> Ich werd ihn brechen.[5]

The effect of the father's pressure on the son is to produce in him a state bordering on insanity; and after a cruel and brutal assault, Walter eventually gives his father a single blow in self-defence. The play ends with the consummation of the sympathetic relations between mother and son in an act of incest, Walter's killing of his father, and his jubilation at his attainment of freedom.

Bronnen's crude play does not treat characterization and motivation with any degree of subtlety; one cannot expect this of an Expressionist drama;[6] but this is the field in which Hauptmann excels. *Das Friedensfest* derives its considerable merits from Hauptmann's evident understanding of the potentiality for love and feeling which, because of its range and intensity, is responsible for both the mutual antagonism and the continued family solidarity of the Scholzes. Hauptmann once wrote: 'There is nothing so terrible as the estrangement of intimates' (VI, 1014); this is the problem he is dealing with in *Das Friedensfest* and the play which most resembles it in this is one by Eugene O'Neill, not *Mourning becomes Electra* (which Hauptmann subsequently came to know and admire) but the more personal *Long Day's Journey into Night*, in which a situation of crisis has the same effect of uniting a deeply discordant family.

There is little opportunity for weighing the conflicting arguments and judgements in *Das Friedensfest*, and so social criticism (of marriage) has only a limited role. We can readily accept that there is some justification for Robert's criticism of his parents' marriage; but as far as Wilhelm and Ida are concerned, this issue is evaded: despite the quarrel which flares up briefly in the final scene, there is no reason to assume that they are mismatched in the way Wilhelm's parents were. The conclusion of the play leaves their future in doubt, but there is some hope for Wilhelm's survival in the environment to be provided by Ida. At the same time the argument between the pessimist, Robert Scholz, and the optimist, Frau Buchner, is not conclusively resolved, despite the apparent defeat of Frau Buchner. In short, the attitude behind the play would seem to be entirely consistent with

---

[5] *Vatermord* (Berlin: Rowohlt, 1925), p. 50.
[6] Cf. Walter H. Sokel, 'Dialogführung und Dialog im expressionistischen Drama', *Aspekte des Expressionismus*, edited by Wolfgang Paulsen (Heidelberg: Stiehm, 1968), pp. 59–84.

Hauptmann's words:

Optimismus an sich hat etwas Verdächtiges... mehr: etwas Vulgäres... mehr: etwas Banales... mehr: etwas Gemeines! – aber der Pessimismus wirkt abgegriffen und in jeder Beziehung als geforderter Gegensatz zu dem vorherigen (VI, 998).	There is about optimism something suspect... worse: something vulgar... worse: something banal... worse: something base – but pessimism seems hackneyed, in all respects an opposite provoked by optimism.

The form of *Das Friedensfest* is that of the typical German Naturalist drama, with Frau Buchner and her daughter sharing the role of *Bote aus der Fremde*, though another way of looking at the play might see Dr Scholz in this role; in any event, the Buchners have very little real influence on the causal structure. What really brings the family together this Christmas Eve is the strength of those bonds which have preserved them as a family until now. There is a certain irrational quality about these bonds, but Hauptmann, treating his subject naturalistically, shows how they operate in the social sphere to produce the family unit and the tensions peculiar to it.

There are a number of signs of affection, strenuously suppressed, beneath the brittle surface of the Scholz family. Ida probes, and Wilhelm concedes that Dr Scholz's behaviour cannot be attributed solely to the desire to dominate over his sons: 'To a certain extent he may perhaps have had good intentions' (I, 131). If this grudging admission means little, there is some evidence that the father's affection was recognized and returned: on different occasions Auguste and Robert speak up for their absent father. Most significant is Frau Scholz's spontaneous reaction when her husband unexpectedly comes through the door:

FRAU SCHOLZ, *den Doktor wie eine überirdische Erscheinung anstarrend.* Fritz! .... *vor Staunen außer sich.* Aber sag mer nur Fritz! sag mer nur... die Gedanken fliegen mer davon. *Ihn weinend umhalsend.* Ach Fritz! was hast du mir für Kummer gemacht in der langen Zeit! (I, 113)	FRAU SCHOLZ, *staring at the doctor like a supernatural apparition.* Fritz! .... *beside herself with astonishment.* But tell me Fritz! just tell me... I'm all confused. *Embracing him in tears.* Ahh, Fritz! What a lot of worry you've caused me all this time!

The same instinctive affection characterizes Frau Scholz's relations with her children. Wilhelm left home some years ago, but in her own petit bourgeois way his mother is still concerned about his future happiness: 'You ought to thank God, you could wait a long time till you found another like Ida!...cautiously, confidentially:...but tell me, are the Buchners well off?' (I, 153). In the past she intervened to protect them from the harshness of their father's discipline; simple person that she was, intellectual persuasion was not a course that was open to her, and so violent scenes resulted. Again it seems that this affection has been returned. Robert, outwardly cynical and cold, has returned every Christmas during the long lonely years to visit his mother and sister; and Wilhelm's account of his feelings at the time of the quarrel suggests an almost guilty excess in his affection for his mother: 'It seemed to me at the time as if he [Dr Scholz] was illegally holding mother prisoner here. I actually wanted her to become separated from him' (I, 132). It was in his mother's name that Wilhelm struck his father; just as it is in his father's name that Robert now hates his brother:

Seh ich ihn..., dann geht alle meine Überlegung zum Teufel, dann bin ich etwas... etwas...na, wie soll ich sagen? dann seh ich nur den Menschen, der meinen Vater – nicht seinen, sondern meinen – Vater ins Gesicht geschlagen hat (I, 122).	If I see him I'm not rational, I become something... something...well, how shall I put it? then I only see the man who struck my father – not his father but my father – in the face.

The strikingly coincidental reunion of the Scholz family is not an implausibility in the action of the play, but an indication that the Scholzes are once again ready to come together as a family, indeed, are irresistibly drawn to do so. There is only the most superficial conflict of interest between them and the Buchners. Christmas for Robert, illness for the Doctor, and the Buchners for Wilhelm, all serve as excuses or provide opportunities for the assertion of an impulse that is normally feared and therefore suppressed. Because Frau Buchner is a superficial woman she does not realize this. A similar situation occurs in a very different play, Racine's *Phèdre*. As the play opens Phèdre is already tormented and dying because of her guilty love for her stepson, Hippolyte; the false report of the death of her husband, Thésée, does not alter the morality of the situation in the least (Phèdre did not need A. W. Schlegel to point this out to her), it merely provides the queen with a reason for seeking out Hippolyte, whom she has hitherto shunned. Without the false report, their meeting could not have taken place, but it is in only the most limited sense the cause of the tragedy.

The Buchners have little real influence in bringing the family together, and equally little on the act of reconciliation itself. The explanation of this is only to be found in the feelings of the various characters, and their continued family devotion.[7] The very fact that the family is assembled is a first step – and the first step towards a family reconciliation is the most difficult one – a tentative admission of affection and mutual dependence, an esoteric signal which can be recognized only within the family, and which itself calls forth the next step.

This second step, the confrontation of father and son, is very nearly thwarted because of Frau Buchner's interference. Wilhelm threatens to leave, suspecting that his father's presence has been engineered by her. When father and son do meet, Wilhelm's behaviour bears little resemblance to the dramatic, almost biblical instructions which Frau Buchner gave him at the end of Act I. From his words and demeanour at this point it does appear to be Wilhelm's intention to do more or less as she instructs him, that is to say to act out the role of Prodigal Son, in which he has been cast – not out of conviction, but for the sake of Ida. It is clear from his conversation with Ida at the beginning of Act II that he is still intellectually convinced of the justice of his attack on his father; he still describes it as a punishment. Yet instead of a pious, but hypocritical plea for forgiveness, we witness an instinctive awakening of sympathy, a relenting by two characters weary of maintaining a cramped and meaningless hostility; and this happens before a single word has been uttered. Unlike Gregers Werle in *The Wild Duck*, Wilhelm agrees to take part in a sentimental 'tableau with father and son' in which he does not fully believe, and then the inherent theatricality of this situation is overcome as the relaxation of tension spreads to involve the whole family in a way which Frau Buchner did not anticipate, because the quality and quantity of the feeling in this particular family is something which is not within the range of her experience, lived or imagined, as she subsequently concedes:

nun habe ich so viel gesehen	I have now seen and
hier und erfahren. Da ist	experienced so much here.
mir vieles von dem, was	I now understand much
Sie [Wilhelm] mir früher gesagt	of what you told me earlier.
haben, erst verständlich	I didn't understand you
geworden. Ich verstand sie	before. I thought you were
nicht. Ich hielt Sie für einen	just prone to look on the

---

[7] The family, of course, is not what it was; thus Margaret Sinden can attribute Wilhelm's 'undue self-castigation' (for having struck his father and broken up his home) entirely to inherited nervous disorder; *Gerhart Hauptmann: The Prose Plays* (Toronto and London: Toronto University Press, 1957), p. 30.

Schwarzseher. Ich nahm vieles gar nicht einmal ernst. Mit einem festen frohen Glauben kam ich hierher. Ich schäme mich förmlich. (I, 155)	gloomy side. There were many things I did not even take seriously. I came here with a firm and joyful faith. I am positively ashamed.

Robert, however, confirms that the brief interlude of peace and happiness was not entirely a surprise; that the potentiality was present before the intervention of the Buchners: 'Now it has come to life in us, so it was in us, why did it not break out sooner?... It was in us!' (I, 138).

Frau Buchner's admission of shame is an admission of excessive trust in the power of the conscious will. In *Das Friedensfest* Hauptmann is very much concerned with exposing the limitations of this force, and with revealing the unconscious motives which lie behind even the most considered words. The spoken words of the Buchners and the Scholzes – even the intelligent Robert's – are seldom effective in helping the characters understand what is driving them; they are only rarely significant for the information they convey directly. This distrust of the spoken word was already evident in *Vor Sonnenaufgang*; Hoffmann, for instance, could be seen rationalizing his designs on Helene with the help of Dr Schimmelpfennig's suggestion that she might make a suitable foster-mother for his second child. This later play probably owes more to Schopenhauer's view of the intellect as an instrument in the service of deeper impulses;[8] there are also traces of Nietzsche's suspicion of the self-gratification derived by the altruist from his task: 'There really still are naive souls, who are not happy unless they can meddle around trying to improve their fellow men' (I, 118), complains Robert. The point is emphasized in the argument between Auguste and Frau Buchner over the dispensation of charity by the local priest:

AUGUSTE. So viel steht fest: wenn ich arm ware, ich hätte auf die Rede des Großmann hin... wahrhaftig den ganzen Bettel hätte ich ihnen vor die Füsse geschmissen. FRAU BUCHNER. Es ist aber doch ein großer Segen für die armen Leute.[9] (I, 108)	AUGUSTE. One thing is certain: if I were poor, when that man spoke... really, I should have chucked all his charity at his feet. FRAU BUCHNER. But it is a great blessing for the poor.

---

[8] See Hans M. Wolff, '*Das Friedensfest*', in K. S. Guthke and Hans M. Wolff, 'Das Leid im Werke Gerhart Hauptmanns', *University of California Publications in Modern Philology*, 49 (1958), p. 55.
[9] Wedekind makes a similar point in a short exchange between Melchior Gabor and Wendla Bergmann in *Frühlings Erwachen*; *Gesammelte Werke*, edited by Artur Kutscher und Joachim Friedenthal, 9 vols (Munich: Georg Müller, 1920–21), II, 114–16.

Frau Buchner's affection for Wilhelm is revealed as a particularly important motive for her actions, her optimism, and her serious underestimation of the task she has taken upon herself. Her first moment of self-awareness is a disastrous blow for her:

FRAU BUCHNER, *unter Tränen.* Ich weiß nicht! Ich weiß das selbst nicht! Ich habe das Kind erzogen. Es ist mir alles in allem gewesen; an seinem Glücke zu arbeiten ist auf der Welt mein einziger Beruf gewesen. Nun kamen Sie in unser Haus. Ich gewann Sie lieb. Ich dachte auch an ihr Gluck, ich... Das hätte ich vielleicht nicht tun sollen... Ich dachte vielleicht ebensosehr an Ihr Glück – und wer weiß – am Ende – zuallermeist – an Ihr Glück. *Einen Augenblick lang starren beide einander bestürzt in die Augen.*
WILHELM. Frau Buchner!!
FRAU BUCHNER, *das Gesicht mit den Händen bedeckend wie jemand der sich schämt, weinend ab durch den Treppenausgang.*
(I, 156)

FRAU BUCHNER, *in tears.* I don't know! I just don't know! I brought the child up. She was everything to me; my sole earthly vocation was to work for her happiness. Then you came into our in house. I became fond of you. I began to think of your happiness too, I... Perhaps I shouldn't have done that... Perhaps I thought equally of your happiness – and who knows – in the end – of your happiness – most of all. *For a moment they both look into each other's eyes in astonishment.*
WILHELM. Frau Buchner!!
FRAU BUCHNER, *covering her face with her hands like someone who is ashamed, goes off in tears, by the staircase-exit.*

This revelation of her hitherto unconscious motives casts a radically different light on the whole of Frau Buchner's behaviour. It ironically underscores her claim: 'I feel that I am acting in a specific cause. That fortifies me' (I, 118). It strengthens the authority of Robert as a judge of character, for he has all along been reluctant to take her actions at their face value: 'I should very much like to know what this Frau Buchner is really doing here' (I, 123); and it lends a greater significance to Auguste's insistence that the Scholz family is not so bad after all: 'We are what we are. Other people, who put on all sorts of airs, are no better than us' (I, 118). For Frau Buchner to judge and to strive to change others is presumption; her self-satisfied equanimity, based as it is on the conviction that she is engaged on an altruistic task, is a fragile delusion. Its sudden collapse and her consequent departure clear the ground for the final confrontation with the real conflict, in much the same way as happens in the concluding section of O'Neill's *The Iceman cometh* after the equally sudden flash of self-awareness in the corresponding character, Hickey.

Yet the progressive devaluation of Frau Buchner's efforts, the justification of the Scholzes' views of the Christmas festivities as 'not really something for adults' (I, 109), and, at first sight, of their pessimistic despair, are not enough to support the interpretation of the play as the tragedy of Frau Buchner's kind of optimism. There is a brief scene, analogous to the one in which we are made aware of Frau Buchner's feelings for Wilhelm, in which Robert's authority is undermined. Knowing himself to be unobserved he creeps stealthily to the table of Christmas gifts and passionately imprints a kiss on the purse which Ida has placed there for Wilhelm. In this unguarded moment he reveals a more yielding side to his character, which is normally masked by his brutal cynicism; a side whose existence Frau Buchner has perceived, declaring: 'It is really not your true face that you are showing' (I, 120). Robert's pessimism is, as Wilhelm remarks, a product of disappointment and envy; he may be right in his assessment of Wilhelm's future prospects, but it is purely coincidental if he is:

Was dich auf den rechten Gedanken gebracht hat, das sag' ich dir ins Gesicht, ist jämmerlicher Neid... das ist einfach tief klägliche Mißgunst!... Du willst mich nicht gereinigt wissen. Warum willst du es nicht? Nun, weil... weil du selbst so bleiben mußt, wie du bist; weil sie mich liebt und nicht dich! (I, 163).	I tell you straight, what has put you on the right lines is pitiful jealousy... sheer, wretched envy!... You don't want to see me healed. And why not? Well, because... because you'll have to stay as you are; because she loves me and not you.

The pessimism of Robert Scholz and the optimism of Frau Buchner are each undermined to such an extent that there can be no talk of a clash of convictions rather than of personalities in *Das Friedensfest*. And it is precisely this lack of ideological discussion and guidance in Hauptmann's works which was to be criticized by the Expressionists; the third critic in Act I of Sorge's *Der Bettler* says:

Wir warten auf einen, der uns unser Schicksal neu deutet, den nenne ich denn Dramatiker und stark. Unser Haupt-Mann, sehen Sie, ist groß als Künstler, aber als Deuter befangen. Es ist sehr an der Zeit: einer muß einmal	We are waiting for someone who will interpret our destiny anew; such a man I will call a dramatist, and a powerful one. Our leading dramatist [Haupt-Mann], you see, is a great artist, but a

wieder für uns alle nachsinnen.[10]	limited interpreter. It is high time: someone must come and think for us all once again.

These younger writers had an ally and an antecedent in Wedekind, for in *Schloß Wetterstein* (1910) (a counterpart to *Das Friedensfest* in that Wedekind here gives his own 'views about the inner necessities on which marriage and the family are based'),[11] he parodies the Naturalists' undermining of intellectual convictions. At the beginning of Act III, the heroine, Effie, is reduced to despair because medical diagnosis has robbed her of the self-assertive individualism to which she felt she owed her happiness:

Mein starkes Verlangenist die Folge, wenn ich recht Verstanden, von Verdauungsstörungen? ... Und meiner Augen Schimmer, Aus dem der Mann sich, was weiß ich verspricht, Verdank ich also einem Leberleiden? ... Und daß so leicht und plötzlich mein Gesicht Die Farbe wechselt, und der matte Ton Der Haut, das alles kommt von Gallensteinen, Wenn nicht ein Lungenleiden gar dran schuld?[12]	My strong desires are, if I have understood aright, the consequence of indigestion?... And the sparkle in my eyes, in which men read promises of I know not what, I owe to a liver complaint?... And the way my face changes colour so easily and suddenly, and the paleness of my skin, all that is the result of gall-stones, if it isn't a disease of the lungs?

Effie pulls herself together when she is assured that, diagnosis notwithstanding, no one will notice any difference in her, and she refuses to be crushed by circumstances. In Wedekind's work it is the strength of the will over such chance circumstances which ensures human dignity; no force, not even love, should be allowed to restrict its free activity: 'As soon as one believes oneself to be bound by something more powerful than one's own free will the whole accursed horror of marriage becomes clear.'[13]

---

[10] R. J. Sorge, *Der Bettler: Eine dramatische Sendung* (Berlin: S. Fischer, 1928; first published 1912), p. 28.
[11] Wedekind, *Gesammelte Werke*, VI, 5.
[12] Wedekind, *Gesammelte Werke*, VI, 59.
[13] Wedekind, *Gesammelte Werke*, VI, 43.

This free and powerful will to self-assertion is very different from the scarcely comprehended force which determines the actions of Hauptmann's characters. As a Naturalist, Hauptmann shows this motive force operating through social phenomena;[14] although in this he does not differ radically from (say) Kleist, for in *Das Erdbeben in Chili* or *Penthesilea*, where a moment of crisis unites all in a common bond of feeling, the consequent harmony produces a complete, if temporary, reorganization of society. Given the more restricted scope of Hauptmann's play, the response of the Scholzes to Wilhelm's collapse before his father amounts to a similar reorganization.

Das Friedensfest resembles the work of Kleist in another important respect: in the limited and tentative evaluation of human conduct which (*pace* Sorge) it does contain. A heroine such as Penthesilea derives much of her beauty and value from the intensity of her feelings, from the totality of her exposure to those forces which, in others, are normally held at bay, from her very inability to restrain herself in the way Prothoe advises. Exposure and suffering can be avoided, but only by restraint or repression. And the difference between the brothers Robert and Wilhelm Scholz lies in the extent to which each is capable of defending himself from suffering. Repression of the self has played a part in the experience of Wilhelm, but it is something which he now rejects: 'I am afraid of myself. To be running away from oneself, can you imagine it? And don't you see, I've been running like this all my life.' (I, 129) He longs for rest from this flight; he remains naively hopeful, and therefore exposed, unable to resist the promise held out by the Buchners. He is willing to risk disappointment in an attempt to change his life; anticipating the optimistic belief of the Expressionist generation in the possibility of moral rebirth he can assert: 'Every man is a new man' (I, 161). After his final conversation with Robert he seems, it is true, to have been convinced by his brother's grim arguments:

Du hast ganz recht! Ich bin ein durch und durch lasterhafter Mensch. Nichts ist mehr rein an mir. Besudelt, wie ich bin, gehöre ich nicht neben diese Unschuld, und ich bin fest entschlossen, kein Verbrechen zu begehen; (I, 164)	You are quite right! I am a thoroughly depraved man. There is no longer anything clean about me. Sullied as I am, I do not belong near this innocent creature and I am firmly resolved not to commit a crime;

---

[14] Wilhelm Emrich plays down the Naturalist side of the play, to concentrate on the 'eternal power-struggle' of love and hate, guilt and reconciliation, etc., which he perceives beneath its surface; 'Der Tragödientypus Gerhart Hauptmanns', *Protest und Verheißung: Studien zur klassischen und modernen Dichtung* (Frankfurt a.M. and Bonn: Athenäum, 1960),

but even so he still gives in to Ida, and to her confident assertion that things will be different.

Robert, too, might well have behaved in this way in these circumstances; but with Ida so strongly committed to his brother, there is no evident escape for him. Intelligence, for a character in his situation, can soon be perverted to provide an excuse for withdrawal; the doctrine of determinism provides a ready justification for inaction. The reproach made to Gabriel Schilling, the hero of a later play by Hauptmann, could, with equal justice, have been made to Robert Scholz: 'One can blame a lot onto destiny' (II, 436). Experience has taught him that emotional involvement means risk; the admission of affection renders one vulnerable. And so Robert's surly behaviour on his first appearance seems to contradict the fact of his having come home to see his family at all. (His father is also reluctant to see any display of emotion when he arrives. He asks for his old manservant, Friebe, and returns to his old room upstairs.) He cynically trivializes any display of emotion; his difficult and moving apology to Wilhelm (I, 139) is followed by a wry comment on his emotional changeability: 'Akrobatenseele'. His every concession to his feelings is costly in terms of personal composure; he cannot therefore bring himself to accept a Christmas gift from Ida; when he comes in to take leave of Wilhelm for the last time, he finds himself stammering with emotion, and rapidly changes the subject:

| Ich habe genug, über und über sogar! Mutter wird künftig... wird künftig die Weihnachtstage ohne, ohne mich auskommen müssen. *Nach dem Ofen umblickend.* Es ist kalt hier (I, 158). | I've had enough, and more than enough! Mother will in future... will in future have to get along at Christmas without, without me. *Looking round at the stove.* It's cold in here. |

In the end Robert's fears prove to have been well-founded. Reconciliation and happiness can only be achieved briefly and with great risk; but it becomes evident that life without the attempt and the risk is a poor thing indeed. In opting for such a life, Robert makes a choice which Wilhelm regards as cowardly; he intends to repress all his feelings in work in a cold urban environment:

| Ich gehe jetzt in ein kleines, geheiztes Comptoirchen, setze | I'm now going into a cosy little heated office, I shall |

---

pp. 193–205. Cf. Neville E. Alexander, *Studien zum Stilwandel im dramatischen Werk Gerhart Hauptmanns* (Stuttgart: Metzler, 1964), p. 36.

mich mit dem Rücken an den Ofen, kreuze die Beine unter dem Tisch, zünde mir diese selbe Pfeife hier an und schreibe, in aller Gemütsruhe hoffentlich... wenn ich da so sitze, siehst du... und die Gasflamme den ganzen Tag so über mir fauchen höre, von Zeit zu Zeit so'n Blick in den Hof – so'n Fabrikhof ist nämlich was Wunderbares! was Romantisches, sag' ich dir... mit einem Wort, da summt mich keine Hummel an.... Soll man sich immerfort aus dem Gleichgewicht bringen lassen, soll man sich denn kopfverwirrt machen lassen? Ich werde sowieso zwei bis drei Tage brauchen, um mich auf mein bißchen Lebensweisheit zu besinnen.[15] (I, 159)	sit with my back to the stove, cross my legs under the table, light this pipe here, and write, peacefully and quietly, I hope... when I sit like that, you see... and listen to the gaslight burning above me, and look out now and again into the yard – a factory yard is something wonderful, something romantic, I tell you... to put it briefly, nothing bothers me... Ought one continually to let oneself be put off balance, ought one to let oneself be driven mad? As it is I shall need two or three days to collect myself again.

The idealism which Wilhelm has inherited from his father, has turned sour in Robert to produce a cynic, not unlike Büchner's Danton:

Vater und du [Wilhelm], ihr ähnelt einander zum Verwechseln. Ihr seid dieselben Idealisten. Anno 48 hat Vater auf den Barrikaden angefangen, und als einsamer Hypochonder macht er den Schluß. – Man muß sich an die Welt und an sich selbst beizeiten gewöhnen, du! – eh' man sich die Hörner abgelaufen hat (I, 159).	You [Wilhelm] and father, you are absolutely alike. You are both idealists. Father began on the barricades in '48, and he's come to the end of the road as a lonely hypochondriac – one has just got to get used to the world and to oneself, don't you see – before one has finished sowing one's wild oats.

---

[15] In Max Halbe's *Mutter Erde* (1897), the hero, Paul Warkentin, echoes Robert Scholz's sentiments about the narcotic effects of working life in the metropolis (*Gesammelte Werke*, 7 vols (Munich: Albert Langen, 1917–23), II, 364). In *Vor Sonnenaufgang*, it will be recalled, alcohol and tobacco provide relief from suffering by numbing the sensibilities; here Robert Scholz is a heavy smoker, and his father smokes and drinks excessively.

Robert's nihilistic mockery corresponds, as a manifestation of the Naturalist period, to the dramas of Otto Erich Hartleben. If we are to believe his friend Cäsar Flaischlen, the bitterness of Hartleben's works is the bitterness of just such a disappointed idealist, and his irony is the defence of a sensitive individual who would rather indulge in mockery than himself become its object.[16] Hauptmann, a greater artist than Hartleben, can do justice to this attitude without adopting it.

Circumstances alone do not explain the difference between the two brothers, for certain innate differences of character explain why their circumstances are so different. Robert possesses a greater share of the discursive, analytical intelligence of his father, whilst Wilhelm has the musical interest of his mother. Robert, without an outlet for his emotions, was forced to fall back on himself when he left home, and pursue a hectic urban career, for which he had no positive inclination. The elder brother's grounds for envy of his more talented and more favoured junior are intensified by their contrasting fortunes in this period. Wilhelm's talent enabled him to approach others on an emotional level, and to gain access to the Buchner household, finding there a second mother-figure and a second home.

The initial natural parity lying deep below the differences is thus disturbed, as it is in the traditional drama of the hostile brothers. Of the works in this tradition Schiller's *Die Braut von Messina*, in which a mother also unsuccessfully tries to use her daughter to bring about a family reconciliation, provides the closest parallel to *Das Friedensfest*, sharing some of the ambiguity of the Naturalist work. The relationship between the two comparatively similar brothers, and especially the envy of the underprivileged for the privileged – ironically perpetuated beyond the death of the latter – provides the motive for Don Cesar's suicide; but, all the same, Schiller seems to evaluate this suicide as he would a voluntary, disinterested, and 'sublime' act. Despite the 'tout comprendre, c'est tout pardonner' which is implicit in the play's motivation, Hauptmann's *Das Friedensfest* ends with what might be read as a declaration of Wilhelm's superiority, an implicit ethical appeal addressed, so to speak, over the head of the on-stage addressee directly to the audience.[17] Ida, now independent of the manipulation of her mother, confident in the intuition that all will be well, proclaims: 'Beside you I am small, oh how small! I am no more than a tiny moth! Without you I am nothing! Through you I am everything! Do not withdraw your hand from me in my misery!' (I, 165). But doubt must remain about this judgement; for what authority can be allowed to the views of a young girl, anxious not

---

[16] *Otto Erich Hartleben: Beitrag zu einer Geschichte der modernen Dichtung* (Berlin: S. Fischer, 1896), p. 20.
[17] Cf. Günther Mahal, *Naturalismus* (Munich: Fink, 1975), pp. 233–34.

to be abandoned by the man she loves, given like her mother, perhaps, to dramatizing a situation, and speaking in a distinctly literary way (which suggests immersion in Novalis' *Heinrich von Ofterdingen*)?[18] What guarantee can there be that Wilhelm is not right to condemn her idealistic hopes as teenage illusions?

It is one of the virtues of this play that Hauptmann has refrained from intruding further at this point, for any authoritative statement would be inconsistent with the scepticism which is characteristic of the rest of the play. As intelligent persuasion Ida's words cannot compete with the devastating analysis of the situation just presented by Robert, and notably his prediction that marriage with Wilhelm will inevitably lead Ida into the situation of their mother; but to be dramatically effective they do not need to compete on the same terms. It is quite plausible that they should have their effect as persuasion, *tout court*. As an expression of Ida's desire to take Wilhelm as he is, without presuming to change him, as an expression of her own anxiety, Ida's words are convincing; just as Wilhelm's response to them, his decision to give in to her, to take his chance, despite his apparent intellectual conviction that he has none, is a convincing response in the context of the drama. One of the most significant advances of *Das Friedensfest* over *Vor Sonnenaufgang* is the realization that decisions are taken in this way, and not in the cold rational way Alfred Loth takes his. This realization is summed up by Hauptmann with a (not entirely appropriate) comment about Ibsen:

Ibsen gibt Gedankenwandlungen, das setzt Personen voraus, die über sich reflektieren. Das tun nur bestimmte Individualitäten. Die Gefühlswandlungen sind die tiefsten.[19]	Ibsen presents intellectual transformations; that presupposes characters who reflect about themselves. Only certain individuals do that. Emotional processes are deepest.

---

[18] Ida's speech recalls some words spoken by Heinrich, shortly after his meeting with Mathilde in Novalis' *Heinrich von Ofterdingen*.
[19] Gerhart Hauptmann, *Die Kunst des Dramas: Über Schauspiel und Theater*, edited by Martin Machatzke (Berlin and Frankfurt a.M.: Propyläen, 1963), p. 189.

7
EINSAME MENSCHEN

The decade of the 1890s saw the beginnings of a decisive retreat from the scientific positivism which had dominated the second half of the nineteenth century and which, in its time, had been one of the most significant factors in the emergence of European Naturalism.[1] It also saw the collapse of the provisional alliance between the German Naturalist writers and organized socialism.[2] These two developments are reflected in a number of the dramas of this period, the best of which is almost certainly Gerhart Hauptmann's third play, *Einsame Menschen*.

Einsame Menschen is a representative work in another, more superficial, but not entirely unconnected sense. Like *Das Friedensfest*, it has a factual basis; the dedication of the first edition runs: 'I place this drama in the hands of those who have lived it', and refers to Hauptmann's elder brother, Carl, his wife Marthe (sister to Gerhart Hauptmann's first wife, Marie Thienemann), and a young Polish student, Josepha Kodis-Krzyzanowska.[3] It also anticipates the problems which subsequently arose in Hauptmann's own marriage, and which he discusses in *Das Buch der Leidenschaft* (1929); and which, according to Max Halbe, were shared by a number of the young writers of the Naturalist generation.[4] The subject of the play, the ever-popular theme of the man between two women, may have had something to do with the play's success; at all events the première of *Einsame Menschen*, on 11 January 1891, provided Hauptmann with his first undisputed success.

---

[1] Cf. H. Stuart Hughes, *Consciousness and Society: The Reorientation of European Social Thought, 1890–1930* (London: MacGibbon and Kee, 1959), Chapter 2, 'The decade of the 1890s', pp. 33–66.
[2] See above, Chapter 4.
[3] Gerhart Hauptmann, *Die Kunst des Dramas: Über Schauspiel und Theater*, edited by Martin Machatzke, (Berlin and Frankfurt a.M.: Propyläen, 1963), pp. 98–102. Cf. also Frederick W. J. Heuser, 'Biographisches and Autobiographisches in "Einsame Menschen"', *Gerhart Hauptmann* (Tübingen: Niemeyer, 1961), pp. 247–58; Karl Musiol, 'Carl Hauptmann und Josepha Kodis: Ihr gegenseitiges Verhältnis im Spiegel des dichterischen Werkes', *Deutsche Vierteljahrsschrift*, 34 (1960), pp. 257–63; and Walter Requardt and Martin Machatzke, *Gerhart Hauptmann und Erkner: Studien zum Berliner Frühwerk* (Berlin: Erich Schmidt, 1980), pp. 168–70.
[4] *Jahrhundertwende: Geschichte meines Lebens, 1893–1914* (Danzig: Kafermann, 1935), pp. 39, 45.

The central character in *Einsame Menschen* is Johannes Vockerat, a brilliant young scholar, the son of devout middle-class parents, struggling in a transitional age to achieve intellectual freedom and moral independence, a representative of the type proclaimed by the contemporary critic, Edgar Steiger, as the characteristic hero of the 'new drama'.[5] His kindred include Ejlert Lövborg in Ibsen's *Hedda Gabler*, *Glockengießer* Heinrich in Hauptmann's own *Die versunkene Glocke*, and even Wilhelm Scholz in *Das Friedensfest*. The play opens shortly after the birth of a son to Johannes and his wife, Käthe. She is six years younger than her husband, and, like Frau Scholz in *Das Friedensfest*, intellectually far from being his equal – although she remains consistently the most sympathetic character in the play. There is a suggestion in the third act that this marriage was arranged without very much reference to the young Käthe, and it soon becomes evident that it has not been a great success. It is the hope of Frau Vockerat, Johannes' mother, that the birth of the child will bring the couple closer together, and give her son some peace of mind, but Johannes' first entry suggests that it is having the opposite effect. For the sake of his parents he has made a compromise: despite his rejection of Christianity he has had the child christened, and he arrives directly from the ceremony in a state of irritability and self-pity; this is not the kind of first entry which will make an audience respond sympathetically. His friend, the sceptical Braun, is there to taunt him still further: 'You old hypochondriac. Stop that nonsense and eat something! It's the sermon that's upset you'; and Johannes' reply sums up, implicitly, the dilemma which forms the central theme of the play: 'Frankly speaking ... you talk like that about baptism ... you know my point of view, and it's not the Christian one. But it is still something which is sacred to many people' (I, 175). This dilemma between respect for traditional beliefs, consideration for the feelings of others on the one hand, and progressive thinking and truth to one's own convictions on the other, is reflected, with all the pedantry of Naturalism, in an introductory stage-direction, which prescribes photographs of Darwin and Haeckel alongside those of theologians on the wall of the room.

Once again it takes Hauptmann no more than a few pages of stage-direction and dialogue to introduce us, in masterly fashion, to a situation charged with tension. The hero, Johannes, is threatened on the one side by the orthodoxy of a conservative generation, by the tyranny of his family; but there is an equal threat from the opposite flank, from the radical socialism of the shaven-headed Braun. Into this tense situation comes the young Anna Mahr, an old acquaintance of Braun, on

---

[5] *Das Werden des neuen Dramas*, 2 vols (Berlin: F. Fontane, 1898), II, 69ff., 299ff.

vacation from her studies in Zürich.[6] She embodies a third attitude which is attractive to Johannes; she is sympathetic towards his work and shares his interests: philosophy, music, love of the open air. Anna supports Johannes in his desire to develop his individual freedom; she appears to be a natural partner for him. But Johannes is indecisive, and will not accept that he must choose between Anna and his wife. This indecision extends over four acts, until Johannes' father returns to assert his authority, and secure his son's assent to Anna's departure.[7] As he hears her train pass, Johannes is overcome with grief, and leaves the house to commit suicide. Käthe's reaction is a reproach to his parents for driving him to this extreme step: 'Mother! Father! You have driven him to the limits. Why did you do it...?' (I, 258).

Käthes judgement of her parents-in-law is the judgement with which the play concludes; her words come in a position of emphasis, and go unchallenged; it is self-evident that they are important words in the design of the play; and it follows that the play ends with the condemnation of the sacrifice of an individual to a rigid moral convention; Paul Schlenther, Gerhart Hauptmann's friend and first biographer, confirms that this was the author's conscious intention. But here, as in *Vor Sonnenaufgang*, Hauptmann's characterizing impulse inhibits the clear development of such a unilinear argument. If one pursues the question, 'why did you do it?', which Käthe asks of his parents, if one examines the complex motivation of all the characters in this play, one discovers, as in *Das Friedensfest*, a primitive trial of strength between characters whose means are devious, and whose ends are only very rarely clear to themselves. It is very much to the advantage of the play that this is so, for this is the ground on which Gerhart Hauptmann moves most surely.

When the play opens the relationship between Johannes and his parents is clouded. The deference which Johannes still shows – for instance by having his child christened – is not enough to pacify them, and they are constantly exerting pressure on him to give up his work. His mother blames all his discontent on his lack of religion, and his espousal of modern ideas: 'Old Haeckel and foolish Darwin – they are

---

[6] The University of Zürich had admitted women since 1864. Ricarda Huch (in voluntary exile for personal and economic reasons) and Rosa Luxemburg (a political refugee) took their doctorates there in the 1890s.

[7] In the first performance the play was shortened by the omission of the fourth act. An obvious comment on this came in the shape of a parody entitled 'Der höhere Zustand', in the *Magazin für die Literatur des In- und Auslandes*, 60 (1891), 204–5. This consisted of a first and a fifth act, and the explanation: 'The second, third, and fourth acts may, with the dramatist's approval, be cut by the director. With the beginning of the fifth act the action continues at the point where we have just left it.' Nevertheless even the omission of the fourth act will significantly flatten the characterization of both Johannes and Anna.

just making you unhappy... Just be a bit religious – do it for the sake of your old mother' (I, 208). The possessive concern of a mother for her young, implicit in these words, is the most striking feature of Frau Vockerat's whole manner: her conversations with Käthe are punctuated with diminutives: 'Käthe', 'Käthinkerle', 'liebes, gutes Kindchen'. She treats her daughter-in-law as a child, and tries to treat Johannes similarly, addressing him as 'alter Junge', thinking back longingly and proudly to the uncomplicated days when he was a brilliant young schoolboy: 'He was a real prodigy'; she even tells him not to wear his best suit so much for Anna's benefit, in case he wears it out, whereupon Johannes feels the need to protest: 'But mother, I'm not a child any longer' (I, 208). Johannes' wife, Käthe, has never represented a threat to Frau Vockerat's possession of her son in the way the newcomer, Anna, does; Anna is not to be treated as a child, she encourages Johannes to think, to assert his independence in every respect, and so to break with the past, with tradition, and with the ties of the family. The conflict between old and new takes the form of a simple struggle for possession of Johannes the man. For the Vockerats Christianity is a weapon in this struggle just as in *Die Weber* it is a weapon in the hands of the property-owning classes. Occasionally Frau Vockerat will use this weapon to assert her own authority: 'You are speaking to your mother in a way which is forbidden by the fourth commandment' (I, 227); but in her moment of profoundest crisis she speaks to Anna more directly, and more honestly:

Ich will nicht richten in diesem Augenblick. Ich will zu Ihnen sprechen, eine Frau zur Frau – und als Mutter will ich zu Ihnen sprechen. *Mit tränenerstickter Stimme*: Als Mutter meines Johannes will ich zu Ihnen kommen. *Sie erfaßt Annas Hand.* Geben Sie mir meinen Johannes. Geben Sie einer gemarteten Mutter ihr Kind wieder! *Sie ist auf einen Stuhl gesunken und benetzt Annas Hand mit Tränen* (I, 243).	I don't want to pass any judgements at this moment. I want to talk to you as one woman to another – and I want to talk as a mother. *In a voice choked by tears*: I come to you as the mother of my Johannes. *She takes Anna's hand.* Give Johannes back to me. Give an unhappy mother her child back! *She has sunk down onto a chair and sheds tears over Anna's hand.*

This sincere and profound affection is so stifling because it forces Johannes off the intellectual ground on which he is reasonably sure of himself; as Anna sees immediately, she cannot justify herself for there is no argument against Frau Vockerat: 'Whatever you say,... I cannot defend myself against you...' (I, 243).

A similar family conflict provides the central theme of Georg Hirschfeld's play *Die Mütter* (first performed by the *Freie Bühne*, 12 May 1895). A young musician, Robert Frey, has been turned out of his home by his authoritarian father, and lives with a working-class girl, Marie Weil. After the death of his father, Robert's mother is anxious that her son should return home: the two women understand much more clearly than Robert what is involved; Marie abruptly rejects the suggestion that she can return with Robert and be accepted into his family; while Robert's mother states unequivocally that if he comes back, this means he has given Marie up.[8]

In these two plays, as in *Das Friedensfest*, the mother tries to act as a buffer between a sensitive son and an authoritarian father. Frau Vockerat therefore sends for her husband only as a last resort. The interview between father and son at the beginning of Act V is only a slight variation on the earlier exchanges between mother and son in the previous part of the play. For the father too orthodoxy is a means of maintaining his authority: when he sees Johannes he announces: 'The will of God has brought me to you', whereupon his son very perceptively asks: 'Did mother send for you?' (I, 248).[9] The old man reveals his stereotypical way of thinking in the clichés with which he addresses his son. There is no argument, no question of the two men reaching any understanding, for what old Vockerat requires is nothing less than total obedience: 'It is not a question of understanding ... It is not a matter of reaching agreement ... I think it is just a question of obedience' (I, 249). He reminds Johannes of the concern his parents bestowed on him when he was young and when he was ill, and demands more than just gratitude in return. And yet there is no question of hypocrisy on the part of Vockerat, any more than there is on the part of his wife. The scene of his return at the end of Act IV, the details of which Hauptmann handles beautifully, reveal him as a thoroughly genuine old man, with a real concern for his family, but with no feeling for the complexities of his son's situation.

His final appeal to his son is a clumsy threat, which is immediately effective, but in the long run proves disastrous. He decides there is nothing left for him to do but to take his wife and go, whereupon Johannes capitulates:

JOHANNES, *nach kurzem Kampf.* Vater!! Mutter!! FRAU VOCKERAT und VOCKERAT *wenden sich.* Johannes	JOHANNES, *after a brief struggle.* Father!! Mother!! FRAU VOCKERAT and VOCKERAT *turn round.*

---

[8] Georg Hirschfeld, *Die Mütter* (Berlin: S. Fischer, 1895), p. 43.
[9] Miller the Musician behaves in a similar way towards his daughter in Schiller's *Kabale und Liebe*, although Luise is less sceptical than Johannes Vockerat.

fliegt in ihre Arme.	*Johannes throws himself*
Johannes! *Pause.*	*into their arms.*
JOHANNES, *mit leiser Stimme.*	Johannes! *Pause.*
Nun sagt, was ich tun soll.	JOHANNES, *in a low voice.*
VOCKERAT. Halte sie nicht.	Now tell me what to do.
Laß sie ziehen, Hannes.	VOCKERAT. Don't keep
JOHANNES. Ich verspreche dir's. *Er*	her. Let her go, Hannes.
ist erschöpft und muß sich auf einen	JOHANNES. I promise. *He*
Stuhl niederlassen. Frau Vockerat	*is exhausted and has to*
eilt freudig bewegt ins	*sit down on a chair. Frau*
Schlafzimmer.	*Vockerat rushes off*
VOCKERAT *streichelt den*	*joyfully into the bedroom.*
Dasitzenden, küßt ihn auf	VOCKERAT *strokes his*
die Stirn (I, 251).	*head, kisses him on the brow.*

This sudden change of heart by Johannes is no tribute to his father's arguments; it is not the kind of response which suggests intellectual conviction. In a moment of physical weakness, which in Hauptmann's works, as in Kleist's, so often indicates a breakthrough to a deeper emotional level, Johannes gives in utterly, to become no more than a child, fearful of being abandoned by its parents.

At the opposite pole to the conservative Vockerats stands the artist, Braun. As an advocate of political commitment he is an example of a type of character who occurs rarely in the work of Hauptmann, and is never treated sympathetically. The altruistic socialism which Braun practises (or at least preaches) represents a stage through which Johannes once passed, but which he now claims to have outgrown; that is to say the friendship between the two men was once a good deal closer than it is when the play opens. Braun is most probably one of the friends to whom Käthe refers when she complains that Johannes has never really belonged to her: 'Have I ever really possessed him? First it was his friends, and now Anna has him' (I, 223). Braun dislikes the compromises Johannes makes – for instance the christening – because they indicate a weakening of his influence over his friend. He is, of course, a natural rival of Frau Vockerat, but shares her hostility to Johannes' work, because this symbolizes his independence of both of them; and he shares her hostility to Anna. Indeed Braun and Frau Vockerat recognize in Anna such a serious threat that they form a provisional alliance against her, combining, in Act IV, to persuade her to depart. Braun makes the first attempt, using the very un-radical argument that she should go for the sake of the Vockerat family; Anna deliberately and scornfully closes her ears to this appeal to her conscience, although she has, in fact, already told Johannes that they must part. Anna, it seems, can see through to Braun's real motives and is not disposed to listen to moral lectures from him. She can see that he is jealous of Johannes' increasing independence and resentful of the encouragement Anna has given him; in Act II she describes Braun as follows: 'Herr Braun is so immature in every respect – I won't say he envies you [Johannes], but it irritates him... The tenacity with which you preserve your independence disturbs him. Maybe it even frightens him' (I, 206).

It has been suggested that Anna is herself a similar character, and that she also contributes to Johannes' destruction by fighting for possession of him; that she is a tough, scheming, emancipated woman, like Laura in Strindberg's *The Father*, who deliberately and maliciously isolates Johannes until she can extract no more from him, whereupon she abandons him to despair and suicide.[10] Such a woman is to be found in the person of Hanna Elias in Hauptmann's later play, *Gabriel Schillings Flucht*, and in Hella in Max Halbe's *Mutter Erde*, who entices the young Paul Warkentin from his provincial home to the city, where he works for the emancipation movement; but Anna is surely a more complex character and her feminism – tentative and moderate – is treated much more sympathetically.[11] Her apparent hardness, like that of Robert Scholz in *Das Friedensfest*, is a mask, a defence against suffering. She is sensitive and lonely; a homeless young girl, with a cosmopolitan background, forced to make her own way in a world which looks with suspicion on self-reliant women, and so forced to toughen herself for the sake of bare survival. Her assertions of the value of independence and the need for ruthlessness are brave rationalizations of a predicament she can do nothing to alter: 'You have to be free in every respect. You can have no fatherland, no family, no friends.' Nevertheless the loneliness of freedom and independence does clearly frighten her: 'I'm going to be back in Zürich too soon. A whole week too soon. If only work were beginning again' (I, 220). Like Robert Scholz, she needs some kind of activity to sublimate her personal anxieties. Aware that she is not wanted in the Vockerat household, she is ready to depart; proudly she resists Käthe's suggestion that she suffers – to admit to others is to admit to oneself – but she is easily persuaded to return to a house in which she has enjoyed some moments of relaxation and happiness. She has enough self-knowledge to appreciate eventually that the *ménage à trois* cannot last; she therefore decides independently that she will bring her association with Johannes to an end, but contrives to

---

[10] Jenny C. Hortenbach, *Freiheitsstreben und Destruktivität: Frauen in den Dramen August Strindbergs und Gerhart Hauptmanns* (Oslo, Bergen, and Tromsö: Universitetsforlaget, 1965), pp. 91–106. *The Father* had been presented by the *Freie Bühne* on 12 October 1890.
[11] The widespread failure among critics of both sexes to recognise elements of a constructive view of women's emancipation in this play is noted – and corrected in the spirit of the present argument – by Raleigh Whitinger, 'Rethinking Anna Mahr: Reflections on the Characterization and Function of the Emancipated Woman in Gerhart Hauptmann's *Einsame Menschen*', *Seminar*, 29 (1993), 233–52.

do so with a sensitivity which leaves Johannes his self-respect; her vision of the future is evoked more for Johannes' benefit than her own.[12] By clumsily interfering after the decision has been reached, Johannes' parents deprive him of this, and to this extent they are responsible for his death. Nevertheless the play does not leave one with a feeling of undivided sympathy for Johannes, as my analysis might hitherto have suggested. The reason for this lies with Hauptmann's treatment of the two remaining characters.

Käthe Vockerat is, it should be remembered, a young wife, obsessed by feelings of inadequacy vis à vis her more intelligent – or at least more educated – husband; she is not only physically weak from the recent birth of her first child, but is also suffering from the depression which affects many women in her situation.[13] She is anxious, unsure of herself, unwilling to accept the responsibility which her husband selfishly forces upon her, almost always on the verge of tears; it is a situation in which she needs the support, the encouragement, and the interest of her husband, but none is forthcoming:

Anstatt daß du mal gut zu mir wärst, mein Zutrauen zu mir selbst – bißchen stärktest... Nein, da werd' ich nur immer kleingemacht – immer klein – immer geduckt werd' ich. Ich bild' mir weiß Gott nichts ein auf meinen großen Horizont. Aber ich bin eben nicht gefühllos. – Nee, wahrhaftig, ich bin kein Licht. Überhaupt: ich hab's schon lange gemerkt, daß ich ziemlich überflüssig bin (I, 211).	Instead of being nice to me, boosting my confidence a bit... No, I'm always being made to feel small – always small – I'm always being belittled. God knows, I don't deceive myself that my horizons are wide. But I'm not exactly without feelings. – No, really, I'm not brilliant. In fact, I've noticed it for some time, I'm more or less in the way here.

Johannes, who makes such great demands on the consideration of others, has himself very little to spare for his wife: 'We are really not suited! I'm doing my work. My work comes first, second, and third,... You have your family interests, and I have universal interests.... I am simply not a family man' (I, 209–10). The arrival of Anna at this time intensifies Käthe's need for her husband's consideration; the added

---

[12] Whitinger, 'Rethinking Anna Mahr', p. 246.
[13] Hauptmann's characterization of Frau Käthe corresponds quite remarkably to Dr Benjamin Spock's description of 'The Blue Feeling' (*Baby and Child Care*, revised edition, 1957, §15); Johannes' behaviour is the opposite of what Spock advises in the section entitled 'The Father's Part' (§18–20).

responsibility of a guest in the house is itself no light matter, but Anna can offer Johannes everything that Käthe cannot. Her very presence reminds Käthe constantly of her own inadequacy, and the cruelty of Johannes' implied comparisons does not help her: 'You ought to be eager to grasp any opportunity for intellectual improvement. You really ought to make the effort. You ought to keep the young lady here. I don't understand how anyone can be so indifferent' (I, 193).

These words reveal not only insensitivity on the part of Johannes, but also a certain lack of honesty with himself, for it is apparent to all the other characters in the play, and to even the most casual reader, that it is for himself that Johannes desires Anna to stay in the house. In *Das Friedensfest* a similar lack of self-knowledge on the part of Frau Buchner was revealed in a sudden flash; the structure of *Einsame Menschen* allows for a more gradual and more subtle illumination. Whereas *Das Friedensfest* and, to a rather lesser extent, *Vor Sonnenaufgang*, related the concluding chapter of a story which depended significantly on events which had taken place in the past, the action of *Einsame Menschen* does add up to a more or less complete story. We therefore see fully and immediately the catalytic effect of Anna's arrival on Johannes. His 'new morality', his sudden aggressive defiance of the philistines, are an ad hoc arrangement, adopted because they suit his present predicament. In a review of the first Frankfurt performance of the play one critic wrote disapprovingly of the behaviour of the audience, complaining that a large part of the public was amused by Johannes' assertion that his interest in Anna Mahr was purely spiritual, and attributing this to what he described as the miscasting of the more attractive actress in the role of Anna.[14] The audience was quicker to perceive Hauptmann's irony than the critic. Johannes speaks rather foolishly and pretentiously of his vision of a new, non-physical relationship between man and woman: 'No longer will the animal have primacy, but the human. No longer will an animal marry an animal, but a human being will marry another human being. Friendship is the basis on which this love will grow' (I, 238); but in doing so he is availing himself of certain ideas associated more with the old Tolstoy than with the German Naturalist movement in order to rationalize an emotional and sexual attraction into a spiritual friendship. He instinctively chooses the easiest line of defence, because an outspoken advocacy of free-love – which would be typical of the Friedrichshagen circle with whom Hauptmann has associated Johannes – would involve him in an immediate head-on clash with his parents.[15] Anna is quicker

---

[14] *Freie Bühne*, 2 (1891), p. 200.
[15] For Tolstoy's views see 'Zweites Nachwort zur "Kreutzersonate"' and 'Von den Beziehungen der Geschlechter zu einander', *Freie Bühne*, 1 (1890), 1009–14 and 11932–95;

to perceive the truth, and to remind Johannes that they are both prone to the same human desires as everybody else: 'In me... in us both, there is something which is hostile to that pure relationship of which we have a glimpse, and ultimately it might be stronger' (I, 240). Braun, too, sees more clearly, and justifiably reproaches Johannes with refusing to face up to the truth: 'You have never liked confronting things clearly and soberly.... You want to reconcile things which simply cannot be reconciled' (I, 230).

Hauptmann's critique of Johannes is twofold; where it depends on the appeal of the unfortunate Käthe, the play tends to that sentimentality which is not an uncommon feature in Hauptmann's work; but where it is concerned with the deflation of a weak and self-deluding man, *Einsame Menschen* has some superb moments. In this play Hauptmann displays an intelligence and an irony which critics have often found wanting in his work; for instance Johannes appeals for support to a new individualist morality which he has not yet made his own, but his phraseology gives him away: 'but *you said yourself* one should not be inhibited by consideration for others' (I, 238; my emphasis). There are moments when one thinks Hauptmann was on the way to creating a literary form of which there is no notable example in German literature, a satirical drama of an artist. It seems, however, that he did not have the nerve to carry through this project consistently; 'Das Wunderkind' ('The child prodigy', the ironic title which Hauptmann originally planned to give his play) became the more pretentious (and cacophonous) *Einsame Menschen*. The play in its final form is a rather ambiguous mixture of criticism and special-pleading on behalf of the artist or outstanding individual. As such it reflects the changing political attitudes among the Naturalist writers, the retreat from social commitment to the cult of individualism, particularly in the Friedrichshagen circle.

One aspect of Johannes' character which is constantly stressed is his restlessness. On the wall of his room is a picture of Jacob struggling with the angel, illustrating the text: 'I will not let thee go, except thou bless me.' (Genesis, XXXII, 26; I, 178). The self-torturing Johannes glorifies in his discontent, saying to his mother: 'Those who are satisfied are the drones in the hive' (I, 182).[16] As I have suggested above, the

---

For the views current among the Friedrichshagen circle of writers see: Julius Hart, 'Freie Liebe: Betrachtungen zu Bebel's "Die Frau und der Sozialismus"', *Freie Bühne*, 2 (1891), 369–72, 396–400, 445–48, and 468–72; and Bruno Wille, 'Moralische Stickluft', *Freie Bühne*, 4 (1893), 816–21.

[16] The extent of the contrast between Hauptmann and his contemporary, Wedekind can be gauged if one compares Hauptmann's treatment of Johannes with Wedekind's unambiguously critical treatment of the self-torturing Ernst Scholz in *Der Marquis von Keith* (*Gesammelte Werke*, IV, 50). In the sketches for a drama, 'Der Niggerjud', Wedekind

action of the play arises out of Johannes' attempts at reorientation. He has broken with the traditional outlook represented by his parents, and has been through a period of socialism in his friendship with Braun. He has now grown beyond this, and is, Anna declares, working his way forward to a new position of independence: 'Familiar paths are not for everyone. Johannes is one of those who are seeking new paths' (I, 196). The discovery of these new paths is threatened equally by the socialism of Braun and the conservatism of Johannes' parents; Anna, however, introduces a ray of optimism:

Auf der einen Seite beherrschte uns eine schwüle Angst, auf der andern ein finsterer Fanatismus. Die übertriebene Spannung scheint nun ausgeglichen. So etwas wie ein frischer Luftstrom, sagen wir aus dem zwanzigsten Jahrhundert, ist hereingeschlagen.... Zum Beispiel, Leute wie Braun wirken doch auf uns nur noch wie Eulen bei Tageslicht (I, 237).	On the one side we were dominated by an oppressive anxiety, on the other by grim fanaticism. The extreme tension now seems to be resolved. A kind of fresh breeze, let's call it a breeze from the twentieth century, is blowing. People like Braun, for instance, now seem to us like owls in the daylight.

The positive end towards which Johannes and Anna are aspiring is not very precisely defined; indeed they are not themselves yet in a position to define it precisely; but we are given a number of hints about its quality. This fresh breeze will bring with it a renewed interest in art. A common interest in music is one of the things which brings Johannes and Anna together. Significantly, Anna has recently taken up music again after having given it up for six years; whereas Braun is moving in the opposite direction, to take the view that in the present social situation art is a luxury which mankind cannot afford: 'There are things to be done which are at present more important than all the painting and scribbling in the world' (I, 201). (This, incidentally, was one objection made by the Social Democrats to the foundation of the *Volksbühnen*.) In Act II Anna gives a summary of a story by Garschin, *Die Künstler*, which leads to a violent disagreement between Johannes and Braun. Johannes takes the view that a work of art does more good for mankind than the active attempt to alleviate human misery. It immediately becomes clear that Johannes sees his own work in this way; although produced in isolation, he claims for it great social value. Its importance is a

---

identifies himself with Keith and Hauptmann with Scholz; see Heuser, 'Hauptmann und Wedekind', p. 245.

justification for the compromises he makes; these are a means of saving energy and preserving the emotional and mental equilibrium which is necessary for artistic creation; as Anna says, 'Conflicts deprive people of their strength' (I, 205). This is, of course, a politically irresponsible view, and it is one of the sadder facts of Hauptmann's life that he himself seems still to have held it in 1932.[17]

Johannes' book is also his only justification for his treatment of Käthe. Her intellectual limitations mean that she cannot give him the support and encouragement he needs in his work, and her practical demands are a distraction. Marie Weil, in Hirschfeld's *Die Mütter*, is a tougher character, who can do more to alleviate the practical burdens of her partner, but she cannot give any positive encouragement to the musical talents of Robert Frey; Wagner is lost on her. Anna, by contrast, is always the understanding, never the demanding, partner and, as a consequence female emancipation is never allowed to become a central issue in this play; it would raise more firmly the question of Anna's rights. The justification for Anna's continued presence is that she can assist Johannes in the process of self-fulfilment, and so enrich his work. Hauptmann is here faced with the perennial problem of the drama whose hero is an artist: he has to make us believe in the value of the work in question. Johannes' statement that the fourth chapter of his *magnum opus* has twelve pages of footnotes is scarcely enough to do that.

A similar special-plea is a feature of Carl Hauptmann's play *Marianne*. The heroine of this play, a young pastor's wife, is encouraged to revolt against the life-denying pietism of her husband and her family by the arrival of the progressive artist, Fritz. They are two young people bound together by a love of nature and the countryside and a passionate hatred of urban civilization. They value personal integrity more highly than consideration for others, and they share a pantheistic love of life, which resembles the quasi-mysticism of Schlaf's *Frühling* (1896) and the lyric effusions of Wille and Bölsche in their Friedrichshagen period: 'Of course everyone would like to experience a miracle, great or small! Indeed – what else does one really want? – but to make what is inconceivable tangible'.[18] It becomes clear from *Marianne* that Carl Hauptmann holds the view that man has an inherent need for some kind of religious experience, and that this is not likely to be explained away by scientific positivism or milieu-theory. Like Johannes Vockerat he respects belief (but not dogma), and to a consistent radical must appear conservative; above all he rejects a 'naturalism' which would presume to explain man in social terms:

---

[17] Josef Chapiro, *Gespräche mit Gerhart Hauptmann* (Berlin: S. Fischer), 1932, p. 40.
[18] Carl Hauptmann, *Marianne* (Berlin: S. Fischer, 1894), p. 60.

Der Naturalismus hat recht, sofern er das Milieu ergriff. Aber nicht, weil er damit ins [sic] Menschen als Naturwesen, sondern nur als Sozialwesen Einblick gewährt. Der Naturalismus ist die Kunst des Menschen als Sozialwesen. Aber wenn er damit die Naturwesen erklären will, so irrt er. Die tiefsten Verborgenheiten unserer Leidenschaften wurzeln in einer anderen Natur, und das Milieu, das sie bilden half, ist längst versunken.[19]	Naturalism was right in turning to milieu. But only in that it thereby provided insight into man as a social being, not as a natural being. Naturalism is the art of man as a social being. But if it thinks it can explain the natural being, then it is wrong. The deepest secrets of our passions are rooted in another nature and the milieu which helped to form it disappeared long ago.

Irrationalist vitalism provides an explicit programme for Carl Hauptmann's play of 1894, and makes for a clear but uninterestingly tendentious drama. Anna Mahr's 'fresh breeze from the twentieth century' blows from the same direction; one obvious symptom of this is Johannes' anti-urbanism: 'I hate the town. My ideal is a large park with a high wall round it. There one can devote oneself to one's aims without being disturbed at all' (I, 189).[20] In view of their origins it is scarcely surprising that there should be this affinity between the two plays, for the character of Johannes is, to some extent, based on Gerhart Hauptmann's elder brother; and it has been shown that Johannes Vockerat shares, in some detail, the theories and attitudes of Carl Hauptmann.[21] Johannes' work corresponds to Carl's planned 'Grundlinien einer allgemeinen Biomechanik'; and Carl's polemic against the psychologist, Wilhelm Wundt, has its counterpart in Johannes' attack on the biologist, Emil Du Bois Reymond, who had, in fact been attacked very vehemently in 1890 by Julius Langbehn in *Rembrandt als Erzieher*.[22] There are other respects in which the hero of the play might be considered a 'Langbehnist': his hostility to Braun's egalitarianism, his hostility to formal education (I, 203) and the high value he places on art. It is true that Johannes appears to be some sort of scientist (Haeckel was one of his teachers) and that a prominent

---

[19] Carl Hauptmann, *Leben mit Freunden: Gesammelte Briefe* (Berlin: Horen-Verlag, 1928), p. 45.
[20] This attitude also allies him with the young aesthetes of Hugo von Hofmannsthal's *Der Tod des Tizian* (1892).
[21] Heuser, 'Biographisches und Autobiographisches in "Einsame Menschen"', p. 251.
[22] *Rembrandt als Erzieher: Von einem Deutschen*, 2nd edition (Leipzig: C. L. Hirschfeld), 1890, pp. 94–95.

feature of Langbehn's project was its anti-modernist challenge to the dominance of science; but Langbehn opposed science because of the fear that the drive to specialization would lead to the fragmentation of life. The way Braun describes Johannes' work in Act I as 'philosophisch-kritisch-psycho-physiologisch' suggests that it ought to be comprehensive enough not to be condemned for specialization.[23]

I would not wish to suggest that *Einsame Menschen* was directly influenced by Langbehn's book, any more than I wished to suggest in my earlier discussion of the political development of the Naturalists that the views of Bruno Wille were a direct result of Langbehn's influence. It is, however, important to recognize that this play was written in a climate of increasing receptivity to anti-rationalist, individualist ideas, but that, unlike *Marianne*, it preserves a certain scepticism about the attitudinizing which such a climate can produce in a basically weak character.

In Anna's eyes, of course, Johannes is a strong character, bold enough to insist on his own individuality, who is attempting to secure some kind of grasp on the world without reducing it by seeing it in terms of some systematic ideology. Johannes is unable to realize his aspirations; Anna thus compares him with a revolutionary hero, who dies for his people (I, 240). But in the final act of the play her comparison is shown to be an egregious one. When the time for Anna's departure comes – that is after his final confrontation with his father – Johannes proves to be anything but the man he was proclaimed to be, pleading for her help as he is left to confront reality alone: 'Give me some support. Give me something to hold on to. A prop. I am breaking down. Help me. Everything within me is breaking down.' (I, 252). Anna recognizes Johannes' need for an ideal which will make life purposeful and – anticipating the end of *Kollege Crampton* – offers him an illusion: 'The prophetic insight which we had into a new state of liberty, a distant state of bliss, let us preserve that. What we once felt shall not be lost, now or in the future.' (I, 253). It is difficult to say how far Anna is aware that what she is offering is an illusion – she has in any case nothing else to offer – but, as far as Johannes is concerned, the illusion is of very short duration. His own response to Anna's departure, the sexual attraction which unmistakeably asserts itself in the parting embrace, shows him finally that he has been deceiving himself about the nature of the bond between them; in reality it was not a new kind of relationship, and it was not characterised by freedom, but very old, very impulsive, and very passionate. Knowledge of this truth proves destructive; Johannes commits suicide.

---

[23] See *Rembrandt als Erzieher*, p. 63.

So Hauptmann ends a trilogy of plays united by their concern for the position of the idealist in a changing world. At his moment of crisis Alfred Loth felt that he was faced with three possible alternatives:

Es gibt drei Möglichkeiten! Entweder ich heirate sie, und dann...nein, dieser Ausweg existiert mcht. Oder – die bewußte Kugel. Naja, dann hätte man wenigstens Ruhe. Aber nein! So weit sind wir noch nicht, so was kann man sich einstweilen noch nicht leisten – also leben! kämpfen! – weiter, immer weiter (I, 94–95).	Either I marry her, and then... No, that cannot be done. Or – a bullet through the head. That would at least bring peace. But no! It's not that bad, that's a luxury we can't yet afford – so live! fight! – forward, ever forward.

Confident – to the point of insensitivity – in his own ideals, Loth opted for the third possibility; Wilhelm Scholz, lacking all confidence, but trusting, despite himself, in the power of love, chose the first; Johannes Vockerat, a man disillusioned by the discrepancy between reality and the ideal he cherishes, takes the second.

8
DIE WEBER

Hauptmann began the first plans of *Die Weber* at the same time as *Vor Sonnenaufgang* when he was in Zürich in 1888. But it was not until 1890 and 1891, when he made two trips into the Eulengebirge, that he first began working seriously on this, his fourth play. The dialect version, *De Waber*, was completed by the end of 1891, and the more familiar version, adapted to make it closer to high German, prepared from it by March 1892. In the meanwhile Hauptmann had completed *Kollege Crampton* with remarkable speed, and had seen it performed at the *Deutsches Theater* on 16 January 1892. He was now an established dramatist and could also have expected a public première for *Die Weber*, but a protracted dispute with the authorities necessitated the resurrection of the *Freie Bühne*, and the play was given its first performance on 26 February 1893.[1]

Hauptmann deeply resented the ban on his play. The label of Socialist was becoming increasingly embarrassing to the Naturalists, and Hauptmann insisted that his drama was 'indeed social, but not socialist'.[2] In his efforts to secure the lifting of the ban Hauptmann's advocate, Richard Grelling, himself the author of a minor social drama, *Gleiches Recht* (1892), went even further than this. He claimed that the author of *Die Weber* was on the side of law and order, for he had allowed the authorities to triumph through the intervention of a few soldiers, and that the play could not be a danger in contemporary circumstances since current legislation for the protection of workers was sufficient to prevent the recurrence of such poverty. For good measure he also pointed out that a performance of the play could do little harm, since three-quarters of the audience in the public theatres came from the upper-classes, and that censorship could, in any case, do nothing to prevent the performance of the play before the working-class audiences of the *Volksbühnen*.[3]

---

[1] There are two detailed accounts of the early reception of the play: Manfred Brauneck, *Literatur und Öffentlichkeit im ausgehenden 19. Jahrhundert: Studien zur Rezeption des naturalistischen Theaters in Deutschland* (Stuttgart: Metzler, 1974), pp. 50–86; and *Gerhart Hauptmanns 'Weber': Eine Dokumentation*, edited by Helmut Praschek, with an introduction by Peter Wruck (Berlin: Akademie Verlag, 1981).

[2] In a letter of 1 August 1893, quoted by C. H. Moore, 'A hearing on "Germinal" and "Die Weber"', *Germanic Review*, 33 (1958), 32.

[3] Grelling's submission to the Prussian *Oberverwaltungsgericht* is reprinted in *Gerhart Hauptmanns 'Weber'*, ed. Praschek, pp. 257–63. A bad harvest in 1890 had caused further trouble among the Silesian weavers, so it is just possible that some of Grelling's words

On appeal the ban was lifted, and *Die Weber* was given its first public performance at the *Deutsches Theater* on 25 September 1894. But the resistance of the conservatives was not over. The Kaiser cancelled his box at this theatre, and local police authorities, using powers which remained even after the introduction of unified Press Laws in 1874, continued to prohibit theatrical performances of the play throughout Germany until after the turn of the century. Even towards the end of Hauptmann's life it remained a source of great bitterness to him that he had once been identified with the forces of disorder; in 1942 he wrote:

Man hat mich wie einen Verbrecher behandelt, wie einen Lumpenhund! Wir mußten mit diesem Stuck, das unter Wilhelm dem Zweiten jahrelang nicht aufgeführt werden durfte, vor die Verwaltungs- und Oberverwaltungsgerichte ziehen. Im Preußischen Landtag wurde ich beschimpft. Ein adliger Herr sagte wörtlich: Der Kerl – damit meinte er mich – der Kerl gehört hinter Schloß und Riegel!⁴	I was treated like a criminal, like a common rogue! Under Wilhelm II this play was banned year after year, and we had to take it before the courts. I was abused in the Prussian Assembly. A member of the nobility said, literally: That fellow – and he meant me – ought to be behind bars!

Understandably *Die Weber* was given a warmer welcome by the political left than any other Naturalist drama. The Social Democratic leaders, Wilhelm Liebknecht and Paul Singer, were in evidence at the première; and the play was subsequently performed three times by Bruno Wille's *Neue Freie Volksbühne*, and seven by Mehring's *Freie Volksbühne*. Wille states that the reception of the play was enthusiastic: 'From my experiences I can only say that *Die Weber*...made a more powerful impact on the working class than any other social drama I have known'.⁵ I say this is understandable without thereby wishing to challenge Hauptmann's own view that this play is not a piece of socialist propaganda. For all its grimness *Die Weber* is a play which has certain positive, even optimistic, features which are lacking from the great majority of Naturalist dramas: it shows a community of people struggling

---

were meant ironically. During the period of the Third Reich Hauptmann was invited to collaborate on a film version of *Die Weber*, which would have made Grelling's point explicit in a conclusion showing how well things were in the contemporary weaving industry; Hauptmann refused. See C. F. W. Behl, *Zwiesprache mit Gerhart Hauptmann: Tagebuchblätter* (Munich: Desch, 1949), pp. 154-5.

⁴ Quoted from Kurt Lothar Tank, *Gerhart Hauptmann in Selbstzeugnissen und Bilddokumenten* (Hamburg: Rowohlt, 1959), p. 28.

⁵ 'Erinnerungen an Gerhart Hauptmann', in *Mit Gerhart Hauptmann: Erinnerungen und Bekenntnisse aus seinem Freundeskreis*, edited by Walter Heynen (Berlin, 1922), p. 108.

against the utmost oppression to maintain a basic human dignity, people whose souls can bear suffering and yet not stifle.

A contemporary social drama, Max Halbe's *Eisgang* (1892), displays the resigned pessimism which is more typical of the Naturalists. In a few scenes – which Franz Mehring admired[6] – the social movement among the working classes is briefly presented, but, as in *Einsame Menschen*, the tone and mood of the play derive more from the predicament of the hero, Hugo Tetzlaff, a young intellectual no longer convinced that his family has an inalienable right to the estates it has inherited for generations, but not yet ready to throw in his lot with the working classes. Tortured by the indecision and impotence characteristic of the heroes of this age of transition, and the hereditary weakness of a decadent family, he drowns in spring, as the frozen river cracks and the ice is carried downstream; the 'Eisgang' of the play's title is thus a symbolic destruction of the past, without very much suggestion of promise for the future.

Hauptmann's *Die Weber* differs from *Eisgang* and other Naturalist social dramas in a further significant respect: it is a genuine working-class drama. For once a Naturalist dramatist goes beyond the fairly narrow limits of most of the works we have so far discussed, which tend to treat social or ethical problems from a bourgeois intellectual standpoint and in a bourgeois setting. Langmann's *Bartel Turaser* (1897), although it is set in a proletarian milieu, works from middle-class assumptions, asking the question whether the poor can afford to conform to the traditional moral code, rather than asking direct questions about the justification of this code. Plays such as *Vor Sonnenaufgang*, *Winterschlaf*, Fulda's *Das verlorene Paradies* (1890), or Sudermann's *Die Ehre* (1889), do touch on the problems of the working classes in a changing society, but they all relate such problems expressly to the socially conscious middle-class intellectual. The same is true of the Naturalist novelists, Hans Land and Felix Hollaender. This bias arises from a basic disagreement between the Naturalists and the socialist movement about what constitutes the characteristic reality of this age. For the young Naturalist writers it was no doubt the *prise de conscience* by the intellectuals, and the consequences this had for them. Even in *Die Weber*, which concentrates on a spontaneous revolt within a working-class community, there is an episode devoted to an idealistic young tutor, Weinhold, who is dismissed by his employer for taking the weavers' part.

A comparison with Hauptmann's other mass-drama emphasizes the singularity of *Die Weber* even further. Despite the careful painting of the historical canvas, the background detail of the Peasants' War,

---

[6] 'Halbe, "Eisgang"', *Gesammelte Schriften*, edited by Thomas Höhle, Hans Koch, and Josef Schleifstein, 12 vols (Berlin: Dietz, 1960–63), XI, 135.

Florian Geyer (1896) remains primarily the story of the agonies of a leader. Geyer is a selfless hero who abandons all the privileges of the aristocrat to take up the task of serving his country, by bringing 'German disharmony' to an end. But of those he has come to serve only a select handful, Löffelholz, Tellermann, Besenmeyer, the prostitute, Marei, recognize their potential saviour. Without a leader the peasants are unable to weld themselves into a unified community, and remain a number of disparate factions. In Geyer's absence the rival leaders order a foolhardy attack on a strongly fortified position, which leads directly to their defeat and the martyrdom of Geyer – for which one leader disclaims responsibility with the words of Pontius Pilate: 'Ich wasche meine Hände in Unschuld' (I, 659). In a strange mixture of nationalism and Christianity, which recalls the ideas of Lagarde, *Florian Geyer* is presented as Messiah and *Führer*. Geyer does not, however, measure up to the claims which are made – by other characters – for his strength and powers of leadership. He is too indecisive and inactive a character to fill satisfactorily the role of *Führer*; he is too scrupulous to seize the leadership when he has the chance. When the play was first performed in 1896 its reception was disastrous; it is difficult to say with any certainty why this was so, but it is interesting that in the successful revival of the play a few years later the leading role was given to Rudolf Rittner, who had played Schäferhans in the earlier production. Rittner – as the portrait by Lovis Corinth seems to confirm – set out to compensate for the inconsistencies in the role, by carefully emphasizing Geyer's vitality:

> Stellen Sie sich vor, unter einem Hundert Menschen ist Florian Geyer der Held, der Mann – jedenfalls reden so die Leute von ihm. Und nun hat Florian Geyer, sehr im Gegensatz zu seinem Ruhm, mehr Passives als Aktives in seinem Wesen... sollte der Zuschauer dasselbe von Florian Geyer glauben, wie seine Bauernschar auf der Bühne, so blieb mir gar nichts übrig, als alle die Stellen in der Rolle herauszuarbeiten, in denen er herrschend, entschlußkräftig, kühn und zur Tat bereit erscheint. Um der inneren Wahrheit willen.[7]

> Imagine, out of a hundred characters Florian Geyer is the man or at least that's what people say. But Florian Geyer, despite his reputation, is more passive than active... if the audience was to have the same opinion of Florian Geyer as his peasant followers on stage, then I had no alternative but to lay special emphasis on those parts of the role in which he appeared commanding, decisive, bold, and ready to act. For the sake of consistency.

---

[7] Quoted from Hans Adolf-Schultze, *Der Schauspieler Rudolf Rittner (1869–1943): Ein Wegbereiter Gerhart Hauptmanns auf dem Theater* (doctoral thesis, Free University of Berlin, 1961), p. 148.

If we read the play without the guidance of Rittner, our attention will not be concentrated on the hero's task, and why he should have failed – this becomes rather obvious – but on his progress as an individual, through suffering and betrayal, to an ultimate transcendence over his unworthy enemies and followers. Nowhere is the other-worldly superiority of Geyer more evident than in the death-scene, which must have been strongly influenced by Hebbel's *Agnes Bernauer*. Like Agnes, Geyer faces his pursuers with the words of Christ: 'Whom seek ye?' (John, 18, iv), and like Agnes he commands the spontaneous respect of his enemies, holding all but the most criminal at bay. He falls to the crossbow of the villainous Schäferhans, and we are explicitly reminded of the messianic pattern of his experiences as Lorenz von Hutten claims Geyer's sword, and reads the inscription: 'Nulla crux – nulla corona' (I, 710).

Nevertheless these symbolic intrusions are in certain respects at odds with the facts of the play. The mass of the peasants take no part in the action and their leaders are presented as an obstacle to the realization of the hero's ideals. The audience's sympathy is thus elicited for Geyer's gradual hardening into an aristocratic attitude, and his vehement denunciations: 'You are trash, muck from the street, a miserable rabble. God would have done better to leave you lying in a dark corner. You're not worth the rope with which you should be hanged' (I, 667–68). These outbursts are the response of a rejected leader; they are the result of disappointment and weakness, not strength; in the context of the play they are given considerable justification; but this indulgence of anger remains incompatible with the symbolic equation of Florian Geyer and Christ.

The remoteness of the historical material of *Florian Geyer* permitted Hauptmann to adapt it and create a play which is very typical of the attitudes of its time, a play which, like *Einsame Menschen*, justifies withdrawal from social commitment. Despite its author's greater familiarity with the conditions of the Silesian weaving industry, *Die Weber* is a much less personal work. In this play the power of the facts with which Hauptmann was working seems to have had a disciplinary effect, as they did perhaps on two other plays, *Das Friedensfest* and *Rose Bernd*, for which Hauptmann was provided with a ready-made and moving story. The actual subject of the play, an account of the spontaneous outbreak of the weavers' revolt of 1844, was thoroughly documented in the historical accounts of Wilhelm Wolff and Alfred Zimmermann.[8] Both accounts provide a story strong enough and dramatic enough not to

---

[8] Wilhelm Wolff, 'Das Elend und der Aufruhr in Schlesien', *Deutsches Bürgerbuch für 1845*, edited by H. Püttmann (Darmstadt, 1845) (this is the Wilhelm Wolff to whom Marx dedicated the first volume of *Das Kapital*); Alfred Zimmermann, *Blüthe und Verfall des Leinengewerbes in Schlesien* (Breslau: Korn, 1885).

need radical changes. As a dramatist Hauptmann's achievement was to recognize and respect this, while making those changes necessary to render the material stageworthy. There is every reason to believe that the consequent restraint, call it Naturalist or not, is responsible for the quality of *Die Weber*. When free of this restraint Hauptmann was capable of writing about these same weavers with a curious mixture of pretentiousness and condescension:

Das Innere dieser halbzerfallenen Berghütten, in deren Mitte das rhythmische Wuchten des Webstuhls, das Schnalzen und Scheppern des Schiffchens tönte, war gleichsam beim ersten Anblick anziehend. Der Webstuhl ist nun einnial ein Ding, an dem zu sitzen die Göttin Kirke nicht verschmäht. Und der musikalische Klang ihrer Arbeit über die Insel Ogygia verknüpft sich mir mit jedem Webstuhle.[9]	The interior of these half-derelict mountain cottages, within which could be heard the rhythmic pulsating of the loom, the clickclack of the shuttle, was, at first sight, somehow attractive. The loom is indeed a thing at which the goddess Circe did not disdain to sit. And the music of her work on the island of Ogygia is associated in my mind with every loom.

In the fifth act of *Die Weber* news of the revolt reaches the old weaver, Hilse, who responds incredulously:

Du kenntest mir meinswegen sagen: Vater Hilse, morgen mußt du sterben. Das kann schonn meeglich sein, werd' ich sprechen, warum denn ni? – Du kennt'st mir sagen: Vater Hiise, morgen besucht dich d'r Keenig von Preußen. Aber daß Weber, Menschen wie ich und mei Sohn, und sollten solche Sachen vorgehabt – nimermehr! Nie und nimmer wer ich das glooben (I, 453).	As far as I'm concerned you could tell me: Father Hilse, tomorrow you're going to die. That may well be, I'd say, why not? – You could say: Father Hilse, tomorrow the King of Prussia's coming to see you. But that weavers, men like me and my son, should have had things like that in their minds – never! I will never ever believe it.

The play itself provides the answer to Hilse's incredulity. It resembles the analytical dramas of Naturalism in that it too provides a full explanation of a striking and improbable event, in this case the outburst of a revolutionary spirit among the weavers after years of oppression and

---

[9] *Breslauer Neueste Nachrichten*, 25 November 1938.

patient suffering. Here Naturalism does not – any more than it did in *Die Familie Selicke* – mean a lack of purpose or structure.

Once again the essential 'gesture' of the drama is captured in a striking opening-scene, as the weavers, present their finished work and wait – symbol of dependence and inability to control their own lives – for scrutiny and payment. The weavers' spirits are low, they are obviously in poor health, over-worked, and underpaid; the treatment they receive from the chief clerk, Pfeiffer, and the cashier, Neumann, is harsh. Resistance to this treatment is shown only by a redoubtable young weaver from Langenbielau, Bäcker, who receives his full payment.[10] But Bäcker's behaviour is symptomatic of an undercurrent of discontent among the weavers, for, as we soon learn, he has been engaged with others in a demonstration against the employers the previous evening. The storm, suggested in the stage direction and in the passing comment of the 'first Weaver', is about to break. This threat is intensified by the second episode in this act, the collapse of a hungry child, which brings Dreißiger into the centre of the stage, and gives him an opportunity to justify himself. He explains his difficulties and offers, magnanimously it would seem, to take on more workers; but when Pfeiffer announces the terms it becomes clear that he is taking advantage of a pool of unemployment to depress wages still further. The curtain falls to the discontented murmurings of the assembled weavers; Hauptmann has skilfully taken us to the point in the story described by the contributor to the *Vossische Zeitung* of 22 June 1844: 'Undeniably there had long been in Peterswaldau a marked restiveness among a large section of the workers, a spirit of discontent, which only needed a chance spark to break out openly in flames.'

This chance impulse is provided in Act II, in which the same pattern of a quiet beginning and steadily rising tension is repeated. The act begins by showing a different aspect of the weavers' life, the home of the Baumert family, where we witness the same mixture of despair and resignation among the wives of the weavers. The function of the returning Moritz Jäger corresponds to that of Bäcker in Act I. A period of military service has broadened his horizons, taken him to the city, and opened his eyes to the misery of the conditions under which the weavers live. Even more important, life in the army has kept him fit; he is dressed in a complete outfit of clean, smart clothes, whereas the weavers are clad in rags; like Bäcker, he is physically distinguished, he is red-cheeked, he stands straight, and has to bend to come through the door, whereas the

---

[10] Hauptmann follows his sources very closely here. Pfeiffer's identification of the Bielau weavers as trouble-makers echoes the report in the *Vossische Zeitung*, 10 June 1844. It is more comfortable for Dreißiger to attribute the revolt to agitators (individuals) than to conditions; cf. above pp. 14–15.

weavers are pale and stoop naturally, so that they seem to fit the low, oppressive houses in which they live. Jäger, then, is shown to be physically up to leadership, and as an ex-soldier he has a primitive idea of the power of a mass of people. Apart from genuine outrage at the way his family and friends have to live, he also has personal reasons for agitating. He had once been regarded as a layabout and a ne'er-do-well; the threat, 'You just wait till you do your National Service' had become depressingly familiar to him (I, 365), but Moritz has made good; he has money and a watch, and he has learnt to 'talk proper' (I, 361). He acts, in part at least, out of a desire for recognition, and recognition is easily won. To the weavers he seems to have accomplished the impossible; he has broken out of the enclosed weaving community, and he brings them the promise of release.

The most important symbol of this promise is the song which he has brought from the world outside. *Das Blutgericht* ('Bloody justice') provides the weavers with a simple articulate assessment of their woes such as they had not previously known. As Moritz Jäger reads it to them they come to feel for the first time that they understand their situation: 'Every word...every word...all that is as true as what is in the Bible' (I, 377). With this feeling resignation and impotence give way to violence and hatred, passivity to activity: 'And all that must change, I say, now this minute. We won't put up with it any more! We won't put up with it any more, come what may' (I, 379). The song is also used most effectively by Hauptmann to indicate, within the limits of the dramatic form, the gradual formation of a mob out of the various individual weavers: in Act I the song is mentioned by Bäcker; in Act II it is introduced to some of the weavers by Moritz Jäger; in the third act a group of weavers leave the inn singing the song; and in the fourth act it is heard off-stage, issuing from the large crowd assembled outside Dreißiger's house. This is a fine example of Hauptmann's faithful, but skilful adaptation of his source; Zimmermann describes the effect of the song as follows:

> for a long time discontent showed itself only in abuse and threats. Then suddenly a song cropped up, which expressed all the general grievances so clearly that it was on everyone's lips in a flash, the weavers' song. The *Vossische Zeitung* wrote: 'It is an explicit manifesto of all the complaints and grievances which until then were only circulating covertly and slowly.... The song sped like a call to arms from house to house; it fell like a lighted fuse among the seething tempers' (p. 351).

Act III follows the pattern established by the two previous acts. The scene changes again, to the village inn, and the action begins with a relatively calm discussion, in which the exploitation and oppression of the weavers by the clergy, the village carpenter, the land-owning nobility, and the farmers is relentlessly revealed, until the weavers march off, the rebellious, threatening mob which invades Dreißiger's house at the end of the fourth act.

The release of this anarchic, animal fury, which amazes some of the weavers themselves, is explained quite fully and quite rationally. The participation of certain individuals, Moritz Jäger, Wittig the smith, is given a quite detailed personal motivation, but underneath the personal reasons, and common to all the weavers, is the ceaseless pressure of social circumstances. The statement of the 'first weaver' in Act I: 'A weaver is also an object' ['Sache'] (I, 329), calls to mind Marx's condemnation of the over-valuation of the material world ('Sachenwelt') and the devaluation of the human world. The confusion of means and ends, whereby what should be made for use is made for its commercial value (the weavers make cloth, but are clad in rags) also recalls Marx's criticism of nineteenth-century bourgeois society; and in the discussion in Act III Hauptmann uses Marx's own example, the theft of wood.[11]

The revolt itself does not, of course, arise from any clear Marxist insight on the part of the weavers. Moritz Jäger is not the kind of messenger from outside, like Ibsen's Lona Hessel, who argues from a carefully thought-out position, he simply helps release the pent-up energies and hatreds of the weavers. The revolt is a despairing outcry or, as old Baumert puts it, a chance to get a breath of fresh air. The weavers do not seriously expect it to bring about any permanent improvement in their conditions. Bäcker and Baumert, two of the most sympathetic and sensible weavers, do not dispute Hilse's assertion that they will end up in prison – they do not care. And this is not just empty bravado, for they have no reason to care: 'In prison is at least better than at home. You are looked after there; you needn't starve' (I, 475). These weavers are not closely related to the class-conscious proletariat of Hauptmann's own day. Like Halbe's *Eisgang*, the play is not even set in the city, but in its author's native province, among the country workers engaged in cottage-industry, whom Hauptmann knew most intimately. Moreover the dramatist's verism, that is to say his fidelity to his sources and his avoidance of anachronism, has excluded any argument for or against organized socialism. There is not in *Die Weber*, as there is in Ernst Toller's *Die Maschinenstürmer* (1922), a single far-sighted figure to whom the future can be said to belong. Hauptmann's is both a better play and a more effective piece of social criticism for this reason. Where the hero, Jimmy Cobbett, is involved, *Die Maschinenstürmer* has a strong thematic

---

[11] Marx, 'Debatten über das Holzdiebstahlgesetz', Karl Marx and Friedrich Engels, *Historisch-kritische Gesamtausgabe: Werke, Schriften und Briefe*, Abt. 1, vol. I, edited by David Borisovic Rjazanov (Frankfurt a.M.: Marx-Engels Archiv Verlagsgesellschaft, 1927), 266 ff.

resemblance to *Florian Geyer* – only, for good measure, the hero is compared to Lord Byron as well as Christ – but the play is more effective where it makes a direct appeal for human pity through its portrayal of the suffering and deprivation of the weavers. It is for this particular aspect of his play that Toller is most indebted to Hauptmann, and it is here that Hauptmann is not to be surpassed. The care and affection with which Hauptmann has depicted all his weavers, and which only rarely borders on sentimentality (the starving child of Act I) is a powerful testimony to Hauptmann's social concern, and constitutes a fierce social attack.

There is every justification for regarding *Die Weber* as a tendentious work. In making the revolt understandable Hauptmann has gone a long way towards making it forgivable. At the same time there is little doubt of his indictment of the employers. Dreißiger is allowed to plead the weak competitive position of the Silesian weaving industry, but, although this is regarded as a fact by the historians, it carries little weight in the drama, because Dreißiger is manifestly concerned only to exploit the situation as best he can. Zimmermann's account singles out the firm of Zwanziger for its reputation for particular harshness (p. 350), but the play goes further than this; the effect of showing just the one firm is to make it a representative of the whole class.

The direction of the play's attack is not substantially altered, as Theodor Fontane argued, by the fifth act.[12] It is true that this act provides the first signs of resistance from among the weavers themselves, but it also introduces another powerful supporter of the revolt in the person of Luise Hilse, an outraged mother, who is the equal of Bäcker, Wittig, and Jäger in terms of fury and energy. Moreover the resistance of Hilse is overcome; his son, Gottlieb, disobeys him and joins the rebels, and the revolt spreads from Peterswaldau to Langenbielau. There is also a certain ambiguity about Hilse's resistance, which requires explanation, for he does not disown the weavers, but prays for their safety (I, 477). Hilse's solidarity with his fellow-weavers in their hostility to their employers is not seriously in doubt, and his clash with them is primarily a clash of personality. Hilse's attitude differs from that of his fellow-weavers because of those differences in character which cannot be fully explained in Marxist terms by environment. Hilse, with his pronounced streak of Silesian pietism, is an example of a man with a strong psychological need for religion; and throughout his life his social situation has reinforced this need. Now an old man, near to death, with little to hope for in this world, he naturally clings more strongly than the other

---

[12] Theodor Fontane, 'Hauptmann, Die Weber', in *Werke, Schriften und Briefe*, 20 vols, edited by Walter Keitel und Helmuth Nürnberger (Munich: Hanser, 1962–94), Abt. II, *Aufsätze, Kritiken, Erinnerungen*, ii, *Theaterkritiken*, edited by Siegmar Gerndt (1969), 858–59.

weavers to the beliefs which have sustained him, to his 'certainty' of happiness in the world to come. His attitude approaches panic when this seems threatened; hence his unreasoning severity towards the child, Mielchen, who has brought into his home a silver spoon which does not rightly belong there: 'Get that devilish spoon out of here' (I, 455). For a man like Hilse it is too much to ask whether he has not been duped by an alliance of Church and bourgeoisie; but his attitude to the revolt is a clear reflection of the teaching of the local pastor, Kittelhaus. In Hilse's eyes the revolt is the work of the devil ('Satansarbeit'), the words of Luise are godless ('gottlose Reden'), Bäcker and his followers are emissaries of Satan: 'Where did the devil bring you from with your staves and axes?' (I, 467). He thus accepts that equation between the prevalent social order and the laws of God, which Kittelhaus made in Act IV, in saying of the angry weavers: 'They are trampling God's laws under foot' (I, 419). The discrepancy between the miserable surroundings in which Hilse lives, and the gratitude he expresses for the goodness of heaven in his prayer at the opening of Act V, strengthens the impression that he has been fobbed off with the promise of an afterlife which will compensate for the misery which is now his lot, that his religion is both an expression of his wretched condition and a protest against it.[13]

Superficially Hilse is distinguished from his fellow-weavers by his firm adherence to his religious beliefs, but a consideration of the quality of these beliefs makes his solidarity with them much clearer. His 'Christianity' is as much a religion of vengeance as of forgiveness:

Fer was hätt' ich denn hier gesessen – und Schemel getreten uf Mord vierzig und mehr Jahr? und hätte ruhig zugesehn, wie der dort drieben in Hoffart und Schwelgerei lebt und Gold macht aus mein'n Hunger und Kummer. Fer was denn? Weil ich 'ne Hoffnung hab'. Ich hab was in aller der Not. *Durchs Fenster weisend*: Du hast hier deine Parte – ich drieben in jener Welt: das hab' ich gedacht. Und ich lass' mich vierteeln – ich hab 'ne Gewißheet. Es ist uns verheißen. Gericht wird gehalten; aber nich mir sein Richter, sondern:	Why should I have been sitting here – treading this loom like mad for forty years or more? quietly watching him over yonder, living in vanity and luxury, and making a packet out of my hunger and misery. Why? Because I have hope. I've got something, despite all this misery. *Pointing out of the window*: You're getting your share here – I'll get mine in the next world: that's what I've been thinking. I'm ready to stake my life on it – I'm certain. We've been promised. The day of judgement will come; but we are not the

---

[13] See Karl Marx, 'Zur Kritik der Hegelschen Rechtsphilosophie', *Gesamtausgabe*, Ser. 1, I, 607.

| mein is die Rache, spricht der | judges; vengeance is mine, saith |
| Herr, unser Gott. (I, 463) | the Lord, our God. |

This attitude, which can hardly have been picked up directly from Pastor Kittelhaus, is just as much a cry of hatred as the inarticulate fury of the other weavers, or their revolutionary song, *Das Blutgericht*. Moreover it is indeed possible that Hilse's speech was in fact suggested to Hauptmann by two verses of the original *Blutgericht*, which Hauptmann did not include in the play:

O euer Geld und euer Gut,	O all your goods will melt away
Das wird dereinst vergehen	And all your riches too,
Wie Butter an der Sonne Glut,	Like butter in the sun's fierce ray,
Wie wirds um euch dann stehen?	And where will that leave you?
Wenn ihr dereinst nach dieser	After your life of ease is done,
Zeit Nach eurem Freudenleben	After your riotous days,
Dort, dort in jener Ewigkeit	When you, before your God alone,
Sollt Rechenschaft abgeben.[14]	Must justify your ways.

Hilse is the one example of a weaver who has an alternative to *Das Blutgericht*, a satisfying and thoroughly coherent assessment of his own situation; his life has purpose and shape. Whether this assessment has any higher validity, is, in dramatic terms, irrelevant; his convictions determine his actions and mean that he is not open to the seductions of Moritz Jäger. Hilse's Old-Testament Christianity is a protest and an expression of suffering similar in intensity to the protest of the outraged mother, Luise Hilse; and even though this protest has about it a certain life-denying character, it is in no way to be likened to the unsympathetic inwardness of Rose Bernd's father. It remains a thing of value, for is it not also evidence of that indomitable spirit to which this play is a tribute, and which makes it a work of admiration as much as a work of pity?

There is about Hilse's attitude a defiant heroism, which contributes to the positive quality of the play – a quality which would have been lost completely if Hauptmann had finished the account, by going on to show how the revolt was crushed and the weavers imprisoned. And before interpreting *Die Weber* as a grimly pessimistic work, we should bear in mind that it was open to the author to make his pessimism much more explicit without in any way abandoning the historical accuracy which informs this play. Even so, there is a finality about

---

[14] Quoted from Gerhart Hauptmann, *Die Weber: Dichtung und Wirklichkeit*, edited by Hans Schwab-Felisch (Frankfurt a.M.: Ullstein, 1959), p. 117. For a discussion of Hilse's religion see H. M. Wolff, 'Der alte Hilse', in Guthke and Wolff, 'Das Leid im Werke Gerhart Hauptmanns', *University of California Publications in Modern Philology*, 49 (1958), pp. 69ff.

Hilse's death; it rounds the play off with an excellent curtain in the conventional sense; and in view of the dominant position which he occupies in this final act, a certain authority does accrue to him and to his utterances. If this is indeed an attempt to make us take Hilse's words at face value, or to suggest that his sufferings have endowed him with a superior insight beyond the reach of his fellow-weavers, then it is an attempt which comes too late in the play. The suspicious rationalist in Hauptmann has done his job too well for us to be able to see in the conclusion of the drama that kind of strong closure.

A much more pronounced ambiguity informs the whole of the short play *Hanneles Himmelfahrt* (1893). The attention to causal details and the consequent undermining of the authority of the religious insight is, if anything, even more scrupulous than in *Die Weber*. The play falls into three parts, showing the objective world of the young Hannele Mattern's present situation, the nightmare world from which she has tried to escape by suicide, and her dream of heavenly bliss. All three worlds are inextricably intertwined, for Hannele's vision of heaven is determined by a strange mixture of earthly hatreds and compensations: a desire for vengeance on a cruel stepfather, a childlike urge for power, attention, and significance, a yearning for maternal affection, and an innate religious humility and piety.[15] The sexual element is particularly strong; the emphasis on physical torment at the hands of the stepfather recalls the masochistic fantasies of Wendla Bergmann in Wedekind's *Frühlings Erwachen*; while the 'stranger', who is played by the same actor as the teacher, Gottwald, is both the figure of Christ, and at the same time the masculine ideal of a young girl whose sexual impulses are just awakening, and who has taken literally the Christian metaphor of the 'bride of heaven'.

In her review of the play, Lou Andreas-Salomé stressed the subjective nature of Hannele's dreams: 'we encounter here a child of this earth, and her earthly longings'.[16] If we are prepared to adopt this standpoint, then the 'sentimentality' of the play is no longer a fault, but part of its overall consistency; the critic Siegfried Jacobsohn describes Hannele's vision, as it was presented in Rittner's production of 1913, in the following words:

> a heaven...which a snob would describe as kitsch, because he forgets that this heaven is not constructed according to his taste, but according to the fairy-tale taste of a young village-girl... By sound and image, by change from earthly to supernatural lighting, he distinguishes between Hannele's dream and reality.[17]

---

[15] Cf. H. M. Wolff, 'Hannele', in Guthke and Wolff, 'Das Leid', pp. 74–82.
[16] 'Hannele', *Freie Bühne*, 4 (1893), 1346.
[17] Quoted from Schultze, *Der Schauspieler Rudolf Rittner*, p. 87.

Hauptmann views the religion of Hannele with the irony and the scepticism which he applied (if only intermittently) to the attitudes of Frau Buchner, Johannes Vockerat, and Hilse – although in *Hanneles Himmelfahrt* the use of verse tends to objectivize the vision to a far greater extent; however, the need of the individual for religion, and the fact and consequence of its existence are acknowledged. By 1893 the Naturalists had begun to develop a considerable interest in religious manifestations, and a greater tolerance towards religious needs.[18] Religion, as it is treated in *Hanneles Himmelfahrt* and, to a lesser extent, *Die Weber*, offers the dramatist an opportunity to extend his range of expression without entirely abandoning the deeply engrained premises of Naturalism. *Hanneles Himmelfahrt* shows how, by the use of the play within a play, the Naturalist drama can be opened up to include the completely subjective vision. Taken together these two plays show Hauptmann developing a style which permits that free activity of the artistic imagination demanded by the now dominant 'individualists' among his Naturalist contemporaries.

---

[18] Cf. Heinrich Hart, 'M. von Egidy', *Freie Bühne*, 3 (1892), 1288; Bruno Wille, 'Der Naturprediger Johannes Gutttzeit', *Freie Bühne*, 2 (1891), 376. Guttzeit was the man who had inspired Hauptmann's short story *Der Apostel* (1890). Edmond de Goncourt, noting a similar development in Zola at this time, dismissed it as opportunism: '[Zola] s'interrompt pour nous dire qu'il a été à Lourdes et qu'il a été frappé, stupifié par le spectacle de ce monde de croyants hallucinés, et qu'il y aurait de belles choses à écrire sur ce renouveau de la foi, qui, pour lui, a amené le mysticisme, en littérature et ailleurs, de l'heure présente. En l'entendant, je pensais au roublard littéraire qui, sentant que le naturalisme est en baisse, songeait un bon tremplin qu'il trouvait lá pour passer mystique', Edmond and Jules de Goncourt, *Journal: Mémoires de la vie littéraire*, edited by Robert Ricatte, 4 vols (Paris: Fasquelle and Flammarion, 1956), IV, 1891–1896, p. 208.

9
THE NATURALIST COMEDY

Comedy was not a field in which the Naturalists – either German or European – were particularly productive, nor was it one in which they particularly excelled. Gerhart Hauptmann did not begin his first comedy, *Kollege Crampton* (1892), until after the completion of *Die Weber*, by which time Naturalism was widely reckoned to be in decline. This is not entirely coincidental, for the veristic doctrine itself necessarily inhibits the exploitation of the conventions and character-types which are inherent in the stylisation of the comic genre.[1] There are, in addition, certain characteristics of the Naturalist ideology as it developed in Germany, which proved peculiarly hostile to the adoption of a comic view. The purpose of this chapter is to show how the relaxation of the earlier aggression, and an increasing tendency to indulge or sentimentality, allowed the movement to embrace a form which had not hitherto received a great deal of attention – except in the form of satirical social criticism – from the earnest young writers of this generation.[2] The results of this, even in the best Naturalist comedy, *Der Biberpelz* (1893), testify to a continuing unease in handling the genre. Like many more famous antecedents in the field, the German Naturalists exploited the comic possibilities in the behaviour of the blind, automaton-like monomaniac (von Wehrhahn in *Der Biberpelz*, Gehrke in Holz's and Ernst's *Sozialaristokraten*), but their comic monomaniacs pale into relative insignificance beside the great sympathetic monomaniacs of Naturalist literature, such as the bigoted old Hilse of *Die Weber*, the self-flagellating Fuhrmann Henschel, or the pathetic Henriette John of *Die Ratten*. There is about the German Naturalist comedy a certain lack of incisiveness which derives, I will suggest, both from an inherent conservatism and from the inhibitions arising from specifically Naturalist convictions; but it is the inherent conservatism, of which I have already spoken on a number of occasions, which prompts the Naturalists to stop short of the ruthless disdain of the greatest exponents of the comic genre.

---

[1] See Wolfgang Trautwein, 'Gerhart Hauptmann: *Der Biberpelz*', in *Interpretationen: Dramen des Naturalismus* (Stuttgart: Reclam, 1988), pp. 179–212 (pp. 182–83).
[2] For an interesting sidelight on the attitude of the Naturalists to satire see Gilbert J. Carr, 'Satire from the German Naturalists? Karl Kraus's Planned Anthology', *German Life and Letters*, N.S. 46 (1993), pp. 120–33.

It was a contemporary of the German Naturalists, Henri Bergson, who saw in the monomaniac the richest source of comedy: 'A comic person is one who automatically follows his own path, without bothering about contact with others. The purpose of laughter is to correct his distraction and awaken him from his dream.'[3] Defined in this way comedy is a genre with an extrinsic purpose, and is thus limited to what we normally tend to describe as satirical comedy. Such comedy might also tend to be conservative, in that it can readily be used to defend the status quo from the threat of fragmentation when the individual is tempted to pursue his own isolated course.[4] One of the clearest examples of this is the use of comedy to ridicule the avant-garde in literature or art; as, for instance, in Molière's *Les Femmes savantes*, or, to take an example from German Naturalism, in Act III, scenes i–v of Otto Ernst's *Jugend von Heute* (1899), where a rather motley collection of individuals holds a poetry-reading (ten lines of one of the poems consist of *Gedankenstriche*).

In comedy of this kind, however – and Bergson's definition does not take sufficient account of this – a point can well be reached where the moral or social purpose of the writer seems to have become subordinate to the simple desire to make the spectator laugh. 'Really it is all tragedy', says a character in Ivy Compton-Burnett's *Mother and Son*, 'comedy is a wicked way of looking at it, when it is not our own'. This 'wicked way of looking at it' is, perhaps, an important ingredient of great comedy. Criticism of Molière, recognizing this, has ceased to place such exclusive emphasis on the social criticism in his work, and has directed our attention rather to his career as a man of the theatre, who earned his living by making people laugh.[5] To this kind of writer the 'faux dévot' (Tartuffe) and the provincial imitators of the 'précieuses' can offer more promising material than the real thing; and the work of such a writer might be more strongly informed with gratitude to the purveyor of comic situations than with any desire to correct his characters' relationship to society. Such detachment is more nearly achieved in the chilly black comedy of Ibsen's *Hedda Gabler* (if one overlooks the rather ineffectual comfort offered by Thea Elvsted) or in the radical nihilism of Schnitzler's *Reigen*, than in the comedies of the German Naturalists.

The social-critical stance of the Naturalists and their desire to engage literature in the problems of the age, made them favourably disposed to satirical comedy; but the theoretical dislike of tendentiousness,

---

[3] *Le Rire: Essai sur la signification du comique* (Paris, 1920; first published 1912), p. 137.
[4] Cf. René König, *Die naturalistische Ästhetik in Frankreich und ihre Auflösung* (Borna and Leipzig: Noske, 1931), pp. 190–91.
[5] René Bray, *Molière: Homme de théâtre* (Paris, 1954). It was a performance of *L'Avare* which prompted Hauptmann to write *Kollege Crampton*, and in the same year he was at work on a play entitled 'Der eingebildete Kranke', which was never completed.

as exemplified in the early critical writings of the Hart brothers, gave rise to certain reservations. In the earlier dramas of Gerhart Hauptmann (satirical) comedy is restricted to a few brief episodes; and in the movement as a whole tragi-comedy, in the widest sense of the term, is felt to be the most congenial genre.[6] Where the dramatist does indulge in a satirical attack the theoretical limits are often stretched, and, particularly among the lesser dramatists, naturalistic characterization readily gives way to caricature. *Hilfsprediger* Boretius in Max Halbe's early play, *Freie Liebe* (1889), the heroine's father and fiancé in Hartleben's *Hanna Jagert* (1893), and the heroine's fiancé in Hirschfeld's *Pauline* (1899), are all caricatured in the course of a satirical attack designed to safeguard certain social values. This strictly functional use of comedy might suggest that the respective dramatists are less than certain about the merits of their cases; and this is not at all surprising, in view of the rapidity with which the Naturalist position is modified in this decade. These three plays do, in fact, provide a rather good barometer of this unsettled period. The earliest, *Freie Liebe*, is ethically 'progressive', defending the right of Ernst Winter and his young friend, Elise, to enjoy life and live together without being married; the second, which dates from the period immediately after the breach with socialism, is less decisive; it defends the right of Hanna to lead her own individual life, but concedes that she has a certain debt of gratitude to both the Socialist and the altruist who were responsible for her liberation from the constraints and conventions of the past, and whom she now deserts; Hirschfeld's play, the latest, is quite unashamedly and unambiguously conservative, advocating the acceptance of the social situation and an underprivileged position in it, provided that decent, humane people are at the top.

Satirical attacks, which tend to be episodic, and tend to become increasingly conservative in character, are further inhibited by the Naturalist doctrine of absolute determinism. Where this operates, it generates a feeling of oppression by uncontrollable external forces, and precludes any possibility of genuine independence or superiority; no one can be free enough to be detached. Just as the belief in relentless laws of causality excludes guilt and inhibits tragedy, so also it excludes ridicule and prevents satirical comedy. The 'moral laxity' which Gustav von Aschenbach so abhorred, the 'tout comprendre, c'est tout pardonner' of Naturalist theory, is a double-edged weapon. Old Thienwiebel in *Papa Hamlet* is a perfect example of the character who is potentially comic because of his *idée fixe*, and Holz and Schlaf do go a long way towards exploiting this potentiality; but they clearly experience the obligation of the Naturalist to make his fantasies plausible, and so they give these fantasies a

---

[6] K. S. Guthke, *Geschichte und Poetik der deutschen Tragikomödie* (Göttingen: Vandenhoeck und Ruprecht, 1961), p. 218.

psychological explanation, relating them (as compensatory delusions) to Thienwiebel's present milieu, and his past experiences and ambitions as an actor. The central figure in this work is therefore at once comic and pathetic. The same is true, though to a lesser extent, of the comic episodes in Hartleben's tragedy, *Rosenmontag* (1900). This play, which was one of the great popular successes of the Naturalist movement, and was given 205 performances at Brahm's *Deutsches Theater*, belongs in the tradition of the *bürgerliches Trauerspiel*. Its hero is a young officer, Hans Rudorff, who is in love with a working-class girl. The Schemer's role is shared by Rudorff's twin cousins, Peter and Paul von Ramberg; this doubling of the role is a stock device, which achieves comic effects without caricature. The interference of the Rambergs breaks up the affair, and leads to Rudorff's suicide, but their motives are honest and they themselves are well-meaning in a way that Schiller's Wurm and Lessing's Marinelli are not. The traditions of a family with a long military tradition, and the stultifying influence of barrack-room life are illuminated in realistic scenes reminiscent of Lenz's *Die Soldaten* which provide the best moments of the play. Here again explanation amounts to a kind of justification; and the Rambergs appear pathetic in their superficial and naive confidence that their scheming will one day earn them their cousin's gratitude.

Ludwig Anzengruber was a dramatist who was close enough to the German Naturalists to earn their admiration, and his plays were very popular with the audiences of the *Volksbühnen*, but he wrote within the tradition of a country richly endowed with comedy, Austria, and at a time when the doctrines of Naturalism had not been formulated. He also preserved a basic belief in individual freedom and human independence. These are clearly factors which enabled him to create in his best comedy, *Die Kreuzelschreiber*, a work which is superior to anything the German Naturalists wrote in this genre. The theme of Anzengruber's play is basically a serious one; interclerical rivalry leads to irresponsible meddling in family-life, and turns wives against their husbands: the priest of one village secures the support of the men for a document proclaiming adherence to the traditions of the Catholic faith and expressing hostility to so-called Lutheran innovations, whereupon the priest of the neighbouring village appeals to the women to make their husbands recant and go on a pilgrimage to Rome in penance for their sins. There is no doubt whatever that Anzengruber's play is a play with a purpose; as always, his attack on the Roman Catholic Church is in earnest, and, typically, he wrings every last drop of emotion from the plight of an old peasant, Brenninger, who kills himself in despair over the futile and unnecessary quarrel with his wife.

Nevertheless there is more to Anzengruber's very amusing play than its overt polemic purpose. The viewpoint of the most important character in the play, Steinklopferhans, is one of detachment, not one of anger, and it is a viewpoint we are encouraged to share. The various events we witness are thus all part of one great comedy in which we are not involved. The message of Steinklopferhans is that man, even at his basest and most exposed can always glory in a certain inviolability.[7] Steinklopferhans has experienced the ultimate in misery and isolation, but even in these depths the restorative power of nature is not eliminated, and he has recovered to assert with confidence that the world is a happy and amusing place.[8]

Secure in the possession of his ultimate truth, he can stand aside from the action of the play as spectator and commentator. He can look on and laugh when the respectably married Anton is suddenly and surprisingly confronted with his former sweetheart; when the prosperous Großbauer von Grundldorf enters the village inn and so easily obtains the signatures of the (mostly illiterate) men for his document; when Josepha, the wife of Anton, successfully follows the example of Lysistrata, and persuades her husband to go to Rome as a penance; or when Josepha pathetically tries to run the farm in her husband's absence. In each case Steinklopferhans is ready with the laconic commentary of the superior, far-sighted observer: 'I stand at my post!... And I have to report that the captain of the cross-signers... has retreated through that window! – Well, tomorrow it's the women who will be on top!'[9]

He intervenes in the action to help Anton clear up the confusion, but, characteristically, he does so in a way which prolongs the amusement of the detached observer. True to his principle, 'As long as there was a joke, I've enjoyed laughing at you.'[10] He organizes the men for the pilgrimage, asks their wives to provide financial support, and enrols a band of devout, young, single women, which includes Anton's former sweetheart, to accompany them. In this final scene the comedian Anzengruber is revealed at his most radical, and the moral purpose behind his play is almost forgotten. Once Anton is back in his customary masculine position of ascendancy he exploits his advantage to the full, sparing his wife no discomfort, until she turns the tables again, by threatening to find herself a man to console her. Equilibrium is restored, and the pilgrimage is called off; whereupon one of the men, Altlechner, who cannot stand his wife, hastily makes a break for Rome. The German Naturalists never pursue their purely comic purpose with quite such consistency.

---

[7] *Sämtliche Werke*, IV, 73.
[8] *Sämtliche Werke*, IV, 70.
[9] *Sämtliche Werke*, IV, 65.
[10] *Sämtliche Werke*, IV, 70.

This kind of detachment is most closely approached in certain episodes of Hauptmann's *Der Biberpelz*, the best comedy of the period and a work which has acquired canonical status within the comic tradition in Germany. The shrewd Frau Wolff perceives the robot-like predictability of the Prussian official, von Wehrhahn, who is so concerned with his defence of 'the highest values of the nation' against socialism that he overlooks all manner of real crimes, and she turns her knowledge of von Wehrhahn's blindness to her own advantage. Beginning with the relatively trivial crime of poaching, she then steals wood from her daughter's employer, Krueger, and finally his beaver-coat; in the sequel, the tragi-comic *Der rote Hahn* (1901), Frau Wolff (now Frau Fielitz) has progressed to arson and fraud. The action of the two plays is therefore repetitive; indeed, the plays depend for their comic effects on repetition, which is emphasized by the regularity of the scene-changes between Frau Wolff's house, where the coups are prepared, and the court-room, where the crimes are investigated. Both plays depend very much on comedy of situation of a fairly basic kind: the outwitting of the slow and foolish by the quick and nimble. The best examples of this are the two most famous examples, the endings of the first and third acts of *Der Biberpelz*; in the former Mitteldorf, an employee of the court, unwittingly assists Frau Wolff and her husband as they set out to steal Krueger's wood; in the latter Krueger brandishes a piece of his own wood, which he has found outside Frau Wolff's house and which he does not recognize, vowing that he will catch the thief.

Hirschfeld's *Pauline* stands in much the same dependent relationship to *Der Biberpelz* as his *Die Mütter* does to *Einsame Menschen*. It shares the same cyclic structure, showing a sequence of events in which the heroine outwits her numerous suitors by playing off one against another. Both plays therefore have a structural resemblance to Molière's *Les Fourberies de Scapin*, a farce consisting of a number of separate episodes in which the central character repeatedly gets the better of a series of dupes. In farce the central character derives his value from the way he acts, the skill, the style, the pace with which he outwits others; the only value which he can be said to embody is the value of comedy itself. In the Naturalist drama, where the portrayal of character for its own sake tends to be more important than action, the momentum which is essential to farce tends to be inhibited by digressive characterisation; at the same time, what the character *does* can be distinguished from what the character *is*. In Hirschfeld's play Pauline's employer says of her: 'for all her cheek, the girl has remained decent, as modest and pleasant as anybody';[11] that is to say those of Pauline's qualities which provide the

---

[11] Georg Hirschfeld, *Pauline* (Berlin, 1899), p. 23.

comic episodes in the play, her vitality, her love of freedom, her selfish philosophy of enjoyment without involvement, are all seen as a threat to her basic humanity; she preserves her value despite these qualities. The same is true of Hauptmann's *Der Biberpelz*, which, more than any other of his plays, is dominated by one single character, Frau Wolff. Her redeeming features are her elemental energy, her good sense, her basic decency and, above all, her almost mythical status as a maternal force, as Mutter Wolff.[12] Hauptmann is most careful to distinguish her transgressions from those of the police-informer, Motes, and his wife. In her basic convictions she conforms to the most important values; in *Der Biberpelz* she commits no crimes which seriously harm others, and one cannot believe she would. However, the ambitions she cherishes for her daughter, Adelheid, recall the foolishness of the mother in many a domestic tragedy, and indicate that her dishonesty is a sign of incipient corruption by a society in which material success is the most important yardstick of achievement. The rather mild foolishness of Frau Wolff's ambitions becomes intensified into the blindness of Frau Fielitz in *Der rote Hahn*, where she undiscriminatingly admires her vain and parasitic son-in-law, Schmarowski: 'that man's got his wits about him! He's a good bet! You mark my words, he'll get on' (II, 23). The destruction of Frau Wolff's humanity as she becomes increasingly dominated by a frantic desire to get on at all costs, which makes the sequel a tragi-comedy, is the aspect of the two plays which Brecht chose to emphasize when he adapted them for performance on a single evening. In order to foreground the changes in her character he encouraged his leading actress to exploit to the full the repetitive structure of the two plays and the similarity between the various situations.[13] But when the two plays are considered as a pair, the later, and weaker, play casts its tragi-comic shadow over the whole. The undermining of the former Frau Wolff's vitality and the weakening of her hold on life as her personal anxiety increases inevitably colour the way in which we view her earlier misdemeanours. *Der Biberpelz* can remain a comedy only if we view it in isolation.

Even when it is viewed in isolation one can sense a certain timidity on the author's part which has prevented a full unfolding of comic effects. The very end of the play, without doubt one of its best

---

[12] See Oskar Seidlin 'Urmythos irgendwo in Berlin', *Deutsche Vierteljahrsschrift*, 43 (1969), pp. 126–46 (p. 130).
[13] Bertolt Brecht, *Schriften zum Theater* (Frankfurt a.M.: Suhrkamp, 1964), VI, 302. Cf. *Theaterarbeit. 6 Aufführungen des Berliner Ensembles* (Dresden, 1952), pp. 171–226. For some comments on the possible influence of *Der Biberpelz* on *Mutter Courage*, see H. W. Reichert, 'Hauptmann's Frau Wolff and Brecht's Mother Courage', *German Quarterly*, 34 (1961), pp. 439–48.

moments, provides a good example of this timidity:

WEHRHAHN. Und so wahr es ist, wenn ich hier sage: die Wolffen ist eine ehrliche Haut, so sag ich Ihnen mit gleicher Bestimmtheit: Ihr Doktor Fleischer, von dem wir sprechen, das ist ein lebensgefährlicher Kerl! FRAU WOLFF. Da weeß ich nu nich... (I, 542).	WEHRHAHN. If, as I can truly say, Frau Wolff is an honest woman, then I can say with equal certainty: that Dr Fleischer, of whom we have been speaking, is a very dangerous fellow! FRAU WOLFF. I wouldn't know about that.

The comic effect of these lines is twofold; in the first instance they show the predictable von Wehrhahn giving vent yet again to his obsession, and secondly they exploit the dramatic irony which naturally arises from von Wehrhahn's blindness. Here, then, is a satirical attack on von Wehrhahn and the society he represents, but an attack whose force is blunted because von Wehrhahn is not totally wrong in his judgement. Indeed, the whole tendency of the play has been to show that Frau Wolff really is, in a very broad sense, 'an honest woman' despite her petty crimes; and the most natural response for an actress in the part to secure from her audience, as Brecht points out, is unthinking approval.[14] If this were not so, if Frau Wolff were clearly and consistently an amoral character, the social criticism of the play would be fiercer, and the conclusion crueller to von Wehrhahn; but above all it would be more comic.

Brecht's appreciation of the role of Frau Wolff distantly recalls some hostile comments which Karl Kraus once made about German comedy in general, and Hauptmann's *Die Jungfern von Bischofsberg* in particular. He condemns a kind of humour 'which humourless people would like to see defined as a metaphysical smile at all the weaknesses of mankind, and which, it is true, is more peaceful and reassuring, but no more praiseworthy than all attempts to bore them to death'.[15] The humour which Kraus is attacking is not harsh and aggressive, but complacent, indulgent, and tolerant. It is the humour which enables us to come to terms with the world in which we live, and which enables us to smile on the activity of Frau Wolff, while still disapproving of the sentiments implied in her statement to her husband that you just have to get on, and no one will ask questions: 'When you've once become rich...and can sit in a coach, no one's going to ask where you got it all from' (I, 501). It is the kind of humour to which Hauptmann was

---

[14] *Schriften zum Theater*, VI, 302.
[15] 'Von Humor and Lyrik' (1921), *Die Sprache* (Munich, 1954), p. 206.

referring in the words: 'Humour is one of the means by which Man either overcomes his fate, or at least learns to bear it',[16] and which is enshrined in his first comedy, *Kollege Crampton*.

Like *Papa Hamlet* and Holz's and Jerschke's tragi-comedy, *Traumulus* (1904), it treats the problem of an individual in an illusory relationship to reality. In the two works on which Holz collaborated – and, indeed, in Hauptmann's own *Schluck und Jau* (1900) – there is a much greater awareness of the fragility and the dangers of illusion. *Kollege Crampton*, however, is almost a plea for the understanding and tolerance of the eccentricities and weaknesses of a creative (male) artist; here, as in *Einsame Menschen*, *Michael Kramer*, and *Die versunkene Glocke*, the artist's wife fails significantly to support him.

Since its first performance, when its success was attributed largely to the contribution of the actor, Georg Engels, in the title-role, *Kollege Crampton* has been regarded as a character-drama. Its episodic action is designed to reveal the protagonist's lack of a will strong enough to resist external circumstances, and his consequent tendency to escape, with the assistance of a vivid imagination and a liberal dose of alcohol, into the easier world of self-delusion. It did not pass unnoticed that Hauptmann's views on alcohol had changed radically since *Vor Sonnenaufgang*. Hartleben wrote a 'sixth act' for Hauptmann's play in which Crampton's pupil and benefactor, Max Straehler, returns from the theatre where he has seen the earlier play, and announces that he cannot now marry Crampton's daughter, Gertrud, because he fears she may have inherited her father's alcoholism.[17]

Kollege Crampton can end happily because Hauptmann sees to it that external circumstances do not resist the imaginative desires of his hero. The wealthy Max helps Crampton along by providing him with an ideal studio and a commission, so that he is completely sheltered from harsh reality; Max's brother enters into the spirit of the game by allowing Professor Crampton to persuade himself that he is to pay rent for the studio. The effect of all this bounty is a sudden urge of resolve by the hitherto inactive Crampton: 'Now we must really work, Max, like two navvies!' (I, 318). There is no Relling, as there is in *The Wild Duck*, to pour cold water on the illusion, but it is, to say the least, doubtful whether this final resolve holds out any real promise; particularly since Crampton spreads the burden of responsibility by his use of the first-person plural. There is no very strong evidence in the play that Crampton's gifts

---

[16] 'Über dramatische Kunst' (1914), *Die Kunst des Dramas: Über Schauspiel und Theater*, edited by Martin Machatzke (Berlin and Frankfurt a.M.: Propyläen, 1963) p. 139.

[17] 'Kollege Crampton, VIer Akt', *Freie Bühne*, 3 (1892), p. 218. Hartleben had been anticipated by a brief note in *Kladderadatsch*, 1890, p. 60: 'News from the Selicke family: a new misfortune, the country parson, Wendt, has written to break off the engagement. Reason: strong suspicion that the old man's alcoholism could be inherited by Toni.'

are not simply part of the illusion, particularly if one holds the view that the ability actually to create something is an integral part of creative ability.[18] There is little reason to believe that Crampton's talent will unfold more productively in his new-found, feather-bedded isolation, and the 'humour' of this play does not require that it should. The point about this kind of humour – and this is what makes it rather feeble – is that it involves an indulgent, patronizing tolerance, such as is extended to the waywardness of a child; and it is a certain childlike innocence which is presented as Crampton's most endearing feature.

In *Kollege Crampton*, as in *Der Biberpelz*, a more radical approach would surely have produced better comedy. What little amusement there is in the conclusion of *Kollege Crampton* derives from the automatic, predictable quality of Crampton's behaviour; from the suspicion, which might have been the certainty, that he will continue to behave as before, to drink, to idle away his time unproductively, and to delude himself that he is a potentially great man, hindered by a hostile and jealous environment.

If, as has been suggested, the satirical attack on the monomaniac – comedy as Bergson defines it – has an inherent conservative tendency, then how much truer is it that the tolerant 'humour' which replaces it, entirely in *Kollege Crampton*, partially in *Der Biberpelz*, tends towards the preservation of the existing social order by smiling on the weakness of those who come to terms with it. This kind of humour emerges in the later stages of Naturalism, along with an increase in tolerance to other means by which the individual can come to terms with a hostile world, for instance the religious compensations of Hilse and Hannele. Both developments take place after the period of greatest political commitment is over.

---

[18] On the evidence of Crampton's productivity it is difficult to agree with Guthke's confident attribution of major talent to him (*Tragikomödie*, p. 256).

10
SOME LATER DRAMAS

By 1898 Gerhart Hauptmann was Germany's most respected dramatist, although the works of Sudermann were more popular with the general public. He had behind him one undisputed and well-deserved success in *Die Weber*, perhaps the finest of all his works, but his other popular successes, *Der Biberpelz*, *Hanneles Himmelfahrt*, and *Die versunkene Glocke*, were much slighter works. The very real merits of the austere *Das Friedensfest* had not been fully appreciated, and his most ambitious play, *Florian Geyer*, had, to Hauptmann's great disappointment, met with a cool response from public and critics alike. It is to the works of the next ten or so years, which include *Und Pippa tanzt!* (1906) and the novel, *Der Narr in Christo Emanuel Quint* (1910), as well as the later Naturalist dramas, that Hauptmann owes his enduring reputation. These dramas, the four most important of which I shall examine in this chapter, were widely regarded as marking a return by Hauptmann to his earlier Naturalist style, perhaps even the culmination of this style, although they were, of course, written when Naturalism had long ceased to exist as a closely-knit literary movement, and when Hauptmann himself was no longer writing exclusively in the Naturalist vein.[1] The purpose of this chapter is to assess the importance of the Naturalist experiment for Gerhart Hauptmann; to consider how much of the original scientific-rationalist impulse remains, and in what way this is responsible for the excellence or the shortcomings of these later works.

These plays do provide something of a bridge between the earliest works and Hauptmann's later, more strenuously 'poetic' works; and they begin to show clearly Hauptmann's preoccupation with the theme of human suffering. They have therefore, more than any other of his plays, been taken by critics as a key to the understanding of the oeuvre of Gerhart Hauptmann. Again and again it is to these works that critics have turned for the clearest – and in the case of *Rose Bernd* probably the finest – examples of Hauptmann's achievement in giving dramatic shape to the painful oppression of the trapped and the pursued; again and again the student of Hauptmann will encounter such quotations as Henschel's fatalistic lament: 'a trap was set for me, and

---

[1] Cf. Peter Sprengel, 'Gerhart Hauptmann: *Die Ratten*', in *Interpretationen: Dramen des Naturalismus* (Stuttgart: Reclam, 1988), pp. 243–82 (pp. 245–46).

I just fell into it' (I, 993); *Rose Bernd's* despairing outcry: 'I have fallen into trap after trap, so that I have just not been able to come back to my senses' (II, 256); Frau John's dull protest at the excruciating pressure she must always endure: 'Fear! Worry! You have no idea what it is' (II, 773).

In order to present a total picture of Hauptmann's world-view, or to support a particular interpretation of his plays, a number of critics have also looked outside his dramas, and considered other of his comments on the problem of suffering, such as the following, from the short essay 'Von den Möglichkeiten des Theaters' (1930):

Der Kampf von Menschen untereinander wird auch im Drama höheren Stiles dargestellt. Über allem jedoch zeigt es den Kampf mit der unsichtbaren Macht, die wir mit dem Namen 'Schicksal' getauft haben. Auf seiner Bühne ist am Ende nicht mehr der Mensch des Menschen Feind. Vielmehr erkennt er sich selbst und erkennt den andern und weiß unter der Hellsicht des Schmerzes meistens, daß sie beide schuldig-schuldlos sind. Sich ihm ergeben ist hier die einzige Form, sich über das Schicksal zu erheben (VI, 813).	The conflict of man against man is also presented in the drama of high style. But it shows primarily the conflict with that invisible power which we call 'Fate'. On this stage man is no longer the enemy of man. Rather he recognizes himself and others for what they are, and generally, in the lucidity occasioned by pain, recognizes that they are both at the same time innocent and guilty. To yield before it is here the only way of overcoming Fate.

There are certain obvious dangers in approaching Hauptmann's work in this way. However interesting and informative Hauptmann's occasional essays and speeches may be – and his greatest admirers would not claim that they are consistently either, for he is not a great theorist or critic – they can only ever be of secondary importance in the interpretation of his dramas. Speculation about the intentions of any author is not often a very rewarding pursuit; and this is especially true where an author of plays like *Vor Sonnenaufgang* and *Einsame Menschen* is concerned. It would, I believe, be mistaken to read Hauptmann's plays in the light of his supposed intentions, and to see in them a pattern of suffering and transcendence, leading to a lucid understanding of the tragic constitution of the universe. In the four plays which I intend to discuss there is still a sufficient residue of the relativism of the Naturalists to call in question the validity of any claims to absolute knowledge. Moreover to insist that all the rich realistic details of these plays are only there as symbols of a deeper level of reality, is to falsify Hauptmann's achievements as a dramatist.

Michael Kramer (1900) is the play which might be said to embody a philosophy of suffering in the most explicit form; it is therefore the least dramatic and, by any standards, the least naturalistic of these four works. It relates the story of Kramer's son, Arnold, who wastes his talent, disappoints his father's hopes, and suffers humiliation and persecution at the hands of a group of bourgeois philistines, until eventually he can bear no more, and commits suicide. Kramer's daughter, Michaline, and a former pupil, Lachmann, have lengthy roles, but no importance in the dramatic action; they never appear on stage at the same time as Arnold (except for one brief moment in the third act, when he rushes past them in his flight from the Bänsch restaurant), and they do not influence the action around him in any way. Their principal and rather obtrusive function is to establish by direct characterization the stature of Michael Kramer, and so the authority of what he says.[2] Their secondary function is to complete the philosophical dialogue, by providing a receptive audience for Michael Kramer. This second function is frequently little more than a formality, for many of Kramer's speeches have a quality which Hauptmann sought to avoid in the ideological speeches of Loth in *Vor Sonnenaufgang,* namely a sententiousness which one associates with speeches aimed, as it were, over the head of the on-stage listener directly at the audience. In the final act, at the climax of his philosophizing, Hauptmann is clearly straining against the limitations of Naturalist doctrine and the conventions of Naturalist practice, for he virtually gives Kramer a monologue: Lachmann, to whom Kramer's words are ostensibly being addressed, retires behind a curtain, taking a candle to set beside the corpse of Arnold, and leaving Kramer alone visible to the audience to make the apparently authoritative judgement: 'When something great appears before us,... then everything petty is, as it were, swept away. That which is petty is divisive, that which is great unifies... Death is always great... Death and love'.

Through his suffering and in his death Arnold is judged to have triumphed over his persecutors: 'That which deigns to crush us is both glorious and monstrous. We feel it, we almost see it...out of suffering we become – great' (I, 1168). But, as so often in the dramas of Hauptmann, there remains a discrepancy between the character's words and the objective evidence (i.e. the evidence of the drama) on which these words are based. Although there is no sign of an attempt to undermine Kramer's authority in the way we have seen the authority of

---

[2] Although one might expect it to have been frowned upon by the theorists, direct characterization occurs quite frequently in the German Naturalist drama: in *Vor Sonnenaufgang* there is Loth's self-characterization, and there is his description of the drunken old Krause; in *Das Friedensfest* Robert provides direct characterizations of all the members of the Scholz family; in *Einsame Menschen* there is Anna's disparaging analysis of Braun; in *Die Familie Selicke,* Wendt's eulogy of Toni.

other characters undermined, his statements do not carry a great deal of conviction. This is very largely because an attempt to make Arnold's triumph all-embracing has, in fact, trivialized it. For what exactly is Arnold's triumph?

Among the characters who assemble in the final act to pay homage to the dead Arnold is Liese, the daughter of the restaurant-proprietor Bänsch, whom Arnold had favoured with so much attention. She, the representative of the philistine world which despised and destroyed Arnold, arrives on the scene just in time to hear Michael Kramer's words of praise for his son's genius: 'I look up to this boy as if he were my oldest ancestor' (I, 1171), words which seem, in retrospect, to justify Arnold's boasts of Act III:

Reisen Sie mal nach München hin und fragen Sie 'rum bei den Professoren... ob die wohl vor mir verfluchten... Respekt haben... Die haben Respekt und die wissen warum. Ich kann mehr, wie die Kerle alle zusammen. Im kleinen Finger. Zehntausendmal mehr. Mein eigner Vater mit inbegriffen (I, 1145).	Just go to Munich and ask the professors... if they damn well respect me. They respect me, and they know why. I can do more than all of them put together. With my little finger. Ten thousand times more. My own father included.

But these were childish boasts, whose adolescent assertiveness is skilfully indicated in the superfluous final reference to the father; and in context they were intended to impress Liese by appealing to her essentially trivial criteria of worldly, and especially financial, success. To contrive a scene which justifies these boasts is to create a triumph of a very insignificant order.

Nor is there, if we consider this too in context, very much substance to the proclamation of a greater triumph made by Arnold's father, for Hauptmann does not seriously attempt to convince us that what Kramer says has any validity outside his own imagination, and it is on this that the meaning of the play ultimately depends. As its title suggests, this play is essentially a character-drama, and it is concerned with the development of Michael Kramer himself, in the face of the great suffering caused him by his son.[3] Disappointed that his son has squandered a precious talent, Kramer has tried to guide him, only to find that

---

[3] Compare the interpretation of this play by Helmut F. Pfanner which decisively places Michael Kramer himself at the centre, and suggests that his two children, the sterile, but stable Michaline, and the gifted, but unstable Arnold, are to be seen as an externalization of his own inner conflict: 'Deutungsprobleme in Gerhart Hauptmanns "Michael Kramer"', *Monatshefte*, 62 (1970), pp. 45–54.

he, too, has failed, and cannot approach his son as a father should. He is not the man to disown his son, and so Arnold's failures, suffering, and eventual death become the father's suffering. Through this experience he comes to change his attitude towards his son, and in the end he ceases to insist that Arnold had wasted his talent. He looks through his dead son's sketches with a tolerance he had not previously practised: 'There are all his persecutors assembled. There they are, you see, as he saw them. And listen, he had eyes. It's a truly evil point of view, but it's a point of view all the same!' (I, 1168).

These sketches are the creation of an imagination distorted by pain and persecution, and Kramer accepts his son's subjective insight on these terms, as a thing of value; he does not suggest that Arnold's suffering has produced a transcendent lucidity. This may prompt us to recall a brief exchange between Michaline and Lachmann in Act III:

LACHMANN. Die Kraft zur Illusion das ist der beste Besitz in der Welt. MICHALINE. Du meinst also eigentlich Phantasie; und ohne die kann ja ein Künstler nicht sein. LACHMANN. Ja. Phantasie und den Glauben daran (I, 1152).	LACHMANN. The power of illusion... that is the dearest possession in the world. MICHALINE. You really mean imagination then; and no one can be an artist without it. LACHMANN. Yes. Imagination, and the belief in it.

The conclusion of the play might well be considered in the light of these words. Michael Kramer's claims about his son's triumphant death might equally well be regarded as an illusion, the creation of an imagination distorted by a sense of failure, and involuntarily compensating. As a father's cry of regret, Kramer's final statements about Arnold have every justification in the structure of the drama, although another dramatist – Ibsen, Brecht, or even the younger Hauptmann – might have treated Michael Kramer less tenderly.

In explaining his change of attitude towards his son, Michael Kramer speaks the following words: 'Pain, pain, pain, pain. Just get a taste of what is in the word. You see, words are like that; they only occasionally come to life; in everyday life they remain dead.' (I, 1168). In the strictest sense (and external to the context), these words imply a rejection of Naturalism, which is, after all, precisely the literature of the everyday. They demand the application of principles of concentration and careful selection of material which are contrary to much early German Naturalist theory, and to most critical preconceptions about this particular literary style. Such principles did, of course, have some influence on the composition of even the first Naturalist dramas – especially on the choice of subject: the situation of crisis – but they were not applied with the consistency with which they are applied in the four plays under discussion in this chapter. Here the dramatist's attention is focussed almost exclusively on those characters whose imaginative power or disposition makes them particularly open to intense mental anguish. This was not immediately appreciated by those of Hauptmann's contemporaries who had turned their backs on Naturalism, and some dismissed his renewed concern with inarticulate (or just lower-class) characters as a retrogressive step, which decisively limited the spiritual content of the drama. Among such critics was the erstwhile pioneer of Naturalism, Julius Hart, who wrote of *Fuhrmann Henschel*: 'we are groping about again in the dark and foggy atmosphere of the old "fate-drama", which was, of course, an essentially naturalist form, and suffered from the deficiency which is so evident in Gerhart Hauptmann's play, the narrowness and constriction of spiritual life.'[4] Such criticism, however, misses Hauptmann's crucial point: Henschel's inarticulateness implies a limitation on his intellect, but not on his imagination. Indeed, the contrast between Henschel and the rationalist Siebenhaar (like the contrast between the brothers Robert and Wilhelm Scholz in *Das Friedensfest*) shows intellect and imagination varying in inverse proportion. Henschel is totally exposed; he has no defence against his destructive imagination. As Hauptmann wrote elsewhere: 'Wer sich der Phantasie ergibt, muß sie beherrschen', ('Whoever gives himself over to the imagination must know how to control it') (VI, 995).

The rigour with which the principles of selection and concentration are applied results in the much tauter dramatic structure of the later as compared to the earlier Naturalist dramas. The basic dramatic technique remains the same; as in *Vor Sonnenaufgang* and plays like it such as Halbe's *Jugend*, Dreyer's *Winterschlaf*, or Schlaf's *Meister Oelze*, the dramatist takes a violent or disturbing act and explains the events leading up to it. Now more experienced in the theatre, he tends to exclude anything which does not bear directly on the outcome. There is a similar moderation of the more radical features of naturalist dramaturgy in the work of Johannes Schlaf. In the revised version of *Meister Oelze*, published in 1909, he tightened the structure of the action considerably by major cuts and he eliminated from the last act everything which delays the approaching death of the central figure.[5] In this

---

[4] 'Hauptmanns jüngstes Bühnenwerk', *Das literarische Echo*, 1 (1898–99), 284.

[5] See Helmut Praschek, 'Zum Zerfall des naturalistischen Stils: Ein Vergleich zweier Fassungen des *Meister Oelze* von Johannes Schlaf', in *Worte und Werte: Bruno Markwardt zum 60. Geburtstag*, edited by Gustav Erdmann and Alfons Eichstaedt (Berlin: de Gruyter,

context it is interesting to note that Hauptmann was prompted to write *Rose Bernd* (1903), the tautest in structure of all his Naturalist dramas, by his experience as a juror at the trial of a village girl for infanticide in April 1903, and that this drama was completed by September and given its première in October of the same year.[6]

Concentration, then, is achieved by the elimination of inessentials, resulting in a tendency towards 'closed' rather than 'open' form.[7] In the earlier works characters did not develop, and a full story could only be told by the (often implausible) compression of a large number of events into a brief period of time; the causal process leading up to these events was revealed – with an implausible rapidity – through the intervention of an inquisitive stranger. The later plays resemble *Einsame Menschen* in that they stretch over a longer period of time. The action of *Rose Bernd* lasts four to five months, that of *Fuhrmann Henschel* (1898) over a year, and so a story can be told in its entirety. The act intervals represent a longer chronological break, and so contain more new events which are revealed retrospectively in the course of the following act: the rape in *Rose Bernd*, the murder of Pauline Piperkarcka in *Die Ratten* (1911). Dramatic action is thus more consistently a reaction by the characters to events which have already taken place, but which the audience has not witnessed. The passage of time seems more uniform; there is no call for those hurried conclusions which the younger Hauptmann tended to impose when it seemed there was no more material left to uncover.

The principle of concentration is also applied in the treatment of character and milieu; but here again the earlier dramatic technique has been refined rather than radically altered. The earliest Naturalist dramas were certainly rich in gratuitous background detail, but the dramatists were seldom guilty of the literal-mindedness of the theatre-director who, following the example of the Duke of Meiningen, played *Wallensteins Lager* in a snowstorm because the history books said the events took place on 22 February.[8] The Christmas setting, which is common to *Die Familie Selicke* and *Das Friedensfest*, the lighting directions in *Einsame Menschen*, have a clearly symbolic function, and are not just gratuitous details. Schlaf's revision of *Meister Oelze* is again symptomatic. The later version omits the directions that Oelze should spit on the stage, but the

---

1961), pp. 315–21; see also Helmut Scheuer, 'Johannes Schlaf: *Meister Oelze*', in *Interpretationen: Dramen des Naturalismus* (Stuttgart: Reclam, 1988), pp. 147–77 (pp. 150–53).
[6] Roy C. Cowen, *Hauptmann-Kommentar zum dramatischen Werk* (Munich: Winkler, 1980), p. 134.
[7] See Volker Klotz, *Geschlossene und offene Form im Drama*, 6th edition (Munich: Hanser, 1972; first published 1969).
[8] Joachim Weno, 'Der Theaterstil des Naturalismus' (unpublished doctoral thesis, Berlin, 1951), p. 210. See also John Osborne, *The Meiningen Court Theatre, 1866–1890* (Cambridge: C.U.P, 1988), p. 160.

tubercular coughing which announces his arrival remains, not as a simple shock effect, but as a means of arousing in the audience a feeling of disgust for Oelze which the conclusion of the play requires.

While the structure of *Fuhrmann Henschel* is still relatively slack and many episodes are not fully integrated – it is, for instance, difficult to see the significance of all the scenes involving Franziska Wermelskirch – most of the detail in *Rose Bernd* can be seen to be functional in theatrical terms: the ominous hum of Streckmann's threshing machine, the oppressive weather of Act III, which suggests the imminent breaking of a storm, and the whole progress of the drama from spring to autumn, from morning to evening, from a fruitful landscape to old Bernd's chilly middle-class parlour.[9] Like the title of *Die Ratten*, all this is evidence of a conscious intensification of the symbolic, and a re-assertion of those elements of Poetic Realism inherited by the German Naturalists.

It is this symbolic aspect of Hauptmann's work which many of his admirers have chosen to emphasize at the expense of the more straightforward realistic elements. In an interpretation of *Rose Bernd*, which is in many ways quite excellent, Hans-Joachim Schrimpf argues, reasonably enough, that Hauptmann has used the Naturalist manner in detailed description, milieu, biological and psychological motivation, but without thereby explaining the real causes of the catastrophe. These, he argues, are to be sought in some incomprehensible fate, while social reality, heredity, milieu, and external circumstances are 'only' [sic] the medium through which this obscure power operates.[10]

The Naturalist theorist, Wilhelm Bölsche, saw man as a victim in a deterministic system whose mainsprings we do not fully understand;[11] because Hauptmann's plays reveal him as sharing this uncertainty they are to some extent open to speculative interpretations as fate-dramas. There is, however, little positive evidence in the plays to support such interpretations. Hauptmann does not make at all clear the precise nature of the destructive force which seems to operate against mankind, and, more important, he does not make it clear whether this force has any objective existence outside the imagination of the victim. In any case, whatever his intention, his achievement, and it is a very considerable achievement, has been to capture the suffering of the victim as it unfolds in the here and now. Hauptmann's understanding of the form this suffering takes, how it works, how it affects the victim and his

---

[9] H. J. Schrimpf, 'Rose Bernd', *Das deutsche Drama*, edited by Benno von Wiese, 2 vols (Düsseldorf: Bagel, 1968), II, 166–85 (p. 178).

[10] Schrimpf, 'Rose Bernd', p. 173.

[11] *Die naturwissenschaftlichen Grundlagen der Poesie: Prolegomena einer realistischen Ästhetik* (Leipzig: Reißner, 1887), p. 3.

fellow men, is more profound than his unclear implications about its first causes or its transcendent significance. This is first and foremost the achievement of a dramatist with an instinctive awareness of the specific characteristics of his chosen medium; but it is also, I would venture to suggest, an achievement which owes a great deal to Naturalist demands for observation and imitation as the first essentials in artistic creation.

In this respect *Fuhrmann Henschel*, *Rose Bernd*, and *Die Ratten* are better plays than the less dramatic *Michael Kramer*, in which a philosophy of suffering is more lucidly expounded. In all four plays, however, the meticulous attention to details of causation implies a rational attempt to explain the catastrophe. In *Michael Kramer* we learn from Michaline that her mother was largely responsible for the alienation of her father and her brother (I, 1166). This takes us right back to the problem of *Das Friedensfest*, the complicated family relationships which arise from an unhappy marriage; but we are given little of the insight into this social situation provided by the earlier play, and no opportunity to assess at first hand the real influence of this factor. Although heredity and environment do not have an absolutely dominant effect on the characters in any of these plays, in the other three their function is much more closely defined.

Economic factors, her humble social origins and her present position of dependence, do much to determine Hanne Schäl's relationship to Henschel. (She closely resembles Helene in Anzengruber's novel, *Der Sternsteinhof*, who starts out as a domestic servant with no means, and vigorously brushes aside all obstacles to become the owner of a farm.) Economic factors also play a part in Henschel's decision to marry Hanne, even if they do little more than assist him to rationalize his strong sexual attraction towards her. And hereditary weakness provides a perfectly logical explanation for the death of Henschel's sickly child, despite the suspicions of Hanne's enemies.

Rose Bernd's relationship to her seducer, Flamm, is also very strongly influenced by her inferior social status. The ambiguities of this relationship are captured very skilfully in the opening scenes of the play; despite Flamm's insistence that she should not address him in a formal way (II, 188), Rose is too unsure of herself to call him 'Christoph' very often, and occasionally she compromises, with 'Herr Christoph'.[12] Old Bernd is materially dependent on his daughter and – therefore – his prospective son-in-law. His desire to have Rose marry soon, and to have her marry August, is very closely connected with the latter's recent purchase of the Lachmann house. Streckmann's loose-living is associated with his peripatetic occupation as the operator of a threshing machine which serves many different farms (II, 197). Whilst it is the infirmity of

---

[12] Cf. W. Butzlaff, 'Die Enthüllungstechnik in Hauptmanns "*Rose Bernd*"', *Der Deutschunterricht*, 13 (1961), 63.

his wife, and the loss of their son, Kurt (of Rose's age), which first directed Flamm's attentions to Rose. The provincial, Silesian setting is an important aspect of *Fuhrmann Henschel* and *Rose Bernd*; but *Die Ratten* takes us back to the Berlin of *Der Biberpelz* and the Naturalist novel of the 1880s. Hauptmann returns to the city in order to condemn it as an environment hostile to the establishment of real contact between people.

The principal and overriding factor in the motivation of these plays is, as it was in the earlier works, the way people are fashioned, their dominant, inherent characteristics: the unfulfilled maternal instinct of Frau John, the robust sensuality of *Rose Bernd*, the sexual pride of Streckmann, the split personality of Henschel, which prompts him in his wife's illness to engage as a maid and, subsequently (like *Bahnwärter Thiel*) to marry, a woman whose whole nature is such as to bring about his disintegration between the two poles of his character. Causal explanations do not go beyond this point. No reason is offered to explain why characters should be so fashioned, or why circumstances should be so delicately balanced; and in these circumstances it is perfectly natural and rationally acceptable that the uncomprehending central figure should feel exposed and helpless, a victim of a cruel external fate; it is not unreasonable that a character such as Henschel should conclude: 'I have seen it clearly in my mind that there was something that had it in for me' (I, 993). There is therefore a set of reasons behind such conclusions which is sufficient to undermine any claim they have to objective truth; and yet there is no clear attempt on the part of the author to distance himself from these conclusions; he does not adopt a superior, ironic standpoint. It appears from this that for Hauptmann, the dramatist, the greater significance lay not with the question of the validity or non-validity of an interpretation of the world, but with the simple fact of its existence, and its consequences for the action of his play.

If the interpretation of the world is really a pained outcry, an expression of the personal feeling of exposure, then the force with which it is communicated to an audience will depend very much on that audience's view of its justification, and therefore on the strength with which the author (or, *faute de mieux*, the actor) endows the central character. It is here that *Fuhrmann Henschel* comes out badly in comparison with *Rose Bernd*, for the primitive Silesian hero, who is presented so much more sympathetically than the limited rationalist, Siebenhaar, and the rootless proletarian, Hanne, has a tendency to persecute himself which trivializes his genuine suffering. Hanne's advice, 'You shouldn't give in so easily' (I, 917), touches directly on his weakness. His very first entry, which is always of immense importance in the theatre, resembles that of Johannes Vockerat in *Einsame Menschen*; it immediately establishes him as a character lacking in any sort of resistance to misfortune: 'God only knows what's the matter: first my wife gets ill! then one of my horses breaks down! It's almost as if someone's got it in for me!' (I, 883). He lacks that indomitable spirit which could assert itself even through the dull resignation of the weavers. And he cannot begin to aspire to the mythological stature of Job, which Alfred Kerr claimed for him.[13]

The desire to lend an emotional depth and an expressive intensity to the drama could (and eventually did) result in the stylized, rhetorical drama of the Expressionists. But so long as this desire is combined with a Naturalist insistence on rational causation and plausibility, the dramatist will find himself increasingly forced to select the unusual and even the abnormal. Hauptmann justifies such selection as follows: 'The sphere of the healthy and normal is left in the height of passion. A drama without high passion is inconceivable, and so it must always reach out to some extent into the pathological' (VI, 1042). The weakness of Hauptmann's statement is one of the fundamental weaknesses of the Naturalist position; he does not here seem disposed to place a different valuation on the response to suffering of a neurotic and prematurely aged man (Henschel) and that of a strong, healthy woman in the prime of life (Rose Bernd). Nevertheless, the breakdown of a character who has shown the will to resist is bound to impress us as more moving, more nearly tragic, than the abject surrender of a person such as Henschel. Although it should be added that, on another occasion, Hauptmann himself seems to have shared this latter view: 'Ibsen generally sees tragedy in life's so-called failures. The tragedy of a fulfilled character is superior' (VI, 1043).

Because of the feebleness of Henschel, Hanne Schäl comes to demand much greater attention, despite her formal subordination in the play. Her strongest impulse is the one that is so deficient in him, the instinct of self-preservation. She ruthlessly strives to suppress all those qualities which might hinder her advance, even to the point of disowning her child. Her social climb is achieved at great cost in human terms, and it remains a precarious achievement. As long as she is struggling purposefully upwards her deeper anxieties are fully sublimated in frantic industry; but once she has arrived her security melts away. She cannot be at ease with her husband, and during his absences she is oppressed constantly by fear of his return. The desires of a hot-blooded young woman married to an older man find an outlet in her affair with the waiter, George, but the tension of expectation and the fear of discovery combine to prevent her from deriving any satisfaction from this affair; all she does derive is nervous irritation:

| Derweil hab ich alleene | And I was sitting here |
| gesessen und hab gewart't | alone waiting till late |

---
[13] 'Fuhrmann Henschel', *Neue Deutsche Rundschau*, 9 (1898), 1315.

bis tief in die Nacht. Eemal – ich weeß nich was das muß gewest sein! A Vogel muß sein ans Fenster geschlagen – da dacht ich du wärscht's, und ging ich ans Fenster und macht es auf. Hernach da ward ich aso verbost, ich konnte die halbe Nacht nich einschlafen. *Sie schlägt mit der Faust schwach auf den Tisch.* Ich weeß nich, ich bin auch noch immer verbost. (I, 943)	at night. Once – I don't know what it can have been! A bird must have bumped against the window – I thought it was you, and went and opened the window. And afterwards I was so irritable, I couldn't sleep for half the night. *She bangs on the table weakly with her fist.* I don't know, I'm always so irritable.

Her frequent outbursts of temper over trivial incidents cause us to wonder how long she can maintain her equilibrium, and they produce a certain sympathy for her, in the way evident weakness arouses sympathy even for Hoffmann in *Vor Sonnenaufgang* and Robert Scholz in *Das Friedensfest*. Despite their tough façade, here are three characters who are not utterly depraved; will they, in fact, stop short of utter depravity? It is speculation about Hanne's subsequent fate, rather than about where Henschel's suffering has led him, which merits our attention as the final curtain falls on this open-ended play.

The same question arises in *Die Ratten*, through the figure of Bruno Mechelke. Here, however, the central character, Henriette John, is a rather stronger character than Henschel, and so Bruno, her younger brother, does not attract a disproportionate amount of attention. His brief appearance in Act IV, after he has murdered Pauline, and the challenging bravado of his reply when his sister suggests that the police might catch him, implies that he, too, is strenuously attempting to conceal an inner disquiet: 'All right, they'll string me up, and then they'll have something else to cut up at the hospital' (II, 813).

In contrast to Henschel, Rose Bernd is a character whose glory is her strength, vigour and energy, as her father boasts – to Streckmann of all people (II, 200). The play, a starkly pessimistic work, reveals the hunting-down of a magnificent young woman, and her reduction to a state of abject despair. The causal process, as I have suggested, appears to begin in the individual make-up of the victim, in the sensuality of Rose, which causes her to become involved with Flamm. Flamm, for his part, is married to an invalid wife; and Rose's father is, for reasons of his own, eager to match her with a physically unequal partner in August. The actual details of the plot are exceedingly complex, because much remains unspoken and therefore misunderstood by the various characters. The crucial point is that once Rose knows she is expecting

Flamm's child she is in a vulnerable position, for she needs both to marry August (to regularise her situation as a mother), and to prevent Streckmann from gossiping about her association with Flamm (which could prevent her marriage). Streckmann, affronted in his sexual pride that Rose is attracted not to him, but to Flamm, will not be bought off with cash, and so Rose has no choice but to go to his cottage, as he suggests. Not knowing of the circumstances which are bearing down on Rose (her pregnancy), he does not realize that she only comes to him out of panic, and interprets her coming in the way one would expect a Streckmann to interpret it:

STRECKMANN. Du bist mir nachgelaufen dahie!	STRECKMANN. You came running after me!
ROSE. Was...?	ROSE. What...?
STRECKMANN. Bist in meine Wohnung gekomm'n und hast mir de Helle heeß gemacht.	STRECKMANN. You came to my house and made things hot for me.
ROSE. Und du...	ROSE. And what about you
STRECKMANN. Nu was denn?	STRECKMANN. Well, what about me?
ROSE. Und du? Und du?	ROSE. And what about you? What did you do?
STRECKMANN. A Kostverächter biin ich halt ni.	STRECKMANN. I never refuse anything tasty.
ROSE. Streckmann!... Ich bin zu dir gelaufa in Himmelsangst! Ich hoa dich um's Himmels wille gebattelt... du sullst m'r mit August'n a Weg freigahn. Ich biin uff a Knien gekruchen vor dir und du sagst itz, ich wär dir nachgelaufa? Asu is: du hust a Verbrecha geton!! Du hust an mir a Verbrecha beganga!! (II, 227).	ROSE. Streckmann!... I came running to you in fear of my life. I begged you for God's sake... to leave me and August alone. I crawled on my knees to you, and you're saying I was running after you? Here's how it was: you committed a crime!! You committed a crime against me!!

The possibility that there might be some way out for Rose is not entirely excluded; the tragedy is that she is unable to see this. Certainly she can expect nothing from Flamm; the end of Act IV shows that sexual jealousy is no less a fault in him than in Streckmann; but he is not a strong character, and Frau Flamm is perfectly willing to help Rose. Act V shows that August, who has matured considerably in the course of the play, is also sympathetic, and he comes forward with a familiar but manifestly sincere proposal: 'We'll go abroad.. I've got an uncle out in Brazil. We'll manage together' (II, 257). Moreover, Rose's father is not the obstacle which Meister Anton is in Hebbel's *Maria Magdalene*, for, although self-righteous and narrow-minded, he is somewhat feeble in the exercise of his authority, and, provided he can go to church he is content to let Rose get on with the work, even on a Sunday.[14]

What prevents Rose from taking, or even trying to take either possibility of escape is the feeling of guilt which clouds her relationship with just those two characters who offer help; she does not expect, and so hardly seems to hear, their offers. She lacks the hardness which enables Hanne Schäl to take from anybody, and is therefore thrown back on herself. Like Hauptmann's weavers, she does not calculate very far ahead; her lies are a primitive attempt at self-defence by an unreflective character, and they only get her more deeply ensnared:

ROSE. 's is nischt zwischen uns gewest, a liegt! FLAMM. Sagt a, daß zwischen euch was gewest ist!? ROSE. Ich sag' weiter nischte, als daß a liegt! (II, 243)	ROSE. There wasn't anything between us; he's a liar. FLAMM. Does he say there was something between you!? ROSE. I'm not saying anything, except that he's a liar.

The climax of the play comes when Rose gives up the struggle, when her lies give way to a shrill condemnation of the world in which she has suffered:

Aus Lieg'n und Trieg'n besteht die Welt.... Da hoa ich wull erntin de Sterne gesehn! Da hoa ich wull ernt geschrien und geruffa! Kee himmlischer Vater hat sich geriehrt.... Itze is halt was ieber uns alle gekomm – ma hat sich dagegen gewohrt und gewohrt (II, 256).	The world is nothing but lies and deceit. I looked up at the stars! And I cried and screamed. No father in heaven stirred.... Something has fallen upon us all – no matter how hard we struggled against it.

Now this is precisely what we would expect from Rose in her particular circumstances of pain and isolation, and we ought therefore to be rather hesitant about interpreting these words as a genuine tragic insight. To be dramatically convincing and humanly significant the words need be

---

[14] Schrimpf, *'Rose Bernd'*, gives a comparison of *Rose Bernd* with *Maria Magdalene* and Wagner's *Die Kindermörderin*. The question of influence is not of major importance, but it is interesting to note that Hebbel's play was in performance at the *Deutsches Theater* from 5 November 1901.

no more than a cry of protest. The last words of the play are spoken by August; he certainly does not accept the universal validity of Rose's pessimistic generalizations, nor does he, after the initial shock, dwell on the horror of her crime, but he cuts instinctively across all moralizing to proclaim with compassion and admiration: 'That girl...what she must have suffered!' (II, 259).

This display of profound sympathy for the character who is by temperament open to suffering is, as we have seen, a feature common to many of Hauptmann's plays. But this openness to suffering is not admired for the tragic insights which it might bring, rather for the human qualities which are complementary to it. Characters like Paul John, old Bernd, and Hanne Schäl can close themselves up in an attempt to protect themselves, but the price they pay in human terms is very high. Hauptmann admires in his open characters their idealism, their preservation of traditional values of unselfishness, generosity, consideration for others; in the domestic dramas this means especially values associated with the family. This is most clearly evident in the case of Henriette John; but it is also true of Michael Kramer, who bitterly regrets his failure as a father; while Henschel, in his concern for Hanne's child, and Rose in her devotion to her father and to Frau Flamm, are contrasted sharply with Hanne, who can deny her own child, and old Bernd, who bigotedly turns his back on his despairing daughter. Hauptmann was sufficiently in tune with the thought and attitudes of his day to know that these old values are fragile, that they are often based on illusions, and that to accept them is to expose oneself to suffering or ridicule, but he shrinks from the alternative.

A brief consideration of Schlaf's play *Meister Oelze* will illustrate the transitional position of Naturalism in a rather different way. The play shows a bitter trial of strength between Oelze and his step-sister, Pauline, in which the latter is trying to extract the confession that Oelze murdered her father and cheated her out of her inheritance. She has justice on her side, but is motivated by the same impulse as her stepbrother, the desire for property for herself and her family. She works ruthlessly on the conscience of the sick Oelze, but he possesses a primitive resilience which enables him to hold out to the end. It was this resilience which Schlaf chose to emphasize in a retrospective Nietzschean interpretation of the conclusion of the play as the victory of a strong masculine will over the extreme tortures of a guilty conscience.[15] Another interpretation of the conclusion is, however, possible, for Oelze's victory is a pyrrhic victory; the struggle to preserve his property costs him his life. However amoral he would like to be, he, like Hanne Schäl, is not secure from the qualms of conscience. The unresolved

---
[15] 'Die Freie Bühne', *Der Greif*, 1, ii, 48.

conflict within and between the two main characters ensures that *Meister Oelze* is more than just another celebration of the Nietzschean superman, and makes it one of the better works by the minor dramatists of German Naturalism.

11
THE DRAMATIC STYLE OF NATURALISM

Diderot, Lessing, auch Goethe und Schiller in ihrer Jugend, wendeten sich in neuerer Zeit vornehmlich der Seite realer Natürlichkeit zu... Diese Art der Natürlichkeit aber kann bei einer Überfülle bloß realer Züge leicht wieder nach einer anderen Seite ins Trockene und Prosaische hineingeraten, insofern die Charaktere nicht die Substanz ihres Gemüts und ihrer Handlung entwickeln, sondern nur, was sie in der ganz unmittelbaren Lebendigkeit ihrer Individualität ohne höheres Bewußtsein über sich und ihre Verhältnisse empfinden, zur Äußerung bringen... Natürliche Menschen verhalten sich in ihren Unterredungen und Streitigkeiten überwiegend als bloß einzelne Personen, die, wenn sie ihrer unmittelbaren Besonderheiten nach geschildert sein sollen, nicht in ihrer substantiellen Gestalt aufzutreten im Stande sind.... Das echt Poetische wird... darin bestehen, das Charakteristische und Individuelle der unmittelbaren Realität in das reinigende Element der Allgemeinheit

Diderot, Lessing, and also the young Goethe and Schiller, are among modern authors who espoused a predominantly naturalistic mode of expression. This kind of naturalism, however, can, because of an excess of merely realistic features, easily fall into the extreme of prosaic flatness, in that the characters are not allowed to develop the essential characteristics of their inner life and action, but express only what they experience directly as individuals, without any higher awareness of themselves or their situation... Real people, in their daily conversations and arguments, generally behave as merely single individuals; if they are to be depicted as such they cannot be seen in their substantive – form... True poetry... will raise the characteristic and individual features of actual reality into the purifying medium of universality and

zu erheben, und beide Seiten	so reconcile the
sich miteinander vermitteln	two sides with one
zu lassen.[1]	another.

Hegel, writing long before the emergence of a Naturalist movement in Germany, or any other country, has provided a basis for much of the criticism of German Naturalism, so his words provide a suitable starting point for this concluding chapter. The purpose of the chapter is to consider two separate aspects of this criticism; that is to consider the charge that the concentration by the German Naturalist dramatists on precise realistic detail has the effect of restricting the scope of their work by lending it the appearance of the purely individual case-history; and, secondly, to consider the further objection, that the characters in a drama of this kind – and particularly the characters in Hauptmann's dramas – lack that awareness of their own predicament which, according to the strictest Hegelians, is a necessary pre-condition of representative stature.

Such criticism has come from widely divergent sources. On the one hand, Wilhelm Dilthey is critical of the association of art and science in Naturalism.[2] Truth, he agrees, should be the object of literature, but the revelation of truth consists in finding a central point of vantage from which life can be comprehended in its totality. Thus the base and the ugly can only figure in art if they are shown in relation to the beautiful and the valuable. Memory is still the mother of the muses, but we come nearer to the artistic act when we cease to try and recall the single, particular impressions of one isolated moment, and use the memory creatively to produce images which represent objects in all their perceivable aspects.[3]

Representative significance, in a social–historical sense, was the principal criterion by which the Marxist critic, Franz Mehring judged the dramas of German Naturalism; he condemns *Einsame Menschen*, recognizing in its hero, Johannes Vockerat, no more than the 'Friedrichshagen type', but praises the characterization of Hoffmann (the bourgeois social-climber) in *Vor Sonnenaufgang*, and the old Heinickes ('Lumpenproletariat') in Sudermann's *Die Ehre* (1889). At the same time he criticizes the amassing of detail which he regards as gratuitous in *Vor Sonnenaufgang*

---

[1] G. W. F. Hegel, 'Vorlesungen über die Ästhetik', *Sämtliche Werke*, Jubiläumsausgabe, edited by Hermann Glockner, XIV (Stuttgart: F. Fromann, 1954), 496.

[2] Wilhelm Dilthey, 'Die drei Epochen der modernen Ästhetik und ihre heutige Aufgabe' (1892), *Gesammelte Schriften*, 19 vols (Leipzig and Berlin: Teubner; Göttingen: Vandenhoeck and Ruprecht, 1914–82), VI, ii (1924), 242–87.

[3] 'Goethe und die dichterische Phantasie', in *Das Erlebnis und die Dichtung* (1877) (Leipzig and Berlin: Teubner, 1922), p. 182.

and *Kollege Crampton*, citing the words of Engels: 'True realism is not built on the minor and coincidental characteristics of individuals.'[4]

Clearly the social realism which a critic such as Mehring would regard as the ideal kind of literature is not the kind of literature which would have appealed to Dilthey, but that need not concern us here. These dissimilar viewpoints converge in rejection of Naturalism; just as in both the early and the later – Marxist – criticism of Lukács, Naturalism is rejected with equal firmness. Holz's statement that art has the tendency to be nature again is not seen in such criticism in the differentiated way of our earlier discussion, but as a programmatic statement of the Naturalists' artistic intentions. The works of the Naturalists are seen as small, individual sections of life, shown in extensive totality, where the presence of detail in description, to the minutest degree, localizes the action, effectively excluding any symbolic intensification or raising to type, and making the Naturalist drama nothing more than the reportage which Wedekind satirizes in *Die junge Welt*.

Among the Marxist critics, Helmut Praschek supports his argument with an original and ingenious analysis of certain plays, which suggests that the German Naturalist dramatists deliberately reinforced the effect of particularization by the systematic exploitation of improbability. Coincidences such as Loth's meeting with two old friends, Hoffmann and Schimmelpfennig in *Vor Sonnenaufgang*, the Christmas reunion of the Scholz family in *Das Friedensfest*, the sudden and violent deaths at the conclusion of *Die Weber* and Halbe's *Jugend*, – in short, all those occurrences which, however fully motivated, strike us as possible, but improbable – are held to emphasize the singularity and so the completely unrepresentative nature, of the 'slice of life' which has been dramatized.[5] A theoretical pendant to this practice could perhaps be found in the words of Bölsche who argued that closer observation could well lead a writer to make more, not less, use of coincidence in his work.[6]

The most cursory examination of the Naturalist dramas will reveal ample evidence for such an interpretation. Indeed, the extent of detail in stage-directions and cast-lists is the feature which strikes most readers most immediately. This applies particularly when – as they frequently are – dramatic characters are based on real-life characters; as,

---

[4] Mehring's comments on the various plays are to be found in *Gesammelte Schriften*, edited by Thomas Höhle, Hans Koch, and Josef Schleifstein, 12 vols (Berlin: Dietz, 1960–63), XI, 190, 191, 199, 245.

[5] H. Praschek, 'Das Verhältnis von Kunsttheorie und Kunstschaffen im Bereich der deutschen naturalistischen Dramatik' (doctoral thesis, University of Greifswald, 1957), p. 30.

[6] *Die naturwissenschaftlichen Grundlagen der Poesie: Prolegomena einer realistischen Ästhetik* (Leipzig: Reißner, 1887), pp. 85–86.

for instance, in the case of Professor Crampton, Robert Scholz, the brothers Friedrich and Wilhelm Kern in Ernst von Wolzogen's *Das Lumpengesindel* (1892), and most of the characters in Holz's and Ernst's *Sozialaristokraten* and Hauptmann's *Der Biberpelz*.[7] As far as the action of the plays is concerned, the diffuseness of the Naturalist drama is very often the direct result of a tendency to compile rather than condense: in *Die Familie Selicke* we witness five different kinds of reaction to the death of Linchen, instead of one typical expression of grief; in *Die Weber* we experience a whole range of possible reactions to the oppression exerted by the factory-owners, from the anger of an outraged mother of starving children, and the self-assertion of the braggart, to the ambiguous quiescence of the pietist, Hilse, and the complacent indifference of the traveller from the town; and Hauptmann's first three plays can be seen as a trilogy, constituting an exhaustive discussion of three possible solutions to one basic problem.[8] The effect of such a style is to undermine the economy normally associated with the dramatic form; instead of that concentrated and intensive presentation of the essential, which Lukács regards as dramatic, we are shown the more extensive picture of reality, which he describes as epic, and which he also criticises in the *description* (as opposed to narration) which he finds in the novels of Zola.[9]

The burden of criticism such as that to which I have been referring is that in a drama the detail of the Naturalist style is superfluous, except on its own misconceived terms as a reflection of the planlessness of life. Even on these terms, however, much of this detail is still dispensable, for it is so minute as to be imperceptible: in *Die Familie Selicke* there is a stage direction which tells us that Walter returns to his room, and that the light shines through a chink in his door until, eventually, it is extinguished. Other stage-directions are, quite simply, unrealizable: Act I of Halbe's *Freie Liebe* contains stage-directions indicating the time registered by a clock on the stage, but it is scarcely

---

[7] Like the brothers Hassenpflug in Hauptmann's novel, *Der Narr in Christo Emanuel Quint*, the Kerns were modelled on Heinrich and Julius Hart. Actors, as well as authors, often used this kind of esoteric detail in their impersonations. Rittner is said to have based his interpretation of the role of Hans in *Jugend* on the play's author, Halbe; and Kainz is said to have impersonated Conrad Alberti when playing Bäcker in *Die Weber*. On *Der Biberpelz* see the detailed investigations by Bruno Fischer, 'Gerhart Hauptmann und Erkner: Quellenkundliche Studien zum 'Biberpelz' und anderen Werken', *Zeitschrift für deutsche Philologie*, 81 (1962), 440–72; and Walter Requardt and Martin Machatzke, *Gerhart Hauptmann und Erkner: Studien zum Berliner Frühwerk* (Berlin: Erich Schmidt, 1980).

[8] Cf. above, p. 133.

[9] *Die Theorie des Romans* (Berlin: Paul Cassirer, 1920), p. 31. See also: 'Grundlagen der Unterscheidung von Epik und Dramatik', *Aufbau*, 9 (1955), 978–91; 'The Zola Centenary' (1940), in *Studies in European Realism: A Sociological survey of the writings of Balzac, Stendhal, Zola, Tolstoy, Gorki and others* (London: Hillway, 1950), pp. 85–96; 'Erzählen oder Beschreiben' (1936), in *Probleme des Realismus* (Berlin: Aufbau, 1955), pp. 103–45.

conceivable that the dialogue Halbe has provided could be stretched to fill the amount of time it ought to fill.[10] It is equally unlikely that an actor could successfully follow all the impressionistic stage-directions of Hauptmann's early plays; and even given a performer such as Eleonora Duse, who could apparently flush or turn pale at will,[11] it is unlikely that such details could have been noticed by the average member of the audience, seated at some distance, in theatres which, in the 1890s were still without technically sophisticated lighting resources, and in which the upward shadows cast by the footlights tended to obscure the face.[12] Nor are such details always the result of great care and great thought on the part of the author; before the collected edition of 1942, the text of Hauptmann's *Die Weber* included a stage-direction that the one-armed Hilse should join his hands in prayer.

If we were to accept the view that the accumulation of detail does limit decisively the scope of the drama, then we must surely be inclined to conclude that all the German Naturalist dramas have no more than cultural–historical value to the modern reader; like old newsreels, they tell us what sort of clothes people used to wear, or how they used to furnish their houses. This is the view of Guthke, but predictably he makes one exception – Hauptmann – for the wrong reason: namely that Hauptmann's plays are coherent entities, which expose a clear meaning ('gegliederte sinntragende Ganzheiten') in a way that the Naturalist milieu-drama, such as *Die Familie Selicke*, does not.[13] While one must agree that the work of Hauptmann does stand out from among that of his contemporaries, it is manifestly not because of his ability to set forth a clear meaning or message; for all their weaknesses, the plays of Sudermann unquestionably do this more evidently than Hauptmann's; even *Die Familie Selicke* is as clearly structured and as consistent as *Vor Sonnenaufgang*. The inferiority of the great majority of the Naturalist dramas, and the relative superiority of the works of Hauptmann, presents the critic with a problem, but this problem is not to be solved by accepting all the objections to Naturalism, and asserting that Hauptmann had nothing to do with the movement.

In fact we need to be wary of accepting as a basic premise that Naturalism was, or even could have been, totally successful in its

---

[10] See Max Halbe, *Gesammelte Werke*, 7 vols (Munich: Albert Langen, 1917–23), I; on p. 21 it is three o'clock, by p. 31 the hands of the clock must have reached five; cf. Praschek, 'Das Verhältnis von Kunsttheorie und Kunstschaffen', p. 45.

[11] See Hugo von Hofmannsthal, 'Eleonora Duse', in *Gesammelte Werke in Einzelausgaben*, edited by Herbert Steiner, 15 vols (Stockholm and Frankfurt a.M.: S. Fischer, 1945–59), *Prosa I* (1956), 71.

[12] Cf. Strindberg's complaints about the theatre of the period in the preface to *Miss Julie*.

[13] Karl Siegfried Guthke, *Gerhart Hauptmann: Weltbild im Werk* (Göttingen: Vandenhoeck und Ruprecht, 1961), pp. 60–61.

supposed intention of presenting the particular, individual 'slice of life'. In his review of *Die Familie Selicke,* Theodor Fontane draws attention to the transformation which the artistic process inevitably brings about:

Es bleibt ein gewaltiger Unterschied zwischen dem Bilde, das das Leben stellt, und dem Bilde, das die Kunst stellt; der Durchgangsprozeß, der sich vollzieht, schafft... eine rätselhafte Modelung, und an dieser Modelung haftet die künstlerische Wirkung, die Wirkung überhaupt.[14]	There remains an enormous difference between the picture which is given by life itself, and the picture given by the work of art; whatever happens in between brings about a strange transformation, and this transformation is responsible for the artistic effect, indeed for any effect.

The theatre, as an art form, has a very strong tendency to mediate between the general and the particular. It is very difficult for any spectator to regard the theatre-set as no more than the actual environment of an individual case-history, for the dramatist, even the Naturalist dramatist, is prevented by considerations of time and space, visibility and audibility, from effectively giving a complete and accurate background; what detail he does provide must necessarily be selective, abstracted. Moreover the dramatist, especially in the 'theatre of illusion', lacks the opportunity, which the epic narrator has, of interrupting his story from time to time to insist on its singularity or documentary truth. Hauptmann's comments on *Vor Sonnenaufgang* suggest that, as far as this play is concerned, he might almost have welcomed such an opportunity. He argues, in effect, that his play is an 'open' drama, and that we do not see in it a complete characterization of Alfred Loth with all his thoughts, feelings and capabilities; all we see is one episode, which shows him (in a less than flattering light) in the conditions which prevail in the drama in which he is a participant.[15]

Yet, as one may well conclude from the fact that Hauptmann found it necessary to offer such an apologia for his character, the drama itself fails to make it sufficiently clear that it is only an episode; and it is the drama in which we, as spectators or critics, are interested. The conditions of the drama are the only conditions under which we know

---

[14] 'Holz/Schlaf, Die Familie Selicke', in *Werke, Schriften und Briefe,* edited by Walter Keitel and Helmuth Nürnberger, 20 vols (Munich: Hanser, 1962–94), Abt. II, *Aufsätze, Kritiken, Erinnerungen,* ii, *Theaterkritiken,* edited by Siegmar Gerndt (1969), pp. 845–48 (p. 847).

[15] Gerhart Hauptmann, *Die Kunst des Dramas: Über Schauspiel und Theater,* edited by Martin Machatzke (Berlin and Frankfurt a.M.: Propyläen, 1963), pp. 94–5.

Loth; our knowledge of his behaviour under these conditions must provide the basis for any deductions we care to make about his possible behaviour in different circumstances. At the very least, Loth's actions will be understood as characteristic of him; and to this extent the events of the play will at once be the basis of a generalization. When we find that emotions are expressed with a degree of intensity that is unusual in our everyday life, and when we perceive that the German Naturalist dramatist – like the French classicists – habitually chooses to present what can best be described in the Abbé d'Aubignac's phrase as a 'jour illustre', then with what degree of conviction can we continue to assert that the events of the German Naturalist drama should be regarded as individual events of no more than average significance?

But just as we should be wary of assuming that the Naturalists could have successfully presented the particular and the individual as the particular and the individual, so should we also be wary of assuming that this was, in fact, their intention. Where the dramatist relies on stage-directions to convey information which is of importance to the understanding of the play, the demands of the theatre count for more than the demands for truth to life. Aware, no doubt, that facial expression was unlikely to convey a great deal in the theatre of the 1890s, Hauptmann endowed an unusually large number of his characters with a propensity for fainting at moments of crisis, in the way Kleist's characters do. In a play such as *Das Friedensfest*, in which the contrast between characters is of immense importance, the contrast in physical appearance (for instance between Frau Scholz and Frau Buchner) is of an exaggerated starkness. This same play also contains a number of examples of the use of mime to replace the monologue, which was abhorrent to Naturalist theory; it is hardly necessary to point out the extent to which mime rests on convention.[16] Naturalism requires a change in acting style; it does not require that acting should cease to have a style.

The Naturalist drama, as it developed in Germany, is a much less simple and consistent phenomenon than is often supposed, and it requires from the critic a more pragmatic approach than it has often received. Too many critics have abstracted from the work of a limited number of writers, and from their own preconceptions about 'naturalism', a theory which they have treated as if it provided a consistent basis to the dramas of the period, and have failed to expose discrepancies between theory and practice. (Thus Helmut Praschek's thesis cleverly reconciles certain implausibilities in the plays with the theory which he has abstracted, but completely overlooks the fact that Schlenther,

---

[16] Cf. Gert Matterklott, *Melancholie in der Dramatik des Sturm und Drang* (Stuttgart: Metzler, 1968), pp. 139–40.

a representative critic and an important theatre director, whose work he does not consider, roundly condemns some of these very implausibilities.[17]) The majority of critics have also failed to give an accurate indication of the range of the theory itself. On a number of occasions I have referred to the views of the Hart brothers, and drawn attention to their moderate demands for an idealised form of realism, emphasizing the closeness of their views to those of the traditional idealist critics. In view of the convergence of idealists and Marxists in the demand for representative characters, it is not surprising that one can also find among the theoretical writings of the Naturalists statements which resemble Marxist demands; for instance, Heinrich Hart's distinction between 'poetic realism' and 'realism of observation' is a re-statement of the views of Engels.[18] But among the Naturalist critics, it is the most distinguished, Otto Brahm, who comes closest to the Marxist position. This emerges most clearly in his interpretation of classical literature. Despite the bitter hostility which prevailed between him and Franz Mehring, there is a great deal of similarity between their respective interpretations of Schiller's *Kabale und Liebe*.

Mehring saw the classical period in German literature as an expression of the struggle of the middle-classes against feudalism, transferred to the literary arena, because the situation of the time inhibited direct political action. He admired in Schiller a more overtly political writer than Goethe, and emphasized in his writings on Schiller his humanist ideals, his hatred of tyranny, his stirring pathos, and his consistent struggle against the political backwardness of Germany, 'die deutsche Misère'.[19] Mehring's admiration even extends to Schiller's aesthetic writings, which he sees as part of an attempt to educate the public towards a political reformation. Mehring shared Brahm's special admiration for the 'revolutionary' play *Kabale und Liebe*, which, he felt, showed in typical form the essential struggle of its age, and he recognized in Miller the Musician the classical embodiment of the German middle-classes. But besides relating the play to its social and economic background, Mehring shows its place in literary history; he points out its resemblance to *Emilia Galotti*, and its relation to the genre, *bürgerliches Trauerspiel*; he traces the genesis of the play itself, and shows Schiller's change in attitude to Lady Milford; and he gives a detailed analysis of the famous ensemble-scene in the house of Miller. Brahm places slightly more emphasis on the purely literary background, giving a more

---

[17] Paul Schlenther, *Gerhart Hauptmann: Sein Lebensgang und seine Dichtung* (Berlin: S. Fischer, 1898), p. 78. See also Max Halbe, *Scholle und Schicksal* (Munich: Knorr and Hirth, 1933), pp. 427–8.

[18] See above, pp. 20–21.

[19] Franz Mehring, 'Schiller: ein Lebensbild für deutsche Arbeiter' (1905), *Gesammelte Schriften*, X, 91–241; 'Kabale und Liebe' (1909), X, 252–58.

detailed comparison of the finished play with earlier drafts; but he too sees the play clearly in the context of its socio-political background, which he interprets in the same way as Mehring; he sees in the ensemble-scene an episode of cultural history: the confrontation of the Swabian court with the Swabian middle-class, in the person of Miller. He even explains Luise's firm religious beliefs, in a way which might be thought more typical of a Marxist, as an imaginative compensation for the misery she must undergo in her real social situation.[20]

Brahm and Mehring can be seen to agree in principle in admiring the art of Schiller as an example of social realism, and they agree in the details of their interpretation, because they recognize the political conflict of bourgeoisie and aristocracy as the characteristic reality of Schiller's age. The Naturalists and the Marxists do not, however, agree about what constitutes the characteristic reality of their own age, and so major disagreements – to which we have already had occasion to refer – emerge in the criticism of contemporary works. The Naturalist works which Mehring singles out for praise are social dramas, such as *Die Weber*, *Der Biberpelz*, Halbe's *Eisgang*, and Ibsen's social dramas from *Pillars of Society* onwards; and Mehring's interpretations squarely emphasize the social dimension of these works, but criticize them where they pessimistically overlook the promise of social reorganization held out by the rising working class movement. Brahm lacked Mehring's confidence in the Social Democratic movement of his day, but this is perhaps not quite the same as saying – as Mehring did – that he was totally deficient in any understanding of history.[21] As his work on Schiller shows, Brahm was fully awake to the social implications of German classical literature, and did not need Mehring to remind him that Schiller's dramas could not be regarded as asocial art for art's sake.[22] In fact Brahm, who was at the centre of the German Naturalist movement from its beginning to its end, was enough of an idealist – Mehring would have said a conservative – to see in Ibsen's dramas an absolute dichotomy of individual and society, but also enough of a realist to admire its treatment most in the social dramas after *A Doll's House*, and thereby to incur the hostility of the more consistently idealist Hart brothers.[23]

Between Heinrich Hart and Otto Brahm German Naturalist theory covers a wide range; and even Brahm has been accused fairly strongly of a tendency to idealize social problems into timeless, existential problems – that is a tendency to abstraction rather than to the

---

[20] *Schiller*, 2 vols (Berlin: Hertz, 1888–92), I (1888), 295–323.
[21] 'Und Pippa tanzt' (1906), *Gesammelte Schriften*, XI, 339.
[22] 'Ibsens Klein Eyolf' (1895), *Gesammelte Schriften*, XII, 92.
[23] Cf. above, p. 35. The Harts themselves provided Mehring with a sitting target; see his review of *Die Weber*, in *Gesammelte Schriften*, XI, 277.

concrete particularization which is generally associated with Naturalism. This suggests quite forcefully that it is erroneous to argue that the demands of the German Naturalist theorists permit of no symbolic intensification, or that they permit the details of description to have no more significance than they would have in normal everyday life. This was not so for the Poetic Realists; it was not so in the theatrical productions of the Meiningen Court Theatre; nor can it be said that Zola and Ibsen used description in this specifically non-symbolic, veristic way; and in view of the cumulative influence of all these, it would be most surprising to find that the German Naturalists did. In fact, in our examination of Naturalist dramas we have already seen that much of that detail, which appears at first sight to figure only as part of an exhaustive catalogue of chance background, is revealed, on closer examination, to have a symbolic function, to create and intensify an atmosphere appropriate to the dramatic situation, or to extend the reference of a story by prompting comparisons and analogies.

There is, however, a great deal of inconsistency here, and this inconsistency, arising from a mixture of symbolism and verism, is one of the major problems presented by the German Naturalist drama. In Flaischlen's *Martin Lehnhardt* (1894) the hero's acquisition of a gun seems to anticipate a despairing suicide, or at least a tragic and significant accident, like the shooting of Annchen in *Jugend*, but it has no significance at all; it is a false trail laid by the dramatist – as if to say that in his drama, as in life, not all tensions are resolved in the way the traditional theatre leads us to expect. But Flaischlen does not always proceed in this way; the accidental breaking of a statuette of Christ does have the symbolic significance which is implied. The veristic principle is therefore called in question; those elements which are not woven purposefully into the structure of the play, begin to look like token offerings to a purely theoretical conviction.

In the later years of Naturalism there are signs of an awareness of this shortcoming, and the unintegrated detail is much reduced. In *Rose Bernd* the principle of dramatic concentration is, as we noticed, completely dominant. By the careful selection of significant episodes a story is told from beginning to end, following a clear pattern, and strongly supported by an equally clear pattern of symbols. Symbolism is also much more easily accommodated with Ibsen's concentrated dramatic style; but even so there are occasions when Ibsen's choice and handling of the symbol is every bit as clumsy as in his German followers.

This inconsistency in the style of the German Naturalists is rooted, I believe, in a basic uncertainty, which is reflected in a number of fields. It appears most strongly in the work of Hauptmann, and it is necessary to emphasize this, because, while many literary historians have been prepared to see the minor Naturalists written off as experimenters in the blind-alley of the individual and the particular, there has been a marked tendency among admirers of Hauptmann to detach him from his contemporaries, and see in his works symbolic, metaphysical statements, which penetrate beneath the level of social reality to some fundamental essence. Analogies have thus been drawn between the work of Hauptmann, and that of Böhme, Schopenhauer, and Hebbel.[24]

'Mitleid', the compassionate expression of solidarity with suffering humanity, is more typical of the German Naturalists than the expression of faith in socio-political remedies; moreover suffering is presented as something constant, which extends across social barriers without becoming different in kind; this might be felt to suggest that social criticism is never more than superficial. In Hauptmann there is even a tendency to regard the capacity for suffering as a significant measure of human worth. But, as I have argued in the previous chapter, Hauptmann's plays do not give an unambiguous answer to the question: what is the purpose of suffering? Is suffering simply a meaningless, but inescapable factor in existence, carrying no promise of redemption, as in the dramas of Büchner; or, arising from the divine, from the very spring of life itself, does it provide the privilege of contact with a deeper reality, a higher, more lucid perception? If the latter, then why should Hauptmann have so meticulously rooted the suffering of his characters in their social and psychological situation? It is because of this scrupulous attention to causal detail that Hauptmann's Naturalist plays are so ambiguous; he once said of *Hanneles Himmelfahrt*: 'Earthly suffering created heavenly bliss' – but as transcendence or compensation?

A useful analogy can, I think, be drawn between the inconsistencies of the German Naturalist movement, and the basic contradiction which Dilthey found in the philosophy of Hegel: namely the contradiction between the stated theoretical conviction of the relativity of any historical reality, and the implicit claim, raised by the Hegelian system itself, to absolute metaphysical completeness.[25] Scientific, theoretical Naturalism does not posit an ideally ordered world, in which man occupies a central position, from which speculative activity can give him a complete,

---

[24] For examples of such interpretations see: Thomas Mann, *Gerhart Hauptmann* (Gütersloh: Bertelsmann, 1953); Karl Siegfried Guthke and Hans M. Wolff 'Das Leid im Werke Gerhart Hauptmanns', *University of California Publications in Modern Philology*, 49 (Berkeley, 1958); Guthke, 'Hebbel, Hauptmann und die Dialektik in der Idee', *Hebbel Jahrbuch 1961* (Heide in Holst., 1962), pp. 71–77; Hans-Joachim Schrimpf, 'Struktur und Metaphysik des sozialen Schauspiels bei Gerhart Hauptmann', *Literatur und Gesellschaft vom 19ten ins 20ste Jahrhundert. Festgabe für Benno von Wiese* (Bonn: Bouvier, 1963), pp. 274–308.
[25] 'Die Jugendgeschichte Hegels', *Gesammelte Schriften*, 19 vols (Leipzig and Berlin: Teubner; Göttingen: Vandenhoeck and Ruprecht, 1914–82), IV (1921), 219. See also Karl Löwith, *Von Hegel zu Nietzsche*, 3rd edition (Stuttgart: Kohlhammer, 1953), p. 138.

absolute spiritual comprehension of that world. The reality of the Naturalists consists, in theory, of the discovered facts of the positive sciences; in such a world there can be no teleological certainty; all is governed by a relentless mechanical causality, which even controls man's spiritual activity. Causality stands in relation to freedom as the relative does to the absolute; a view caused by a given set of circumstances cannot aspire to absolute validity, but can only be expected to be valid as a function of those circumstances. But under this theoretical acceptance of rational, scientific relativism, there still lurks a continued need for absolute, metaphysical certainties, derived through religious or artistic insight.

It was this theoretical conviction which demanded a revolution in the drama: the development of an anti-heroic milieu-drama, in which man more or less disappears in his environment.[26] The characters in such a drama would tend to be victims, unfree and incapable of responsibility, therefore incapable of incurring the idealists' tragic guilt, or developing 'the essential characteristics of their inner life and action' (Hegel). Interpersonal conflicts, expressed fully and completely in dialogue form, must give way where an active role is allowed to extra-personal forces, whose overall purpose the dramatist himself does not feel able to explain adequately, and which therefore resist containment in the rounded, complete, symbolic framework of the traditional closed dramatic form.[27] If the audience is to understand that the dramatic clash is not brought about by an active exercise of will, an epic manner is required: through a profusion of stage-directions an implied narrator can tell us that his characters are a direct product of a certain set of circumstances, which have their own independent existence in the empirical world. The drama must be a sequence of tableaux, which reveal milieu and character, but without relating to any pre-ordained purpose, such as a plot structure; it must therefore contain no complete, rounded action, but be 'open' at both beginning and end.[28]

The clearest and most constructive exposé of a theory of epic drama on these lines occurs in a rather obscure review of *Vor Sonnenaufgang*, which appeared shortly after the first performance of Hauptmann's play in 1889.[29] The reviewer, who uses the pseudonym Kaberlin, praises

---

[26] Schlaf, 'Vom intimen Drama', *Neuland*, I (1896–7), 35.

[27] Here, as elsewhere, Naturalist drama stands at the opposite pole to Greek tragedy, which offers a tendentious interpretation of an otherwise incomprehensible myth; see Walter Benjamin, *Ursprung des deutschen Trauerspiels* (Frankfurt a.M.: Suhrkamp, 1969; first published 1928), p. 108.

[28] Cf. Szondi, *Theorie des modernen Dramas* (Frankfurt a.M.: Suhrkamp, 1959), pp. 52–61; Schrimpf, 'Struktur und Metaphysik', pp. 285–95.

[29] Kaberlin, 'Eine Fortentwicklung des deutschen Dramas', *Das Magazin für die Literatur des In- und Auslandes*, 58 (1889), 696–700. For a slightly fuller discussion of this, see John Osborne, 'Naturalism and the dramaturgy of the open drama', *German Life and Letters*, 23 (1969–70), 119–28.

especially the first three acts of the play for the absence of any active conflict of wills, and the consequent lack of theatrical tension, which, he argues, is redressed by a feeling of excited participation arising from the spectator's freedom to associate for himself ideas and images, to link cause and effect in a way the individual characters within the drama cannot. Anticipating Brecht, Kaberlin requires dramatic presentation to be more passive, the spectator to be more active. Not surprisingly, he is highly critical of the conclusion of *Vor Sonnenaufgang*; anticipating Brechtian dramaturgy again, he condemns the re-emergence of a conventional theatrical tension to which the mood of social sympathy becomes subordinated. As an alternative ending to the play, he suggests that Loth might have married Helene in the knowledge that he would have been unhappy. As in his subsequent review of *Papa Hamlet*, he shows a preference for an 'open' ending, which would permit the basic mood of social sympathy to continue in its effect after the curtain had fallen: 'The young realists continue to believe that dramatic effect can be intensified by a completely unprepared tragic conclusion, but they forget that a sudden concentration of the action after a looser style of presentation only disturbs the unity of the basic mood'.[30]

The kind of drama outlined by Kaberlin is epic in that subject and object are clearly present and separable as two distinct viewpoints; the spectator has a horizon wider than that of the characters in the drama, and is better able to understand the forces which determine the action. But the characters in such a drama, who are so far beneath us, and who are 'without any higher awareness of themselves or their situation' (Hegel), cannot, according to the strictest Hegelians, figure as our representatives in a tragic scheme.[31] In Kaberlin's epic drama, however, identification takes place on a different level: not between audience and character, but between the audience and the implied narrator; the spectator becomes a fellow-dramatist. Limited characters are necessary in order that there should be a drama at all, for in the context of the determinist beliefs of the Naturalists, knowledge and action are incompatible; knowledge of the superiority of external forces will cripple the will to react against them; awareness in the Naturalist drama must therefore take the form of passive, and therefore undramatic contemplation. In its optimistic form this will appear as wonder at the

---

[30] 'Neurealistische Novellen', *Magazin für die Literatur des In- und Auslandes*, 58 (1889), 713.
[31] Cf. G. Lukács, 'Hauptmanns Weg', *Die Schaubühne*, 7 (1911), 253: '[Hauptmann's] tragic heroes resemble hunted animals: deeply moving though they are in their dark despair they cannot be symbolic representations of our entrapment and persecution', 'Hauptmanns Weg', *Die Schaubühne*, VII (1911), p. 253. It can, of course, be argued that this is a source of the originality and strength of Hauptmann's dramas; see Edward McInnes. *Das deutsche Drama des 19. Jahrhunderts*, Grundlagen der Germanistik, 26 (Berlin: Erich Schmidt, 1983), pp. 181–82.

grandiose, planless majesty of life, such as is expressed in the novels of Zola; in its more common, negative form it will appear as despair and resignation, the lyric moments for which Lukács praised those dramatically weak plays, *Florian Geyer* and *Michael Kramer*. Only the Marxists have an answer; for while they still adhere to the determinist belief, they insist that their awareness is not incompatible with social action. Brecht, in his adaptation of *Der Biberpelz* and *Der rote Hahn*, introduces a new character, Rauert, with a Marxist awareness, who is therefore a 'representative' Socialist revolutionary.

The dichotomy knowledge-action is as important for the Naturalists as it was for their near-contemporaries Thomas Mann and Hugo von Hofmannsthal. The latter's comments on the characters in Ibsen's dramas show his understanding of this affinity:

| Alle diese Menschen leben ein schattenhaftes Leben; sie erleben keine Taten und Dinge, fast ausschließlich Gedanken, Stimmungen und Verstimmungen. Sie wollen wenig, sie tun fast nichts. Sie denken übers Denken, fühlen sich fühlen und treiben Autopsychologie, das Reden und Reflektieren ist ihr eigentlicher Beruf.[32] | All these people live a shadowy life; they do not experience deeds and objects, but almost exclusively thoughts, moods, and depressions. They barely exercise their wills; they do almost nothing. They think about thinking, they feel themselves feeling, and they are constantly analysing themselves; their real vocation is talking and reflecting. |

In consequence of this dichotomy the characters in the Naturalist drama fall into two basic categories, anticipated in Büchner's two tragedies, *Dantons Tod* and *Woyzeck*. A bourgeois, intellectual strain, reinforced by the influence of Ibsen, biases the earlier works towards the Danton-type, the intelligent, withdrawn, inactive man, exemplified by Robert Scholz (although in *Das Friedensfest* the unreflective Buchners are necessary to precipitate the action); while the later works, *Rose Bernd* and *Die Ratten* (and the earlier works in their treatment of some female characters), are more concerned with the uncomprehending suffering of less educated, but still active persons.[33]

---

[32] 'Die Menschen in Ibsens Dramen', *Gesammelte Werke, Prosa I*, 88.
[33] As Szondi points out, the Naturalists tended to draw their active characters from among the lower classes, finding only there unbroken expressions of will and passionate commitment, uninhibited by self-doubt (*Theorie des modernen Dramas*, p. 71).

Where a character's knowledge still permits action, consistency with the determinist view means that this knowledge must be false or insufficient. Awareness of this kind, I have suggested, is not important as insight, but as expression, the response to a stimulus, a cry of pain; what is said is not identical with what is true, or even with what the speaker really means. The epic manner enables the dramatist to make some sort of intervention, and reveal the causality which makes the awareness only a relative awareness. This can also be true of that resigned, passive awareness, which more nearly corresponds to the theoretical views of the Naturalists themselves; we frequently encounter characters who express what sounds very like the determinist case, and yet who do not have the authority of the conventional *raisonneur*. If, in *Das Friedensfest*, Robert Scholz is presented as substantially correct in many of his insights, it is quite clear that this is coincidental, and that his opinions are just as much emotional expressions as those of other characters. The result of this is what Schlaf called the 'intimate drama'; knowledge, opinion, argument, do not arouse interest as such, but only in so far as they reveal a more primitive struggle; in the words of Maeterlinck, the purpose of the drama is: 'de faire entendre par dessous les dialogues ordinaires de la raison et des sentiments, le dialogue plus solennel et ininterrompu de l'être et de sa destinée'.[34]

Such a drama requires that intelligence and irony which are indeed present in Hauptmann's work,[35] but which have often been overlooked, because they are not consistently present, and because they are balanced by the diametrically opposite tendency: the continued desire, despite all theoretical convictions, to express through his characters a view of life which is not merely relative or predominantly social; to continue to use the drama as a closed, symbolic, even metaphysical form. This ambiguity is among the most important characteristics of the German Naturalist drama: to refer for the last time to two crucial examples: in *Die Weber* and *Hanneles Himmelfahrt* it seems that the author recognized, as a Naturalist, the existence of individuals with a need for religion, which, because of a combination of historical and psychological circumstances, directs them to the Christian religion; and that then, in a thoroughly inconsistent way, he sought to re-establish the absolute validity of their Christian faith. More than any of his contemporaries, and increasingly in his later plays, Hauptmann continues to elevate various individual views, despite their dubious origins, because, we must conclude, he is so deeply impressed by intensity of expression, that he is not disposed to differentiate between the pathological and the mystical.

---

[34] *Le Trésor des humbles* (Paris: Mercure de France, 1896), p. 181.
[35] Schrimpf, 'Struktur und Metaphysik', p. 197.

In the later verse-drama, *Der weiße Heiland* (1920) we find the lines:

Worte sind verwirrte Sprache.	Words are a confused form of speech.
Schrei ist Klarheit!	The scream is clarity!
Schrei ist Wahrheit!	The scream is truth!
Wahre Lust und wahre Pein!	True joy and true pain!
Wutgeheul und Lustgestöhne Pressen Götter aus den Seelen. (II, 1297)	Howls of rage and sighs of joy forcibly release the gods from within.

In the wake of Expressionism the balance has clearly changed for Hauptmann, but it is a change we cannot look back on with much satisfaction. The value set on the ecstatic and the irrational here seems unconditional – but by the standards of Naturalistic theory the words are, of course, still ambiguous. Circumstances force the emergence of the 'gods'; 'truth' is not attained by the free activity of the independent spirit, but it is realized under intense pressure; there is a causality at work which might be held to limit or condition the 'truth' proclaimed, and so even these words can be said to contain evidence of both the impulses which go to make up the style of the German Naturalists as it actually was. This can best be defined in a formula which itself attempts to reconcile opposites: an essay at scientific, analytical understanding, which does not exclude the aim of metaphysical comprehension.

Conclusion

Closely knit artistic movements are not given to longevity. German Naturalism is no exception. The two full seasons of the *Freie Bühne*, 1889–90 and 1890–91, represent the creative peak; but at the same time they signal the beginning of the end, in that Brahm's policies provoked hostility among both the Berlin and the Munich Naturalists. As soon as it became a creative rather than a theoretical-critical movement, German Naturalism was bound to fall apart, for the theorizing which took place in the preceding decade was so extensive, and, in many instances, so contradictory, that no conceivable creative literary movement could have met its demands. Yet even though the practice does not exactly accord with the theory, if we attempt to view both as a whole, it is possible to recognize a certain family likeness. Seen as a whole, German Naturalist theory does not propose an extreme and revolutionary kind of literature; and, seen as a whole, the German Naturalist movement does not provide an extreme and revolutionary kind of literature. Rather both combine, often in a perplexing way, such features as the traditional distaste of German literature for social and political reality, a pronounced nationalism, a distrust of the rational, on the one hand, with a commitment to precise, scientific observation and mimesis, on the other. German Naturalism compromises between inward, German conservatism and outward-looking, European radicalism.

Any development is in the conservative direction. The Naturalists' progressive political aspirations are not sufficiently deep-rooted to overcome one set-back; and it takes little (Julius Langbehn!) to capture the enthusiasm of some of them for out-and-out reaction. The same is true of the creative work. Their critical satire is muted, and their comedies are tolerant and, on the whole, feeble; their dramas tend increasingly to compromise in the face of the demands of the traditional theatre, and they tend to revert to the closed, symbolic form of the classical drama. Nevertheless, the German Naturalists asserted the will to experiment and the will to reorganize the theatre themselves in such a way as to accommodate their experiments. It is here that Expressionism and other forms of theatrical modernism take over.

APPENDIX I
PLAYS PRESENTED BY THE FREIE BÜHNE

(i) Under the direction of Otto Brahm

1889

29 Sept.	Ibsen	*Gespenster* (*Ghosts*)
8 Oct.	Hauptmann	*Vor Sonnenaufgang* (*Before Sunrise*)
17 Nov.	E. & J. de Goncourt	*Henriette Maréchal*
15 Dec.	Björnson	*Ein Handschuh* (*The Glove*)

1890

26 Jan.	Tolstoi	*Die Macht der Finsternis* (*The Power of Darkness*)
2 Mar.	Anzengruber	*Das vierte Gebot* (*The Fourth Commandment*)
7 Apr.	Holz and Schlaf	*Die Familie Selicke* (*The Selicke Family*)
	Alexander Kjelland	*Auf dem Heimwege* (*The Way Home*)
4 May	Arthur Fitger	*Von Gottes Gnaden* (*By the Grace of God*)
1 Jun.	Hauptmann	*Das Friedensfest* (*The Celebration of Peace*)
12 Oct.	Strindberg	*Der Vater* (*The Father*)
30 Nov.	Hartleben	*Angèle*
	Marie von Ebner-Eschenbach	*Ohne Liebe* (*Loveless*)

1891

11 Jan.	Hauptmann	*Einsame Menschen* (*Lonely People*)
15 Feb.	Henri Becque	*Die Raben* (*The Ravens*)
15 Mar.	Anzengruber	*Der Doppelselbstmord* (*The Double Suicide*)
3 May	Zola	*Thérèse Raquin*

1892

3 Apr.	Strindberg	*Fräulein Julie* (Miss Julie)

1893

26 Feb.	Hauptmann	*Die Weber* (The Weavers)
30 Mar.	Ernst Rosmer (Else Bernstein)	*Dämmerung* (Twilight)

(ii) Under the direction of Paul Schlenther

1895

12 May	Georg Hirschfeid	*Die Mütter* (The Mothers)

1897

11 Apr.	Emil Marriot	*Gretes Glück* (Meg's Joy)
	Ebner-Eschenbach	*Am Ende* (At the Last)

(iii) Under the direction of Ludwig Fulda

1898

15 May	Ernst Hardt	*Tote Zeit* (Time Suspended)
	Hofmannsthal	*Die Frau im Fenster* (The Woman at the Window)

1899

12 Nov.	Eduard von Keyserling	*Ein Frühlingsopfer* (A Spring Sacrifice)

1901

19 May	Ernst Rosmer	*Mutter Maria* (Mother Mary)

APPENDIX II
PLAYS PRESENTED BY THE VOLKSBÜHNEN, 1890–5

(i) Die Freie Volksbühne, 1890–2 (Bruno Wille)

1890
Ibsen	*Stützen der Gesellschaft* (Pillars of Society)
Hauptmann	*Vor Sonnenaufgang*
Ibsen	*Der Volksfeind* (An Enemy of the People)
Heinrich Hart	*Tul und Nahila* (a reading)

1891
Schiller	*Kabale und Liebe* (Intrigue and Love)
Sudermann	*Die Ehre* (Honour)
Pissemski	*Der Leibeigene* (The Serf)
Fulda	*Das verlorene Paradies* (Paradise Lost)
Reuter	*Kein Hüsung* (Homeless)
Schiller	*Die Räuber* (The Robbers)
Anzengruber	*Der Doppelselbstmord*
Ibsen	*Bund der Jugend* (The League of Youth)
Hebbel	*Maria Magdalene*
Gogol	*Der Revisor* (The Government Inspector)

1892
Halbe	*Eisgang* (Thaw)
Anzengruber	*Der Pfarrer von Kirchfeld* (The Priest of Kirchfeld)
Zola	*Thérèse Raquin*
Fulda	*Die Sklavin* (The Slave Girl)
Ibsen	*Gespenster*
Ludwig	*Der Erbförster* (The Forester)
Ibsen	*Nora* (A Doll's House)

(ii) 1892–5 (Franz Mehring)

(a) Plays from the repertoire of the *Lessingtheater*:

Anzengruber	*Das vierte Gebot*
	Der Meineidbauer (The Perjurous Peasant)
	Die Kreuzelschreiber (The Cross-Signers)

Sudermann	*Die Ehre* (Honour)
	Heimat (Home, or *Magda*)
	Sodoms Ende (The Fall of Sodom)
Lessing	*Nathan der Weise* (Nathan the Wise)
	Emilia Galotti
Grillparzer	*Der Traum ein Leben* (Life is a Dream)
Kleist	*Der zerbrochene Krug* (The Broken Jug)
Augier	*Die arme Löwin* (The Poor Lioness)
Blumenthal and Kadelburg	*Großstadtluft* (City Air)
Björnson	*Fallissement* (Bankruptcy)
Ibsen	*Stützen der Gesellschaft*

(b) Special productions:

H. Faber	*Der freie Wille* (Free Will)
Goethe	*Egmont*
Calderon	*Der Richter von Zalamea* (The Mayor of Zalamea)
Schiller	*Kabale und Liebe*
Molière	*Der Geizige* (The Miser)
Verga	*Sizilianische Bauernehre* (Peasant Honour in Sicily)
P. Bader	*Andere Zeiten* (Different Times)
Hauptmann	*Die Weber*
Mellesville and Duveyrier	*Michel Perrin*
Edgreen and Leffler	*Wie man wohltut* (How To Do Good)
Held	*Ein Fest auf der Bastille* (Celebration in the Bastille)
Hauptmann	*Der Biberpelz* (The Beaver Coat)
Heyse	*Ehrenschulden* (Debts of Honour)
Westenberger and Croissant	*Hildegard Scholl*
Reuter	*Kein Hüsung* (Homeless)
Augier	*Der Pelikan* (The Pelican)

(iii) Die Neue Freie Volksbühne, 1893–5 (Bruno Wille)

Goethe	*Faust I*
Wolzogen	*Das Lumpengesindel* (The Rabble)
Anzengruber	*Der G'wissenswurm* (Pangs of Conscience)
Reuter	*Kein Hüsung*
Tolstoi	*Die Macht der Finsternis*
F. Lange	*Der Nächste* (The Neighbour)
Anzengruber	*Der Meineidbauer*
Molière	*Tartüff*

Hartleben	*Die Erziehung zur Ehe (Education for Marriage)*
Hauptmann	*Die Weber*
Ostrowski	*Gewitter (The Storm)*
Halbe	*Jugend (Youth)*
Anzengruber	*Die Kreuzelschreiber*
Ibsen	*Der Volksfeind*
Lessing	*Emilia Galotti*
Erckmann-Chatrian	*Die Rantzau (The Rantzaus)*
Guinon and Dénier	*Die Dummen (The Idiots)*
Freytag	*Die Journalisten (The Journalists)*
Anzengruber	*Das vierte Gebot*
Hauptmann	*Einsame Menschen*
Becque	*Die Raben (The Ravens)*
Vischer	*Schlimme Saat (The Bad Seed)*
Benedix	*Die zärtlichen Verwandten (The Tender Cousins)*
Meyer-Förster	*Unsichtbare Ketten (Invisible Bonds)*
L'Arronge	*Mein Leopold (My Leopold)*
A. Agrell	*Einsam (Loneliness)*
Schiller	*Don Karlos*

SELECT BIBLIOGRAPHY

I Dramatic texts of the Naturalist period

Dramen des deutschen Naturalismus: Von Hauptmann bis Schönherr, edited by Roy C. Cowen, 2 vols, Munich: Winkler, 1981.
Dramen des Naturalismus, edited by Artur Müller and Helmut Schlien, Emsdetten: Lechte, 1962.
Einakter des Naturalismus, edited by Wolfgang Rothe, Stuttgart: Reclam, 1973.

Alberti, Conrad, *Brot! Ein soziales Schauspiel in fünf Akten*, Leipzig: W. Friedrich, 1888.
Anzengruber, Ludwig, *Sämtliche Werke*, edited by Rudolf Latzke and Otto Rommel, 15 vols, Vienna and Leipzig: Anton Schroll, 1920–22.
Bahr, Hermann, *Die neuen Menschen*, Zürich: Schabelitz, 1887.
Bleibtreu, Karl, *Dramatische Werke*, 3 vols, Leipzig: Friedrich, 1889.
Dehmel, Richard, *Der Mitmensch*, Berlin: S. Fischer, 1909 [first published 1895].
Dreyer, Max, *Winterschlaf*, Leipzig and Berlin: Georg Heinrich Meyer, 1904 [first published 1894].
Ernst, Otto, *Jugend von Heute: Eine deutsche Komödie in vier Akten*, Hamburg: Kloss, 1900 [first published, Leipzig: Straakmann, 1899].
Ernst, Paul, *Lumpenbagasch – Im chambre separée: Zwei Schauspiele von Paul Ernst*, Berlin and Paris: Sassenbach, 1898.
Flaischlen, Cäsar, *Martin Lehnhardt: Ein Kampf um Gott*, Berlin: Fleischel, 1895.
——, *Toni Stürmer: Eine Alltagsgeschichte*, Berlin: Fleischel, 1891.
Fulda, Ludwig, *Das verlorene Paradies*, Stuttgart: Cotta, 1892.
——, *Die Kameraden*, Stuttgart: Cotta, 1895.
Halbe, Max, *Gesammelte Werke*, 7 vols, Munich: Albert Langen, 1917–23.
——, *Jugend*, edited by Edward McInnes, New German Studies Texts and Monographs 7, Hull: New German Studies, 1984.
Hardt, Ernst, *Tote Zeit*, Berlin: S. Fischer, 1898.
Hart, Heinrich, *Gesammelte Werke*, edited by Julius Hart, 4 vols, Berlin: Fleischel, 1907.
Hartleben, Otto Erich, *Ausgewählte Werke*, 3 vols, Berlin: S. Fischer, 1909.
Hauptmann, Carl, *Marianne*, Berlin: S. Fischer, 1894.

Hauptmann, Gerhart, *Sämtliche Werke*, Centenar-Ausgabe, edited by Hans-Egon Hass and Martin Machatzke, 11 vols, Frankfurt a.M. and Berlin: Propyläen, 1962–74.
——, *Die Weber*, edited by Mark Boulby, London: Harrap, 1962.
——, *Die Weber: Dichtung und Wirklichkeit*, edited by Hans Schwab-Felisch, Frankfurt a.M.: Ullstein, 1959.
Held, Franz, *Ein Fest auf der Bastille*, Berlin: Rosenbaum and Hart, 1889.
Hirschfeld, Georg, *Die Mütter*, Berlin: S. Fischer, 1896.
——, *Pauline*, Berlin: Schottlaender, 1899.
Holz, Arno, *Das Werk*, edited by Hans W. Fischer, 10 vols, Berlin: Dietz Nachfolger, 1924–5.
Holz Arno and Oskar Jerschke, *Traumulus*, Munich: Piper, 1905.
Holz Arno and Johannes Schlaf, *Die Familie Selicke*, Berlin: Issleib, 1890.
Ibsen, Henrik, *The Oxford Ibsen*, 8 vols, edited by J. W. McFarlane, London: O.U.P, 1960–77.
Langmann, Philipp, *Bartel Turaser*, Leipzig: Friese, 1897.
Rittner, Rudolph, *Narrenglanz*, Berlin: Oesterheld, 1906.
Rosmer, Ernst [Else Bernstein], *Dämmerung*, *Freie Bühne*, 4 (1893), 609–29, 737–52, 882–99, 1000–08.
Schlaf, Johannes, *Die Feindlichen*, Minden: Bruns, 1899.
——, *Meister Oelze*, Berlin: S. Fischer, 1892.
——, *Meister Oelze*, 2nd edition, Munich and Leipzig: Georg Müller, 1909.
Sudermann, Hermann, *Dramatische Werke*, 6 vols, Stuttgart and Berlin: J. G. Cotta'sche Nachfolger, 1923.
Wedekind, Frank, *Gesammelte Werke*, edited by Artur Kutscher and Joachim Friedenthal, 9 vols, Munich: Georg Müller 1920–21.
Weigand, Wilhelm, *Der Vater*, Munich: Lukaschik, 1894.
Wolzogen, Ernst von, *Das Lumpengesindel*, Berlin: F. Fontane, 1892.

II Other Literary and Theoretical Works by Naturalist Writers and their Contemporaries

Literarische Manifeste des Naturalismus, 1880–1892, edited by Erich Ruprecht, Stuttgart: Metzler, 1962.
Literarische Manifeste der Jahrhundertwende, edited by Erich Ruprecht and Dieter Bänsch, Stuttgart: Metzler, 1970.
Naturalismus: Manifeste und Dokumente zur deutschen Literatur 1880–1900, edited by Manfred Brauneck and Christine Müller, Stuttgart: Metzler, 1987.
Naturalismus-Debatte, 1891–1896: Dokumente zur Literaturtheorie und Literaturkritik der revolutionären deutschen Sozialdemokratie, edited by Norbert Rothe, Texte zur frühen sozialistischen Literatur in Deutschland, 25, Berlin: Akademie Verlag, 1986.

Prosa des Naturalismus, edited by Gerhard Schulz, Stuttgart: Reclam, 1973.
Theorie des Naturalismus, edited by Theo Meyer, Stuttgart: Reclam, 1973.

Bahr, Hermann, *Zur Überwindung des Naturalismus*, edited by Gotthart Wunberg, Stuttgart: Kohlhammer, 1968.
Berg, Leo, *Der Naturalismus*, Munich: Poessel, 1892.
——, *Der Übermensch in der modernen Literatur*, Paris, Leipzig, and Munich: Albert Langen, 1897.
Bergson, Henri, *Le Rire: Essai sur la signification du comique*, Paris: Alcan, 1900.
Bleibtreu, Karl, *Revolution der Literatur*, edited by Johannes J. Braakenburg, Deutsche Texte, 23, Tübingen: Niemeyer, 1973 [reprint of the 3rd edition, Leipzig: Wilhelm Friedrich, 1886; first published 1886].
Bölsche, Wilhelm, *Die naturwissenschaftlichen Grundlagen der Poesie: Prolegomena einer realistischen Ästhetik*, Leipzig: Reißner, 1887.
——, *Hinter der Weltstadt*, Leipzig: Diederichs, 1901.
Brahm, Otto, *Kritische Schriften*, edited by Paul Schlenther, 2 vols, Berlin: S. Fischer, 1913–15.
——, *Theater, Dramatiker, Schauspieler*, edited by Hugo Fetting, Berlin: Henschel, 1961.
——, *Briefe und Erinnerungen*, edited by Georg Hirschfeld, Berlin: Stilke, 1925.
——, 'Henrik Ibsen', *Deutsche Rundschau*, 49 (1886), 193–220.
——, *Heinrich von Kleist*, Berlin: Allgemeiner Verein für deutsche Literatur, 1884.
——, *Schiller*, 2 vols, Berlin: Hertz, 1888–92.
[Brahm, Otto] *Der Briefwechsel Arthur Schnitzler–Otto Brahm*, edited by Oskar Seidlin, Deutsche Texte, 35, Tübingen: Niemeyer, 1975.
Brandes, Georg, 'Emil Zola', *Deutsche Rundschau*, 54 (1888), 27–45.
Bulthaupt, Heinrich, *Dramaturgie des Schauspiels*, 4 vols, Oldenburg and Leipzig: A. Schwartz, 1897–1902, IV, *Ibsen, Wildenbruch, Sudermann, Hauptmann* (1901).
Conrad, Michael Georg, *Von Emil Zola bis Gerhart Hauptmann: Erinnerungen zur Geschichte der Moderne*, Leipzig: Seemann Nachf., 1902.
Dilthey, Wilhelm, 'Die drei Epochen der modernen Ästhetik und ihre heutige Aufgabe' [1892], in *Gesammelte Schriften*, 19 vols, Leipzig and Berlin: Teubner; Göttingen: Vandenhoeck and Ruprecht, 1914–82, VI, ii, (1924) 242–87.
Flaischlen, Cäsar, *Otto Erich Hartleben: Beitrag zu einer Geschichte der modernen Dichtung*, Berlin: S. Fischer, 1896.
Fontane, Theodor *Werke, Schriften und Briefe* (first published as *Sämtliche Werke*), 20 vols, edited by Walter Keitel and Helmuth Nürnberger, Munich: Hanser, 1962–94.

Goncourt, Edmond and Jules de, *Journal: Mémoires de la vie littéraire*, edited by Robert Ricatte, 4 vols, Paris: Fasquelle and Flammarion, 1956.
Halbe, Max, *Jahrhundertwende: Geschichte meines Lebens 1893–1914*, Danzig: Kafermann, 1935; repr. Munich: Langen-Müller, 1976.
Halbe, Max, *Scholle und Schicksal: Geschichte meines Lebens*, Munich: Knorr and Hirth, 1933.
Hanstein, Adalbert von, *Das jüngste Deutschland*, 3rd edition, Leipzig: Voigtländer, 1905 [first published 1901].
Hartleben, Otto Erich, *Briefe an Freunde*, edited by Franz Ferdinand Heitmüller, Berlin: S. Fischer, 1912.
Hauptmann, Carl, *Leben mit Freunden: Gesammelte Briefe*, Berlin: Horen-Verlag, 1928.
Hauptmann, Gerhart, *Die großen Beichten*, Frankfurt a.M. and Berlin: Propyläen, 1966.
——, *Die Kunst des Dramas: Über Schauspiel und Theater*, edited by Martin Machatzke, Frankfurt a.M. and Berlin: Propyläen, 1963.
Hofmannsthal, Hugo von, *Gesammelte Werke in Einzelausgaben*, edited by Herbert Steiner, 15 vols, Stockholm and Frankfurt a.M.: S. Fischer Verlag, 1945–59, *Prosa I* (1956), *Prosa II* (1959).
Holmsen, Bjarne P. (see Holz, Arno and Johannes Schlaf).
Holz, Arno, *Briefe: Eine Auswahl*, edited by Anita Holz and Max Wagner, Munich: Piper, 1949.
Holz Arno and Johannes Schlaf, *Neue Gleise*, Berlin: F. Fontane, 1892.
[Holz Arno and Johannes Schlaf], Bjarne P. Holmsen, *Papa Hamlet*, übersetzt und mit einer Einleitung versehen von Dr. Bruno Franzius, Leipzig: Reißner, 1889.
Ibsen auf der deutschen Bühne: Texte zur Rezeption, edited by Wilhelm Friese, Deutsche Texte 38, Tübingen: Niemeyer, 1976.
James, Henry, 'The Art of Fiction' (1884), in *Partial Portraits*, London: Macmillan, 1919, pp. 373–408.
Kerr, Alfred, *Die Welt im Drama*, 5 vols, Berlin: S. Fischer, 1917.
Kollwitz, Käthe, *Aus meinem Leben*, Munich: List, 1957.
Kraus, Karl, 'Von Humor und Lyrik' (1921), in *Die Sprache*, edited by Hans W. Fischer, 2nd edition, Munich: Kösel, 1954, pp. 201–13.
Lamprecht, Karl, *Alte und neue Richtungen in der Geschichtswissenschaft*, Berlin: Gaertner, 1896.
——, *Deutsche Geschichte*, 14 vols, Berlin: Gaertner, 1895–1909.
Landauer, Gustav, 'Gerhart Hauptmann' *Die neue Zeit*, 10 (1891–2), 612–21.
[Langbehn, A. Julius], *Rembrandt als Erzieher: Von einem Deutschen*, 2nd edition, Leipzig: C. L. Hirschfeld, 1890.
Lindau, Paul, *Dramaturgische Blätter*, 2nd edition, Stuttgart and Leipzig: Simon, 1877.

——, *Nur Erinnerungen*, 2 vols, Stuttgart and Berlin: Cotta, 1917–19.
Maeterlinck, Maurice, *Le Trésor des humbles*, Paris: Mercure de France, 1896.
Mann, Heinrich, *Im Schlaraffenland: Ein Roman unter feinen Leuten*, Leipzig: Kurt Wolff, [1917; first published 1900].
Mehring, Franz, *Gesammelte Schriften*, edited by Thomas Höhle, Hans Koch, and Josef Schleifstein, 12 vols, Berlin: Dietz, 1960–63.
Meyer, Richard M., *Die deutsche Literatur des neunzehnten Jahrhunderts, Das neunzehnte Jahrhundert in Deutschlands Entwicklung*, vol. 3, edited by Paul Schlenther, Berlin: Bondi, 1900.
Moderne Dichtercharaktere, edited by Wilhelm Arent, Leipzig: W. Friedrich, [1885].
Nordau, Max, *Die konventionellen Lügen der Kulturmenschheit*, Leipzig: Elischer, 1883.
Schlaf, Johannes, 'Die Freie Bühne und die Entstehung des naturalistlschen Dramas', *Der Greif*, 1 (1913–14), i, 403–13, 480–89, ii, 38–48.
——, *Maurice Maeterlinck*, Berlin: Marquadt, 1906.
Schlenther, Paul, *Gerhart Hauptmann: Sein Lebensgang und seine Dichtung*, Berlin: S. Fischer, 1898.
——, *Theater im neunzehnten Jahrhundert*, edited by Hans Knudsen, Berlin: Gesellschaft für Theatergeschichte, 1930.
——, *Wozu der Lärm? Genesis der Freien Bühne*, Berlin: S. Fischer, 1889.
Schmoller, Gustav, 'Die Entwicklung und die Krisis der deutschen Weberei im 19. Jahrhundert', *Deutsche Zeit- und Streitfragen*, 2, Berlin, 1873.
Spitteler, Carl, 'Die Familie Selicke', in *Gesammelte Werke*, 10 vols, edited by Gottfried Bohnenblust and others, Zürich: Artemis, 1945–58, IX (1950), 331–9.
Steiger, Edgar, *Das Werden des neuen Dramas*, 2 vols, Berlin, F. Fontane, 1898.
Volkelt, Johannes, *Ästhetische Zeitfragen*, Munich: Beck, 1895.
Wille, Bruno, *Philosophie der Befreiung durch das reine Mittel*, Berlin: S. Fischer, 1894.
Zimmermann, Alfred, *Blüthe und Verfall des Leinengewerbes in Schlesien*, Breslau: Korn, 1885.
Zola, Emile, *Les Oeuvres complètes*, texte de l'édition Eugène Fasquelle, 50 vols, Paris: Bernouard, 1927–29.

III Secondary Sources

Alexander, Neville Edward, *Studien zum Stilwandel im dramatischen Werk Gerhart Hauptmanns*, Stuttgart: Metzler, 1964.
Bab, Julius, 'Gerhart Hauptmann als Regisseur', *Gerhart-Hauptmann-Jahrbuch*, N.F. 1 (1948), 147–53.

Batley, Edward M., 'Functional Idealism in Gerhart Hauptmann's "Einsame Menschen"', *German Life and Letters*, 23 (1969–70), 243–54.
Behl, Carl Friedrich Wilhelm, *Gerhart Hauptmann: Überblick über sein Leben und Werk*, Würzburg: Holzner, 1956.
——, *Zwiesprache mit Gerhart Hauptmann: Tagebuchblätter*, Munich: Desch, 1949.
Behl, Carl Friedrich Wilhelm, and Felix A. Voigt, *Chronik von Gerhart Hauptmanns Leben und Schaffen*, Munich: Bergstadtverlag, 1957.
Berger, Paul, *Gerhart Hauptmanns Ratten: Interpretation eines Dramas*, Winterthur: Schellenberg, 1961.
Bock, Hans Manfred, 'Die Literaten- und Studenten-Revolte der Jungen in der SPD um 1890', *Das Argument*, 13 (1971), 22–41.
Böckmann, Paul, 'Der Naturalismus Gerhart Hauptmanns', in *Gestaltprobleme der Dichtung: Festschrift für Günther Müller*, edited by Richard Alewyn and others, Bonn: Bouvier, 1957, pp. 239–58.
Boulby, Mark, 'Optimism and Pessimism in German Naturalist writers,' 2 vols (doctoral thesis, University of Leeds, 1951).
Brauneck, Manfred, *Literatur und Öffentlichkeit im ausgehenden 19. Jahrhundert: Studien zur Rezeption des naturalistischen Theaters in Deutschland*, Stuttgart: Metzler, 1974.
Brecht, Bert., *Schriften zum Theater*, edited by Werner Hecht, 7 vols, Frankfurt a.M.: Suhrkamp, 1963–64.
[Brecht, Bert.] *Theaterarbeit: 6 Aufführungen des Berliner Ensembles*, edited by Berliner Ensemble and Helene Weigel, 2nd edition, Berlin and Frankfurt a.M.: Suhrkamp, 1961.
Brinkmann, Richard, *Wirklichkeit und Illusion*, Tübingen: Niemeyer, 1957.
Bronnen, Arnolt, *Vatermord*, Berlin: Rowohlt, 1925 [first published 1920].
Butzlaff, W., 'Die Enthüllungstechnik in Hauptmanns "Rose Bernd",' *Der Deutschunterricht*, 13 (1961), H.4, 59–70.
Carr, Gilbert J., 'Satire from the German Naturalists? Karl Kraus's Planned Anthology', *German Life and Letters*, N.S. 46 (1992–93), 120–33.
Chapiro, Josef, *Gespräche mit Hauptmann*, Berlin: S. Fischer, 1932.
Chevrel, Yves, *Le Naturalisme*, Paris: Presses Universitaires de France, 1982.
Claus, Horst, *The Theatre Director Otto Brahm*, Theatre and Dramatic Studies, 10, Ann Arbor, Michigan: UMI Research Press, 1981.
Cowen, Roy C., *Das deutsche Drama im 19. Jahrhundert*, Stuttgart: Metzler, 1988.
——, *Der Naturalismus; Kommentar zu einer Epoche*, Munich: Winkler, 1973.
——, *Hauptmann-Kommentar zum dramatischen Werk*, Munich: Winkler, 1980.
Demetz, Peter, *Marx, Engels und die Dichter: Zur Grundlagenforschung des Marxismus*, Stuttgart; Deutsche Verlags-Anstalt, 1959.

Demler, Leopold, *Arno Holz: Kunst und Natur* (doctoral thesis, University of Vienna, 1938).
Dietzel, Thomas and Hans-Otto Hügel, *Deutsche Literarische Zeitschriften, 1880–1945: Ein Repertorium*, 5 vols, edited by Deutsches Literaturarchiv, Marbach am Neckar, Munich, New York, London, Paris: Saur, 1988.
Döblin, Alfred, 'Der Geist des naturalistischen Zeitalters', *Die neue Rundschau*, 35 (1924), 1275–93.
Doucet, Fernand, *L'esthétique de Zola et son application à la critique*, Paris: Nizet, 1930.
Dreifuß, Alfred, *Deutsches Theater in Berlin, Schumannstraße 13a: Deichmann, L'Arronge, Brahm, Reinhard, Hilpert; 5 Kapitel aus der Geschichte einer Schauspielbühne*, [East] Berlin: Henschel, 1983.
Emrich, Wilhelm, 'Arno Holz und die moderne Kunst', 'Der Tragödientypus Gerhart Hauptmanns', in *Protest und Verheißung: Studien zur klassischen und modernen Dichtung*, Frankfurt a.M. and Bonn: Athenäum, 1960, pp. 155–68, 193–205.
Fick, Monika, *Sinnenwelt und Weltseele: Der psychophysische Monismus in der Literatur der Jahrhundertwende*, Studien zur deutschen Literatur, 125, Tübingen: Niemeyer, 1993.
Fischer, Bruno, 'Gerhart Hauptmann und Erkner: Quellenkundliche Studien zum "Biberpelz" und anderen Werken', *Zeitschrift für deutsche Philologie*, 81 (1962), 440–72.
Fischer-Lichte, Erika, *Kurze Geschichte des deutschen Theaters*, Tübingen and Basel: Francke, 1993.
Die Frauenfrage in Deutschland, 1865–1915: Texte und Dokumente, edited by Elke Frederiksen, Stuttgart: Reclam, 1988 [first published 1981].
Fried, Michael, *Absorption and Theatricality: Painting and Beholder in the Age of Diderot*, Berkeley and Los Angeles: University of California Press, 1980.
Fülberth, Georg, *Proletarische Partei und bürgerliche Literatur*, Neuwied: Luchterhand, 1972.
Garten, Hugo F., *Gerhart Hauptmann*, Cambridge: Bowes and Bowes, 1954.
Genette, Gérard: *Figures III*, Paris: Editions du Seuil, 1972.
George, David E. R., *Henrik Ibsen in Deutschland: Rezeption und Revision*, Göttingen: Vandenhoeck und Ruprecht, 1968.
Gerhart Hauptmann und sein Werk, edited by Ludwig Marcuse, Berlin and Leipzig: Schneider, 1922.
Gerhart Hauptmann, Wege der Forschung, 207, edited by Hans-Joachim Schrimpf, Darmstadt: Wissenschaftliche Buchgesellschaft, 1976.
Gerhart Hauptmann: Leben und Werk, Gedächtnisausstellung des deutschen Literaturarchivs zum 100. Geburtstag des Dichters, edited by Bernhard Zeller [exhibition catalogue], Stuttgart: Schiller-Nationalmuseum, 1962.

Gerhart Hauptmanns 'Weber': Eine Dokumentation, edited by Helmut Praschek, with an introduction by Peter Wruck, Berlin: Akademie Verlag, 1981.

Glass, Emil, *Psychologie und Weltanschauung in Gerhart Hauptmanns 'Fuhrmann Henschel': Ein Beitrag zur Wesenserkenntnis Gerhart Hauptmanns*, Emsdetten: Lechte, 1933.

Gooch, George P., *History and Historians in the 19th Century*, 2nd edition, London: Longmans, Green, 1920.

Grimm, Reinhold, 'Pyramide und Karussell', in *Strukturen: Essays zur deutschen Literatur*, Göttingen: Sachse und Pohl, 1963, pp. 8–43.

Grothe, W., 'Die neue Rundschau des Verlags S. Fischer', *Börsenblatt für den deutschen Buchhandel*, 17 (1962), 2171–266.

Guthke, Karl Siegfried and Hans M. Wolff 'Das Leid im Werke Gerhart Hauptmanns', *University of California Publications in Modern Philology*, 49, Berkeley, 1958.

Guthke, Karl Siegfried, 'Gerhart Hauptmanns Menschenbild in der "Familienkatastrophe" Das Friedensfest', *Germanisch-Romanische Monatsschrift*, N.F. 12 (1962), 39–50.

——, 'Hebbel, Hauptmann und die Dialektik in der Idee', *Hebbel Jahrbuch* (1961), Heide in Holst., 1962, 71–77.

——, 'Probleme neuerer Hauptmannforschung', *Göttingsche Gelehrte Anzeigen*, 216 (1960), 84–107.

——, *Gerhart Hauptmann: Weltbild im Werk*, Göttingen: Vandenhoeck und Ruprecht, 1961; 2nd edition, Munich: Francke, 1980.

——, *Geschichte und Poetik der deutschen Tragikomödie*, Göttingen: Vandenhoeck und Ruprecht, 1961.

Hamann, Richard and Jost Hermand: *Epochen deutscher Kultur von 1870 bis zur Gegenwart*, 5 vols, Munich: Nymphenburger Verlagshandlung, 1971–73, I, *Gründerzeit* (1971), II, *Naturalismus* (1972). [First published under the title *Deutsche Kunst und Kultur von der Gründerzeit bis zum Expressionismus*, Berlin: Akademie Verlag, I, *Gründerzeit* (1965), II, *Naturalismus* (1959)].

Hauptmann: Centenary Lectures, edited by Kenneth G. Knight and Frederick Norman, London: Institute of Germanic Studies, 1964.

Hays, Michael, *The Public and Performance: Essays in the History of French and German Theater*, Theatre and Dramatic Studies, 6, Ann Arbor, Michigan: UMI Research Press, 1974.

Henze, H., *Otto Brahm und das Deutsche Theater in Berlin*, Berlin: Mittler, 1930.

Hermand, Jost, 'Zur Literatur der Gründerzeit', *Deutsche Vierteljahrsschrift*, 41 (1967), 202–31; repr. in Hermand, *Von Mainz nach Weimar (1793–1919): Studien zur deutschen Literatur*, Stuttgart: Metzler, 1969, pp. 211–49.

Heuser, Frederick W. J., *Gerhart Hauptmann*, Tübingen: Niemeyer, 1961.

Hoefert, Sigfrid, 'Emile Zola dans la critique d'Otto Brahm', *Les Cahiers naturalistes*, 30 (1965), 145–52.
——, *Das Drama des Naturalismus*, 2nd edition, Stuttgart: Metzler, 1973.
——, *Gerhart Hauptmann*, 2nd edition, Stuttgart: Metzler, 1982.
Hortenbach, Jenny C., *Freiheitsstreben und Destruktivität: Frauen in den Dramen August Strindbergs und Gerhart Hauptmanns*, Oslo, Bergen, and Tromsö: Universitetsforlaget, 1965.
Hughes, H. Stuart, *Consciousness and Society: The Re-orientation of European Social Thought, 1890–1930*, London: MacGibbon and Kee, 1959.
Interpretationen: Dramen des Naturalismus, Stuttgart: Reclam, 1988.
Jelavich, Peter, *Munich and Theatrical Modernism: Politics, Playwriting, and Performance, 1890–1914* Cambridge, Mass. and London: Harvard U.P., 1985.
Kafitz, Dieter, *Johannes Schlaf – Weltanschauliche Totalität und Wirklichkeitsblindheit: Ein Beitrag zur Neubestimmung des Naturalismus-Begriffs und zur Herleitung totalitärer Denkformen*, Studien zur deutschen Literatur, 120, Tübingen: Niemeyer, 1992.
Kaiser, Gerhard, 'Die Tragikomödien Gerhart Hauptmanns', in *Festschrift für Klaus Ziegler*, edited by Eckehardt Catholy and Winfried Hellmann, Tübingen: Niemeyer, 1968, pp. 269–89.
Kayser, Wolfgang, 'Zur Dramaturgie des naturalistischen Schauspiels', in *Die Vortragsreise: Studien zur Literatur*, Bern: Francke, 1958, pp. 214–31.
Klotz, Volker, *Geschlossene und offene Form im Drama*, Munich: Hanser, 1960.
König, René, *Die naturalistische Ästhetik in Frankreich und ihre Auflösung*, Borna and Leipzig: Noske, 1931.
Lidtke, Vernon L., 'Naturalism and Socialism in Germany' *The American Historical Review*, 79 (1974), 14–37.
——, *The Alternative Culture: Socialist Labor in Imperial Germany*, New York and Oxford: O.U.P., 1985.
Literatur und Theater im wilhelminischen Zeitalter, edited by Hans-Peter Bayerdörfer, Karl Otto Conrady and Helmut Schanze, Tübingen: Niemeyer, 1978.
Löb, Ladislaus, *From Lessing to Hauptmann: Studies in German Drama*, London: University Tutorial Press, 1974.
Löwith, Karl, *Von Hegel zu Nietzsche*, 3rd edition, Stuttgart: Kohlhammer, 1953.
Lukács, Georg, *Deutsche Literatur im Zeitalter des Imperialismus: Eine Übersicht ihrer Hauptströmungen*, Berlin: Aufbau, 1947.
——, 'Grundlagen der Scheidung von Epik und Dramatik', *Aufbau*, 11 (1955), 978–91.
——, 'Hauptmanns Weg', *Die Schaubühne*, 7 (1911), 253–5.
——, *Probleme des Realismus*, Berlin: Aufbau, 1955.

──, 'Das Problem des untragischen Dramas', *Die Schaubühne*, 7 (1911), 231–34.

──, *Studies in European Realism: A Sociological survey of the writings of Balzac, Stendhal, Zola, Tolstoy, Gorki and others*, London: Hillway, 1950.

──, *Die Theorie des Romans*, Berlin: Paul Cassirer, 1920.

Mahal, Günther, *Naturalismus*, Munich: Fink, 1975.

Mann, Thomas, *Gerhart Hauptmann*, Gütersloh: Bertelsmann, 1953.

Marshall, Alan, *The German Naturalists and Gerhart Hauptmann: Reception and Influence*, Historisch-kritische Arbeiten zur deutschen Literatur, 2, Frankfurt a.M. and Bern: Peter Lang, 1982.

──, 'Naturalism and Nationalism', *German Life and Letters*, 37 (1983–84), 91–104.

──, 'Recent Trends in Naturalist Research', *German Life and Letters*, 33 (1979–80), 276–90.

Martersteig, Max, *Das deutsche Theater im neunzehnten Jahrhundert: Eine kulturgeschichtliche Darstellung*, 2nd edition, Leipzig: Breitkopf und Härtel, 1924.

Martini, Fritz, *Deutsche Literatur im bürgerlichen Realismus*, 3rd edition, Stuttgart: Metzler, 1974.

──, 'Gerhart Hauptmanns *Der Biberpelz*: Gedanken zum Bautypus einer naturalistischen Komödie', in *Lustspiele und das Lustspiel*, Stuttgart: Klett, 1974, pp. 213–35.

──, 'Soziale Thematik und Formwandlungen des Dramas', *Der Deutschunterricht*, 5 (1953), 73–100.

──, *Das Wagnis der Sprache*, 5th edition, Stuttgart: Ernst Klett, 1964.

Matthews, J. H., *Les deux Zola: Science et personnalité dans l'expression*, Geneva: Droz, and Paris: Minard, 1957.

May, Kurt, 'Die Weber', in *Das deutsche Drama*, edited by Benno von Wiese, 2 vols, Düsseldorf: Bagel, 1968, II, 157–65.

Mayer, Hans, 'Gerhart Hauptmann und die Mitte', in *Von Lessing bis Thomas Mann*, Pfullingen: Neske, 1959, pp. 338–55.

McInnes Edward, *Das deutsche Drama des 19. Jahrhunderts*, Grundlagen der Germanistik, 26, Berlin: Erich Schmidt, 1983.

──, 'Continuity and Change in German Drama', *Forum for Modern Language Studies*, 8 (1972), 261–68.

──, 'The Image of the Hunt in Hauptmann's Plays', *German Life and Letters*, n.s., 19 (1965–66), 190–96.

──, 'The Domestic Dramas of Gerhart Hauptmann: Tragedy or Sentimental Pathos?', *German Life and Letters*, n.s. 20 (1966–67), 53–60.

──, 'Die naturalistische Dramentheorie und die dramaturgische Tradition', *Zeitschrift für deutsche Philologie*, 93 (1974), 161–86.

McKenzie, John R. P., *Social Comedy in Austria and Germany, 1890–1933* Bern: Lang, 1992.

Die Meininger: Texte zur Rezeption, edited by John Osborne, Tübingen: Max Niemeyer, 1980.
Mendelssohn, Peter de, 'Die Geschichte der "Neuen Rundschau" [I]', *Die neue Rundschau* 80 (1969), 597–615.
Mit Gerhart Hauptmann: Erinnerungen und Bekenntnisse aus seinem Freundeskreis, edited by Walter Heynen, Berlin: Stilke, 1922.
Moore, C. H., 'A Hearing on "Germinal" and "Die Weber"', *Germanic Review*, 33 (1958), 30–40.
Münchow, Ursula, *Deutscher Naturalismus*, Berlin: Akademie Verlag, 1968.
Musiol, Karl, 'Carl Hauptmann und Josepha Kodis', *Deutsche Vierteljahrsschrift*, 36 (1960), 257–63.
Naturalismus/Ästhetizismus, edited by Christa Bürger, Peter Bürger, and Jochen Schulte-Sasse, Frankfurt a.M.: Suhrkamp, 1979.
Naturalismus: Bürgerliche Dichtung und soziales Engagement, edited by Helmut Scheuer, Stuttgart: Kohlhammer, 1974.
Nestriepke, Siegfried, *Geschichte der Volksbühne Berlins, 1890–1914*, Berlin: Volksbühnen Verlags- und Vertriebsgesellschaft, 1930.
Osborne, John, 'Gerhart Hauptmanns "Vor Sonnenaufgang": Zwischen Tradition und Moderne', *Der Deutschunterricht*, 40 (1988), II, 77–88.
——, 'Naturalism and the Dramaturgy of the Open Drama', *German Life and Letters*, n.s. 23 (1969–70), 119–28.
——, *The Meiningen Court Theatre, 1866–1890*, Cambridge: C.U.P., 1988.
Pfanner, Helmut F., 'Deutungsprobleme in Gerhart Hauptmanns "Michael Kramer"', *Monatshefte*, 62 (1970), 45–54.
Praschek, Helmut, 'Das Verhältnis von Kunsttheorie und Kunstschaffen im Bereich der deutschen naturalistischen Dramatik' (doctoral thesis, University of Greifswald, 1957).
——, 'Zum Zerfall des naturalistischen Stils', in *Worte und Werte: Bruno Markwardt zum 60. Geburtstag*, edited by Gustav Erdmann and Alfons Eichstaedt, Berlin: de Gruyter, 1961, pp. 315–21.
Rasch, Wolfdietrich, 'Zur dramatischen Dichtung des jungen Gerhart Hauptmanns' in *Festschrift für Franz Rolf Schröder*, edited by Wolfdietrich Rasch, Heidelberg: Winter, 1959, pp. 241–53.
Reichart, Walter A., 'Grundbegriffe im dramatischen Schaffen Gerhart Hauptmanns', *PMLA*, 82 (1967), 142–51.
Reichert, Herbert W., 'Hauptmann's Frau Wolff and Brecht's Mother Courage', *German Quarterly*, 34 (1961), 439–48.
Requardt, Walter and Martin Machatzke, *Gerhart Hauptmann und Erkner: Studien zum Berliner Frühwerk*, Berlin: Erich Schmidt, 1980.
Ritter, Gerhard A., 'Die Arbeiterbewegung im wilhelminischen Reich: Die Sozialdemokratische Partei und die Freien Gewerkschaften', *Studien zur europäischen Geschichte aus dem Friedrich-Meinecke Institut der Freien Universität Berlin*, 3, Berlin: Colloquium Verlag, 1959.

Root, Winthrop H., *German Criticism of Zola, 1875–1893*, New York: Columbia U.P., 1931.
Ruttmann, Irene, 'Zwischen Distanz und Identifikation: Beobachtungen zur Wirkungsgeschichte von Gerhart Hauptmanns *Der Biberpelz* und *Der rote Hahn*', *Germanisch-Romanische Monatsschrift*, N. F. 30 (1980), 49–72.
Scherer, Herbert, *Bürgerlich-oppositionelle Literaten und sozialdemokratische Arbeiterbewegung nach 1890*, Stuttgart: Metzler, 1974.
Scheuer, Helmut, *Arno Holz im literarischen Leben des ausgehenden 19. Jahrhunderts (1883–1896): Eine biographische Studie*, Munich: Winkler, 1971.
Schickling, Dieter, *Interpretationen und Studien zur Entwicklung und geistesgeschichtlichen Stellung des Werkes von Arno Holz* (doctoral thesis, University of Tübingen, 1965).
Schlawe, Fritz, *Literarische Zeitschriften, 1885–1910*, Stuttgart: Metzler, 2nd edition, 1965.
Schley, Gernot, *Die Freie Bühne in Berlin*, Berlin: Haude und Spener, 1967.
Schrimpf, Hans-Joachim, 'Rose Bernd', in *Das deutsche Drama*, edited by Benno von Wiese, 2 vols, Düsseldorf: Bagel, 1968, II, 166–85.
——, 'Struktur und Metaphysik des sozialen Schauspiels bei Gerhart Hauptmann', in *Literatur und Gesellschaft vom 19ten ins 20ste Jahrhundert: Festgabe für Benno von Wiese*, edited by Hans-Joachim Schrimpf, Bonn: Bouvier, 1963, pp. 274–308.
——, 'Das unerreichte Soziale: Die Komödien Gerhart Hauptmanns "Der Biberpelz" und "Der rote Hahn"', in *Das deutsche Lustspiel*, edited by Hans Steffen, 2 vols, Göttingen: Vandenhoeck und Ruprecht, 1969, II, 25–60.
Schroeder, P., 'Arno Holz's "Die Kunst" and the Problem of "Isms"', *Modern Language Notes*, 66 (1951), 217–24.
Schultze, Hans-Adolf, *Der Schauspieler Rudolf Rittner (1869–1943): Ein Wegbereiter Gerhart Hauptmanns auf dem Theater* (doctoral thesis, Free University of Berlin, 1961).
Schwerte, Hans, 'Deutsche Literatur im wilhelminischen Zeitalter', *Wirkendes Wort*, 14 (1964), 254–70.
Seidlin, Oskar, 'Otto Brahm', *German Quarterly*, 36, (1963), 131–40.
——, 'Urmythos irgendwo in Berlin', *Deutsche Vierteljahrsschrift*, 43 (1969), 126–46.
Seltzer, Mark, *Henry James and the Art of Power*, Ithaca, London: Cornell U.P., 1984.
Sengle, Friedrich, 'Wunschbild Land und Schreckbild Stadt', *Studium generale*, 16 (1963), 619–30.
Shaw, Leroy R., 'Witness of Deceit: Gerhart Hauptmann as Critic of Society', *University of California Publications in Modern Philology*, 50, Berkeley, 1958.

——, *The Playwright and Historical Change: Dramatic Strategies in Brecht, Hauptmann, Kaiser, and Wedekind*, Madison, Milwaukee, and London: University of Wisconsin Press, 1970.
Shepherd, William A. G., 'Social Conscience and Messianic Vision: A Study in the Problems of Gerhart Hauptmann's Individualism' (doctoral thesis, University of Edinburgh, 1962).
Sinden, Margaret, *Gerhart Hauptmann: The Prose Plays*, Toronto and London: Toronto University Press, 1957.
——, 'Marianne and Einsame Menschen', *Monatshefte*, 54 (1962), 311–17.
Soergel, Albert, *Dichtung und Dichter der Zeit: Eine Schilderung der deutschen Literatur der letzten Jahrzehnte*, Leipzig: Voigtländer, 1911.
—— and Curt Hohoff, *Dichtung und Dichter der Zeit: Vom Naturalismus bis zur Gegenwart*, 2 vols, Düsseldorf: Bagel 1964, [first published 1961; revised version of the preceding and two further volumes].
Sokel, Walter H., 'Dialogführung und Dialog im expressionistischen Drama', *Aspekte des Expressionismus*, edited by Wolfgang Paulsen, Heidelberg: Stiehm, 1968, 59–84.
Sorge, Reinhard Johannes, *Der Bettler: Eine dramatische Sendung*, Berlin: S. Fischer, 1928 [first published 1912].
Sprengel, Peter, *Gerhart Hauptmann: Epoche – Werk – Wirkung*, Munich: Beck, 1984.
Stern, Fritz, *The Politics of Cultural Despair*, Berkeley and Los Angeles: University of California Press, 1961.
Stern, Joseph Peter, *Re-interpretations: Seven Studies in Nineteenth-Century German literature*, London: Thames and Hudson, 1964.
Szondi, Peter, *Theorie des modernen Dramas*, Frankfurt a.M.: Suhrkamp, 1959.
Tank, Kurt Lothar, *Gerhart Hauptmann in Selbstzeugnissen und Bilddokumenten*, Hamburg: Rowohlt, 1959.
Thalmann, Jörg, *Wege zu Kafka: Eine Interpretation des Amerikaromans*, Frauenfeld and Stuttgart: Huber, 1966.
Toller, Ernst, *Die Maschinenstürmer*, Leipzig: Tal, 1922.
Trilling, Lionel, 'The morality of inertia', in *A Gathering of Fugitives*, London: Secker and Warburg, 1957, pp. 31–40.
Turner, David, 'Die Familie Selicke and the drama of Naturalism', in *Periods in German Literature: Texts and Contexts*, II, edited by James Macpherson Ritchie, London: Oswald Wolff, 1969, pp. 193–219.
Voigt, Felix A. 'Grundfragen der Gerhart-Hauptmann-Forschung', *Germanisch-Romanische Monatsschrift*, 27 (1949), 271–86.
——, *Hauptmann Studien*, Breslau: Maruschke and Berendt, 1936.
Wais, Kurt, 'Zur Auswirkung des französischen naturalistischen Romans in Deutschland', in *An den Grenzen der Nationalliteraturen: Vergleichende Aufsätze*, Berlin: de Gruyter, 1958, pp. 215–36.

Weber, Max, *Schriften zur theoretischen Soziologie, zur Soziologie der Politik und Verfassung*, edited by Max Graf zu Solms, Frankfurt a.M.: Schauer, 1947.

Weno, Joachim, 'Der Theaterstil des Naturalismus,' (doctoral thesis, University of Berlin, 1951).

Whitinger, Raleigh, 'Gerhart Hauptmann's *Vor Sonnenaufgang*: On Alcohol and Poetry in German Naturalist Drama', *German Quarterly*, 63 (1990), 83–91.

——, 'Rethinking Anna Mahr: Reflections on the Characterization and Function of the Emancipated Woman in Gerhart Hauptmann's *Einsame Menschen*', in *Seminar*, 29 (1993), 233–52.

Wiese, Benno von, 'Wirklichkeit und Drama in Gerhart Hauptmanns Tragikomödie "Die Ratten"', *Jahrbuch der deutschen Schillergesellschaft*, 6 (1962), 311–25.

Wölfflin, Heinrich, *Kunstgeschichtliche Grundbegriffe: Das Problem der Stilentwicklng in der neueren Kunst*, Munich: Bruckmann, 1915.

Wunberg, Gotthart, 'Utopie und fin de siècle', *Deutsche Vierteljahrsschrift*, 43 (1969), 685–706.

Zander, Rosmarie, *Der junge Gerhart Hauptmann und Henrik Ibsen*, Limburg, 1947.

Ziegelschmidt, A., 'Gerhart Hauptmanns Ikarier', *Germanic Review*, 13 (1938), 32–39.

Zimmermann, Alfred, *Blüthe und Verfall des Leinengewerbes in Schlesien*, Breslau: Korn, 1885.

INDEX

Alberti, Conrad   3, 11, 27, 39, 178
   Brot   10, 11
   Riesen und Zwerge   25
Alcoholism   88, 90, 98, 115
Andreas-Salomé, Lou   147
Anti-Aristotelian drama   27, 186–87
Antoine, André   13, 14, 38
Anzengruber, Ludwig   4, 32, 34, 152
   Die Kreuzelschreiber   152, 153
   Der Sternsteinhof   167
   Das vierte Gebot   34, 103
Augier, Emile   6

Baake, Kurt   66
Baginski, Richard   66
Bahr, Hermann   41, 78
   'Die Überwindung des Naturalismus'   77
Bassermann, Alfred   42
Bebel, August   70, 75
Berg, Leo   34, 81
Bergson, Henri   150, 158
Berlin   7, 8, 27, 32, 38, 64, 70, 73, 75, 80, 87, 101
Bernard, Claude   20
Bernstein, Else
   Dämmerung   39, 104
Bernstein, Max   37
Bertens, Rosa   42
Bie, Oskar   41
Bierbaum, Otto Julius   17, 41, 81
Birch-Pfeiffer, Charlotte   64
Bismarck, Otto von   4, 11, 64, 66
Bleibtreu, Karl   3, 10, 11, 16, 29, 32, 39, 63

Ein Faust der Tat   10
Größenwahn   25
Das Halsband der Königin   10
Harold der Sachse   10
Schicksal   10
Weltgericht   10
Blumenthal, Oskar   6, 38, 72
Böcklin, Arnold   48
Bölsche, Wilhelm   41, 65, 66, 71, 72, 78, 88, 130
   Die naturwissenschaftlichen Grundlagen der Poesie   19, 23, 166
'Bote aus der Fremde'   64, 89, 106
Bourget, Paul   78
Brahm, Otto   3, 8, 10, 13, 14, 17, 18, 28, 30, 31, 33, 34, 35, 38–42, 43, 66, 71, 77, 152, 182, 183, 190
   'Henrik Ibsen'   27, 36, 37
Brand, Julius   20
   Thomas Münzer   10
Brandes, Georg   22, 45, 68, 69, 81
Brecht, Bertolt   155, 156, 163, 187, 188
Brinkmann, Richard   54
Bronnen, Arnolt
   Vatermord   104, 105
Büchner, Georg   66
   Dantons Tod   72, 115, 188
   Woyzeck   188
'bürgerliches Trauerspiel'   152, 182
Burgtheater, Vienna   9, 13, 30
Burns, Rob   47, 56

Cabet, Étienne   67
Calderon de la Barca   29

Censorship   14, 34, 37, 38, 39, 135, 136
Chandler, Raymond   51–53
Chevrel, Yves   91
Comte, Auguste   14
Conrad, Michael Georg   3, 8, 11, 21, 68
  Was die Isar rauscht   25
Conradi, Hermann   11, 63
Cowen, Roy C.   2, 94, 165

Dahn, Felix   4, 10
  Ein Kampf um Rom   10
Darwin, Charles   120, 121
Dehmel, Richard   71
  Der Mitmensch   36
Deutsche Monatsblätter   3
Deutsche Rundschau   20, 22, 31, 33
Deutsches Theater, Berlin   13, 17, 27, 30, 31, 39, 40, 41, 77, 135, 136, 152
Devine, George   42
Diderot, Denis   175
Dilthey, Wilhelm   176, 177, 185
Dingelstedt, Franz von   10, 13
Döblin, Alfred   80
Dreyer, Max   64
  Winterschlaf   89, 95, 96, 137, 164
Du Bois Reymond, Emil   131
Dumas, Alexandre, fils   6, 20
Dupont, Paul   71
Duse, Eleonora   179

Ebers, Georg   4
Eckstein, Ernst   4
Emrich, Wilhelm   47, 113
Engels, Friedrich   177
Ernst, Adolf   31
Ernst, Otto
  Jugend von Heute   150
Ernst, Paul   41, 70, 75
Expressionism   104, 105, 113, 169, 190

Fischer, Samuel   38, 41
Fitger, Arthur   4, 32
  Von Gottes Gnaden   34
Flaischlen, Cäsar   116
  Martin Lehnhardt   37, 184
Fontane, Theodor   9, 10, 31, 32, 66, 67, 81, 144, 180
Freie Bühne   11, 28, 29, 31, 34, 37–40, 65, 66, 87, 101, 103, 135, 190, 193–94
Freie Bühne für modernes Leben   8, 40, 41, 73, 77, 81
Freie Volksbühne   65, 66, 71, 72, 97, 136, 195–96
Frenzel, Karl   32, 38
Freytag, Gustav   9, 14
  Bilder aus der deutschen Vergangenheit   8
Friedrich, Wilhelm   25
Friedrichshagen   77, 78, 81, 127, 130, 176
Fulda, Ludwig   8, 37, 39
  Das verlorene Paradies   137

Garborg, Arne   17
Die Gartenlaube   64
Geibel, Emanuel   8, 10, 44
  Brunhild   9
Genette, Gérard   52
George, Stefan   77
Die Gesellschaft   8, 11, 21, 32, 39, 43
Goethe, Johann Wolfgang von   6, 17, 29, 33, 63, 175, 182
  Egmont   72
Gogol, Nikolai   66
Goncourt, Edmond de   35, 148
Goncourt, Jules de   35
Gotthelf, Jeremias   80
Gourmont, Remy de   78
Greif, Martin   4
Grelling, Richard   135
  Gleiches Recht   135
Grisebach, Eduard   4

Guthke, Karl Siegfried 93, 151, 158, 179, 185

Haeckel, Ernst Theodor 24, 120, 121, 131
Halbe, Max 37, 64, 68, 71, 77, 79, 89, 119
  Eisgang 137, 143, 183
  Freie Liebe 151, 178, 179
  Jugend 89, 177, 178, 184
  Mutter Erde 115, 125
Hamerling, Robert 4
  Ahasver in Rom 5
Hanstein, Adalbert von 72
Harden, Maximilian 38, 68, 101
Hardt, Ernst
  Tote Zeit 89, 178, 182, 183
Hart, Heinrich 3, 5, 6, 8, 11, 17, 18, 19, 20, 22, 28, 29, 30, 31, 33, 37, 38, 39, 41, 48, 53, 64, 65, 69, 70, 71, 151, 178, 182, 183
  'Das Deutsche Theater des Herrn L'Arronge' 27–29
  'Für und gegen Zola' 16, 17, 19
  Sedan 11
  see also *Kritische Waffengänge*
Hart, Julius 4, 7, 33, 38, 39 40, 41, 64, 65, 66, 71, 72, 151, 164, 178, 182, 183
  see also *Kritische Waffengänge*
Hartleben, Otto Erich 72, 116, 157
  Hanna Jagert 77, 151
  Rosenmontag 152
Hauptmann, Carl 64, 119, 131
  Marianne 24, 37, 130, 131
  Sonnenwanderer 77
Hauptmann, Gerhart 2, 3, 5, 10, 30, 32, 38, 39, 40, 41, 42, 43, 46, 56, 60, 64, 66, 67, 75, 79, 151–159, 185
  Das Abenteuer meiner Jugend 65, 76
  Der Apostel 148

Bahnwärter Thiel 43, 57, 58, 78, 168
Der Biberpelz 149, 154–56, 158, 159, 168, 178, 183, 188
Das Buch der Leidenschaft 119
Einsame Menschen 35, 36, 39, 56, 76, 77, 81, 92, 99, 101, 119–33, 137, 148, 154, 157, 160, 161, 165, 168, 176
Fasching 43
Das Friedensfest 24, 92, 98, 101–117, 119, 120, 121, 125, 127, 133, 148, 159, 161, 164, 165, 167, 170, 177, 178, 181, 188, 189
Florian Geyer 10, 29, 159, 188
Fuhrmann Henschel 57, 149, 164–69, 173
Gabriel Schillings Flucht 114, 125
Germanen und Römer 10
Hanneles Himmelfahrt 42, 132, 147–48, 158, 159, 185, 189
Die Jungfern von Bischofsberg 156
Kollege Crampton 39, 60, 135, 149, 157, 158, 177, 178
Michael Kramer 157, 161–63, 167, 173, 188
Der Narr in Christo Emanuel Quint 159, 178
Die Ratten 42, 149, 160, 165–68, 170, 173
Rose Bernd 146, 159, 160, 165–73
Der rote Hahn 154–55, 188, 184
Schluck und Jau 157
Und Pippa tanzt! 159
Der weiße Heiland 190
Die versunkene Glocke 77, 120, 157, 159
Vor Sonnenaufgang 10, 24, 32, 34, 39, 43, 61, 67, 68, 69, 79, 87–99, 101, 115, 109, 117, 121, 127, 133, 135, 137, 157, 160, 161, 164, 170, 176, 177, 179, 180, 181, 186, 187

'Von den Möglichkeiten des
  Theaters' 160
Die Weber 14, 15, 35, 39, 40, 92
  72, 82, 122, 135–47, 149, 158, 159,
  177, 178, 179, 183, 189
Hebbel, Friedrich 8, 9, 185
  Agnes Bernauer 8
  Maria Magdalene 172
  Die Nibelungen 9
Hegel, Georg Wilhelm Friedrich 8,
  14, 175, 176, 185, 186, 187
Heimatkunst 11
Heine, Heinrich 63
Held, Franz 81
  Ein Fest auf der Bastille 10
Henckell, Karl 67, 68
Hermand, Jost 4
Heyse, Paul 4, 8, 10, 33, 70
  Kinder der Welt 5
Hillebrand, Karl 20, 21
Hirschfeld, Georg
  Die Mütter 76, 77, 123, 130, 154
  Pauline 151, 154, 155
Historical drama 8, 10, 11, 29
Historiography 8, 9, 14
Hofmannsthal, Hugo von 41, 45,
  53, 179
  'Ballade des äußeren Lebens' 53
  'Der Dichter und diese Zeit' 53
  'Die Menschen in Ibsens
  Dramen' 188
  Der Tod des Tizian 131
Hollaender, Felix 137
Holz, Arno 1, 10, 17, 23, 34, 41,
  43–62, 63, 64, 67, 75, 93, 177
  Das Buch der Zeit 44
  Deutsche Weisen 44
  Die Kunst: Ihr Wesen und
  ihre Gesetze 48, 54
  Emanuel Geibel: Ein
  Gedenkbuch 44
  Klinginsherz 44
Holz, Arno and Johannes Schlaf 52,
  53

Der erste Schultag 56, 104
Die Familie Selicke 3, 58–62, 96,
  141, 157, 161, 165, 178, 179, 180
Papa Hamlet 43, 54–56, 59, 89,
  151, 152, 157, 187
Die papierne Passion 59
Ein Tod 50, 56–57, 62
Holz, Arno and Oskar Jerschke
  Traumulus 104, 157
Holz, Arno and Paul Ernst
  Sozialaristokraten 75, 82, 149,
  178
Huch, Ricarda 121
Huysmans, Joris Karl 78

Ibsen, Henrik 3, 8, 10, 25, 27, 30,
  32, 33, 34, 35, 37, 38, 39, 40, 41,
  43, 63, 66, 68, 78, 89, 101, 117,
  163, 169, 183, 184, 188
  Brand 8
  A Doll's House 3, 8, 32, 33, 38, 91
  An Enemy of the People 36, 38, 75
  Ghosts 3, 13, 32, 34, 35, 37, 38,
  92, 101
  Hedda Gabler 120, 150
  The Lady from the Sea 38
  The League of Youth 41
  Peer Gynt 8
  Pillars of Society 3, 8, 32, 38,
  72, 143
  The Pretenders 13
  Rosmersholm 38, 101
  When we dead awaken 41
  The Wild Duck 38, 96, 97, 98,
  108, 157

James, Henry 21, 46
Jensen, Wilhelm 4
Jordan, Wilhelm 4, 10
  Die Nibelungen 5
Jugendbewegung 104

Kaberlin 186, 187
Kafka, Franz 54

Kainz, Josef   13, 101, 178
Kastan, Dr Isidor   91
Kaulbach, Wilhelm von   9, 10
Kean, Charles   9
Keller, Gottfried   18, 33
Kerr, Alfred   169
Key, Ellen   104
Kirchbach, Wolfgang   24
Kleist, Heinrich von   13, 29, 33, 34, 124, 181
  Das Erdbeben in Chili   113
  Penthesilea   113
Klotz, Volker   165
Kodis-Krzyzanowska, Josepha   119
Kraus, Karl   149, 156
Kretzer, Max
  Die beiden Genossen   67, 68
  Die Betrogenen   25
  Die Verkommenen   25
Kritische Waffengänge   5, 7, 8, 11, 18, 27, 28, 32, 33, 64
Kruse, Heinrich   4, 32

L'Arronge, Adolf   6, 13, 27, 30, 31, 38, 40
Lamprecht, Karl   14, 49
Land, Hans   137
Landauer, Gustav   69, 72, 83
Langbehn, Julius   191
  Rembrandt als Erzieher   80, 81, 82, 104, 131, 132
Langmann, Philip
  Bartel Turaser   137
Laube, Heinrich   9
Ledebour, Georg   72
Lehmann, Else   42
Lenz, Jakob Michael Reinhold
  Die Soldaten   152
Lessing, Gotthold Ephraim   29, 31, 175
  Emilia Galotti   72, 91, 99, 152, 182
Lessingtheater, Berlin   33, 39, 40, 41, 71, 72, 87

Leuthold, Heinrich   4
Liebknecht, Wilhelm   136
Lienhardt, Fritz   11
Liliencron, Detlev von   17, 41
Lindau, Paul   5, 6, 7, 8, 9, 11, 31, 32, 38, 64
  Marion   6
Lindner, Albert   4
Lingg, Hermann   4
Lubliner, Hugo   6
Ludwig, Otto   20, 66
Lukács, Georg   21, 177–78, 187–88
Luxemburg, Rosa   121

Maeterlinck, Maurice   41, 78, 189
Makart, Hans von   9, 10
Mann, Heinrich   12
  Professor Unrat   104
Mann, Thomas   21, 151, 185, 188
  Buddenbrooks   64
Marx, Karl   14, 69, 75, 139, 143
Mauthner, Fritz   71
Mayer, Hans   75
McFarlane, James Walter   35
McInnes, Edward   2, 187
Mehring, Franz   44, 70, 71, 72, 74, 75, 76, 137, 176, 177, 182, 183
Meiningen Court Theatre   9, 12, 13, 14, 30, 31, 37, 165, 184
Menzel, Adolf von   48
Meyer, Conrad Ferdinand   4
Moderne Dichtercharaktere   44, 63
Moeller van den Brück, Arthur   82
Molière, Jean-Baptiste   150, 154
Münchener Dichterschule   8, 10
Munich   8, 10, 38, 64

Nationalism   4, 6, 11, 12, 28
Neue deutsche Rundschau   41
  see also *Freie Bühne für modernes Leben*
Neue Freie Volksbühne   72, 136, 196–97
Die neue Rundschau   41

see also *Freie Bühne für modernes Leben*
Nietzsche, Friedrich 4, 11, 65, 68, 69, 70, 75, 109, 174
Nissel, Franz 4
Novalis
   Heinrich von Ofterdingen 117

O'Neill, Eugene
   The Iceman cometh 110
   Long Day's Journey into Night 105

Pascal, Roy 56
Philippi, Felix 37
Piloty, Karl von 9
Ploetz Alfred 88
Poetic Realism 20, 182, 184
Praschek, Helmut 164, 177, 179
Proust, Marcel 23
Przybyszewski, Stanislaw 17

Racine, Jean
   Phèdre 107
Reicher, Emanuel 30
Reinhardt Max 30, 40, 41, 42
Richter, Jean Paul Friedrich 80
Riehl, Wilhelm Heinrich 9, 14, 17
   Die deutsche Arbeit 8
Rilke, Rainer Maria 63
Rittner, Rudolf 42, 79, 80, 147, 178
Rodenberg, Julius 31
Rosmer, Ernst, see Bernstein, Else
Sauer, Oscar 42
Schack, Adolf, Graf von 4, 11
Schaufert, Heinrich
   Vater Brahm 7
Scherer, Wilhelm 31
Scheuer, Helmut 2, 61, 68, 75, 77, 164
Schiller, Friedrich von 13, 18, 20, 28, 29, 175, 183
   Die Braut von Messina 116
   Kabale und Liebe 72, 123, 152, 18–83
   Wallenstein 83
   Wallensteins Lager 165
Schlaf, Johannes 12, 41, 48, 54, 55, 63, 64, 68, 78, 79, 82, 164, 186, 189
   Ein Dachstubenidyll 55
   Frühling 130
   Mainacht 59
   Meister Oelze 89, 164, 165, 166, 173, 174
   see also Holz, Arno and Johannes Schlaf
Schlenther Paul 30, 31, 32, 33, 38, 39, 43, 121, 181
Schmidt, Conrad 66
Schmidt, Erich 31
Schmoller, Gustav 14, 15
Schnitzler, Arthur 41
   Reigen 150
Schopenhauer, Arthur 65, 109, 185
Schrimpf, Hans-Joachim 166, 172, 185, 186, 189
Scribe, Eugène 6
Servaes, Franz 76
Shakespeare, William 13, 29
Singer, Paul 136
Social drama 3, 8, 28, 32, 33, 36, 37, 82, 87, 92, 135, 183
Socialism 5, 44, 63–83, 119, 120, 124, 129, 135, 151, 183
   anti-Socialist legislation 64, 65
   Independent Socialists 71
   Social Democratic Party 44, 66, 68, 70–73, 129
   socialist realism 74
Sorge, Reinhard Johannes 113
   Der Bettler 111
Spielhagen, Friedrich 8
Spitteler, Carl 4, 60
Sprengel, Peter 39, 159
Stanislavsky, Constantin 13, 14

Steiger, Edgar 73
Stern, Fritz 81, 82
Stern, Joseph Peter 23
Stifter, Adalbert 80
Storm, Theodor 4
Strindberg August 39, 41, 78
   The Father 125
   Miss Julie 39
   Preface to *Miss Julie* 179
Sudermann, Hermann 8, 159, 179
   Die Ehre 137, 176
   Sodoms Ende 92, 186, 188
Szondi, Peter 90, 91

Taine, Hippolyte 14, 48
Theatre 5, 8, 9, 12, 13, 14, 25, 27, 38, 73, 180
Théâtre Libre, Paris 38
Toller, Ernst
   Die Maschinenstürmer 143, 144
Tolstoy, Leo 66, 127
   The Power of Darkness 34, 92
Trilling, Lionel 61
Türk, Julius 66, 71

Verein Deutsche Bühne 39
Volkelt, Johannes 16, 18
Volksbühnenbewegung 29, 39, 65, 73, 75, 129
Voß, Richard 4, 8

Wedekind, Frank 39, 41, 77, 102
   Erdgeist 102
   Frühlings Erwachen 92, 104, 109, 147
   Die junge Welt 102, 177
   Schloß Wetterstein 112
   Der Marquis von Keith 128
Weigand, Wilhelm
   Der Vater 104
Whitinger, Raleigh 125, 126
Whitman, Walt 78
Wilbrandt, Adolf 4, 32
Wildberger, Karl 66
Wilde, Oscar 41
Wildenbruch, Ernst von 4, 11, 32
Wilhelm II, German Kaiser 136
Wille, Bruno 65, 66, 70, 71, 72, 75, 78, 130, 132, 136
   Philosophie der Befreiung durch das reine Mittel 69, 82
Wolff, Eugen 27
Wolff, Julius 4
Wolff, Theodor 38
Wolter, Charlotte 10
Wolzogen, Ernst von 72
   Das Lumpengesindel 178
Women's emancipation 93, 121, 125
Wundt, Wilhelm 131

Ziegler, Klara 10
Zimmermann, Alfred 15, 144
Zola, Emile 1, 3, 7, 10, 12, 16, 17, 19, 20, 21, 22, 25, 28, 32, 33, 34, 37 45, 46, 47, 50, 54, 66, 68, 78, 89, 98, 148, 178, 184, 188
   Germinal 135
   Le Roman expérimental 19
   Thérèse Raquin 3
Zürich University 121

For Product Safety Concerns and Information please contact our EU
representative GPSR@taylorandfrancis.com
Taylor & Francis Verlag GmbH, Kaufingerstraße 24, 80331 München, Germany